Encyclopedia of Bird Reference Drawings

by

David Mohrhardt

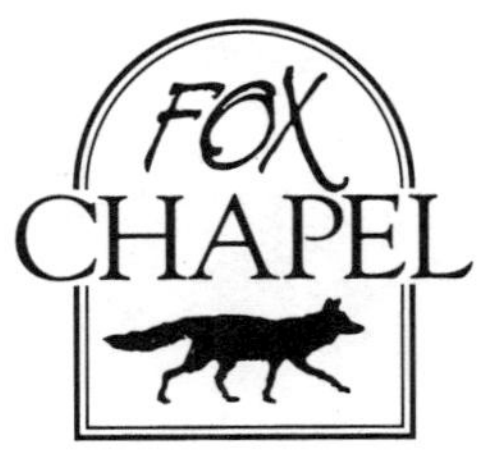

Fox Chapel Publishing
Box 7948
Lancaster, Pennsylvania
USA , 17604

Library of Congress #92-70301

ISBN # 1-5623-009-4

To order your copy of this book, please send $14.95 plus $2.50 shipping and handling . Try your bookseller first.

Fox Chapel Publishing
Box 7948
Lancaster , Pennsylvania 17604

Large quantity purchases of this title by corporations, nature groups, clubs and others may qualify for special discounts, Contact the Special Sales Manager.

Manufactured in the United States of America.

Foreword

Originally published by the artist in 1985 , this book has quickly become an underground classic among birders and artists - popularized almost exclusively by word of mouth. The limited number of copies from the first printing sold out and the book had been unavailable for several years.

We are pleased to bring you this excellent sourcebook once again by arrangement with Mr. Mohrhardt. These detailed studies make bird anatomy fascinating and will add depth to your knowledge and appreciation for nature.

Write and let us now how you've found this book helpful , we'll be glad to hear from you.

About the Author

Wildlife artist David Mohrhardt successfully captures the beauty of nature in his paintings and sketches.

After earning a university degree in biology from Michigan State University, he entered the museum field to learn more about nature while developing his skills as an artist.

David has spent 20 years in museum work as an artist-preparator working for institutions such as the Kalamazoo Nature Center , Kellogg Bird Sanctuary , Montana State University and the Maryland Department of Natural Resources. Mohrhardt now pursues painting full time.

Largely a self-taught artist, David has won numerous honors and awards from Ducks Unlimited and other prestigious competitions. He is a frequent exhibitor at the "Birds in Art" show of the Leigh Yawkey Woodson Museum in Wausau , Wisconsin. David has illustrated many books and articles, including work for Readers' Digest and Time Life Books . The author-artist of nine books, David Mohrhardt's commitment to precise detail is legendary in his field. Mr. Mohrhardt lives in Michigan.

TABLE OF CONTENTS

ABOUT THE DRAWINGS

The open wing drawings were originally done for personal art reference. The wings were drawn as they appeared with no attempt to make the contour uniform or to even up new growth feathers. The upper and under sides of the wings were done separately which accounts for the differences in size, angle and perspective. Feather vanes were eliminated in some cases so the shape would be more apparent. No effort was made to separate and count the upper and under wing coverts. Because of uniform color or pattern, these coverts on some wings blend together and have little or no individual definition. After examining several specimens of the same species, it was noted that there was not only a color and size variation, but minor feather shape differences for the same feathers within the species. Many feathers are only in prime condition for a short time due to function or habitat, e.g., ragged tails on woodpeckers and frayed wings on marsh birds. The drawings are as accurate as possible. However, they were not meant to be treated as scientific illustrations. The purpose of these drawings is an aid. For complete accuracy, there is no substitute for the specimen in hand.

The open wing drawings are original, all other illustrations are reproduced from; Birds of North and Middle America, by Robert Ridgway, et. al., Bulletin 50 of the U.S. National Museum, Parts 1 thru 11, 1901 - 1950.

WING TOPOGRAPHY

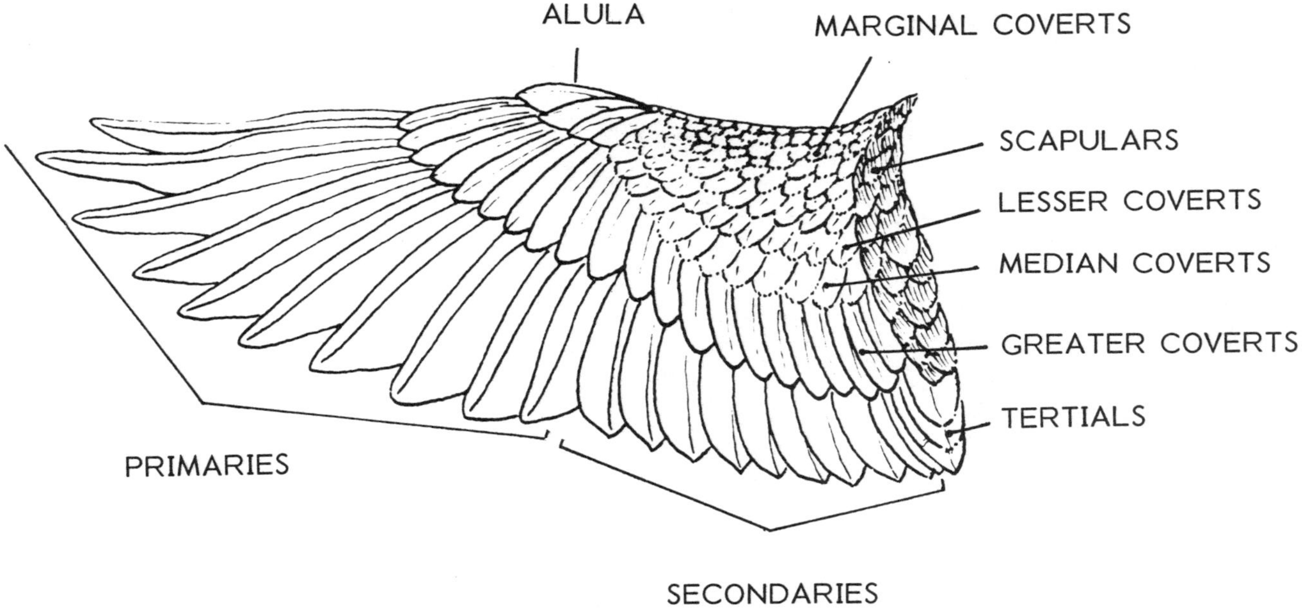

ALULA

MARGINAL COVERTS

SCAPULARS

LESSER COVERTS

MEDIAN COVERTS

GREATER COVERTS

TERTIALS

PRIMARIES

SECONDARIES

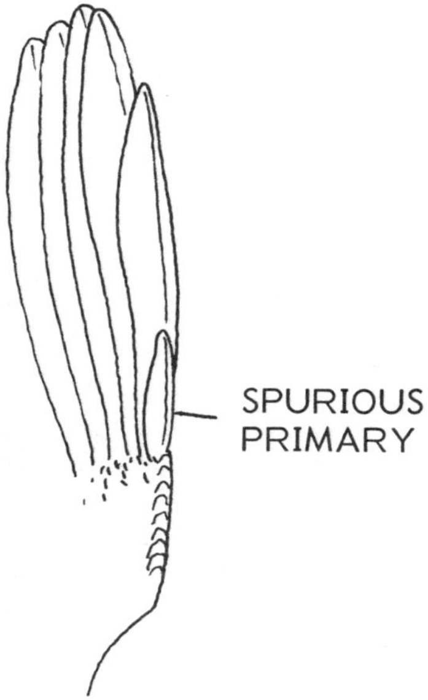

SPURIOUS PRIMARY

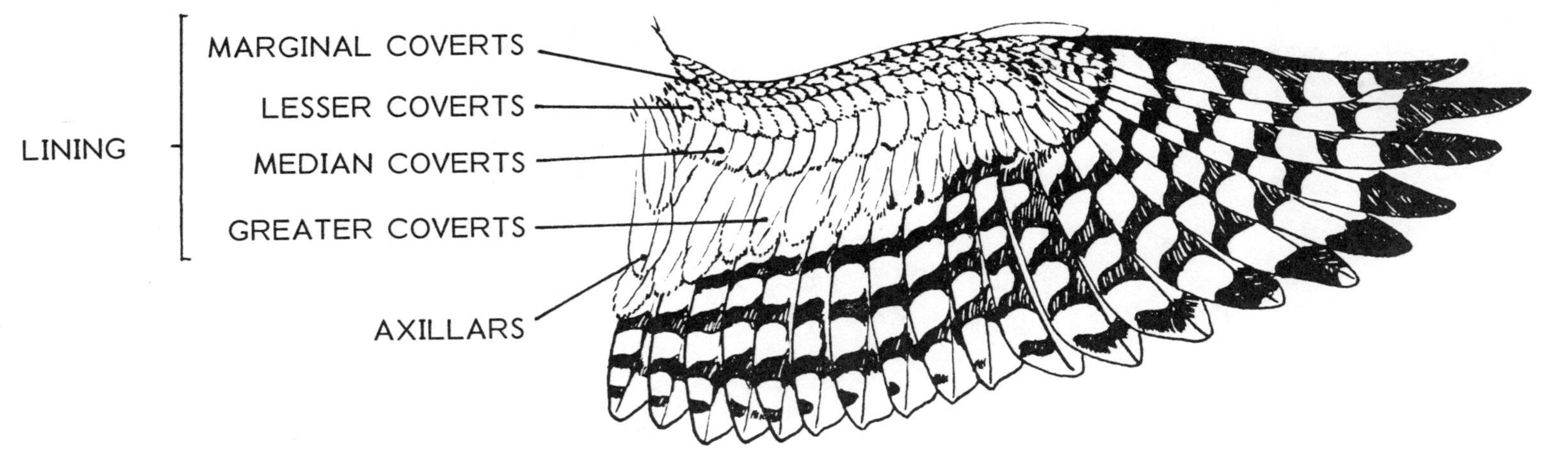

HOW THE WING FOLDS

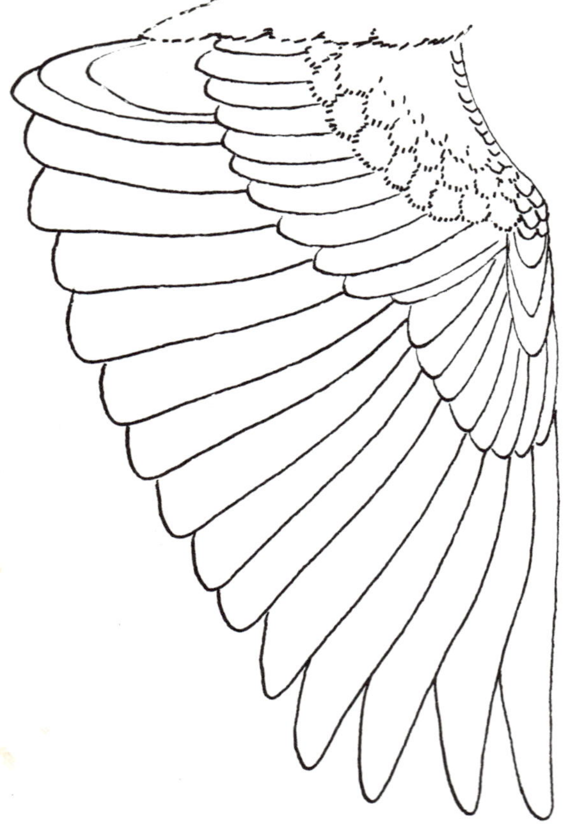

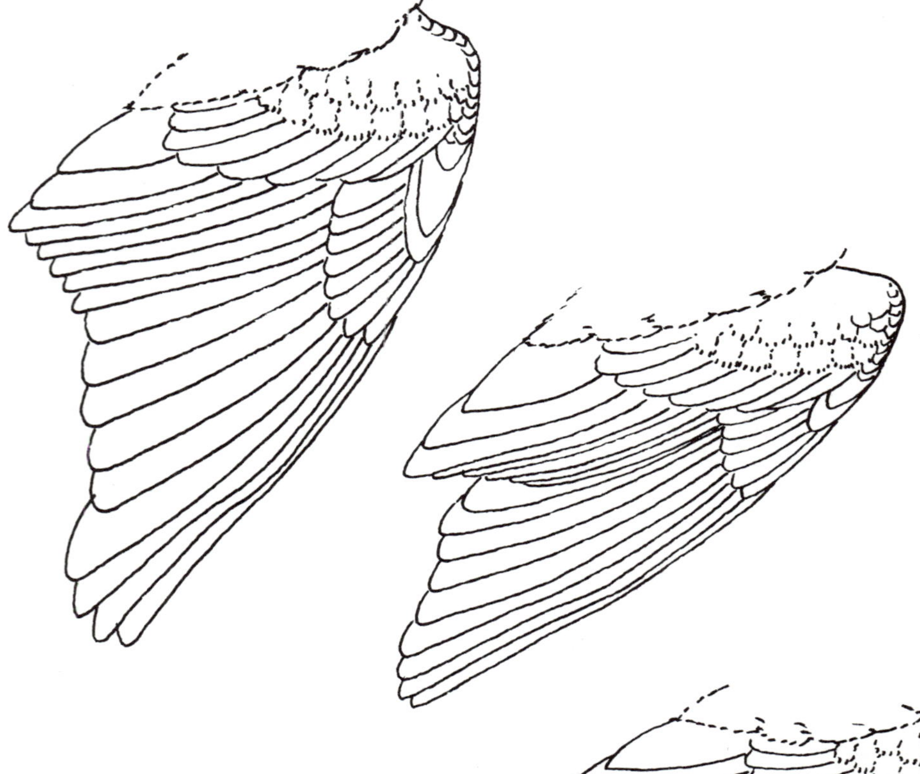

THE PRIMARIES & SECONDARIES SLIDE CLOSED UNDER THE GREATER COVERTS

WITH THE WING FOLDED THE SECONDARIES OVERLAP THE EDGES OF THE LAST FEW PRIMARIES

THE NUMBER OF MIDDLE & LESSER COVERTS SHOWING DEPENDS ON HOW FAR THE WRIST IS TUCKED IN

TYPES OF FEET

The tarsus is part of the birds foot, its skin is a horny covering which, in different species, takes on various patterns, the most common are booted, scutellate and reticulate.

The hallux, or first toe, is pointed backwards and may be elevated, on the same level as the other toes or nonexistant.

SMOOTH OR BOOTED TARSUS
e.g., ROBIN

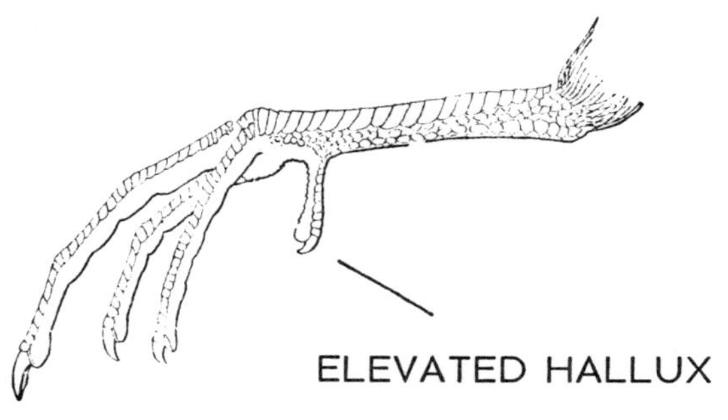

ELEVATED HALLUX

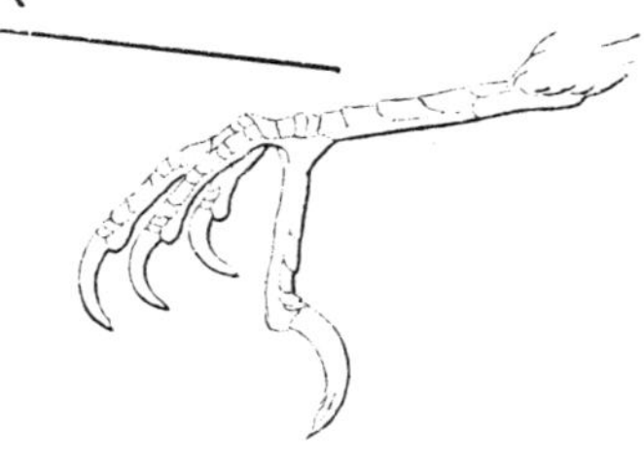

OVERLAPPING SCALES OR SCUTELLATE TARSUS
e.g., NUTHATCH

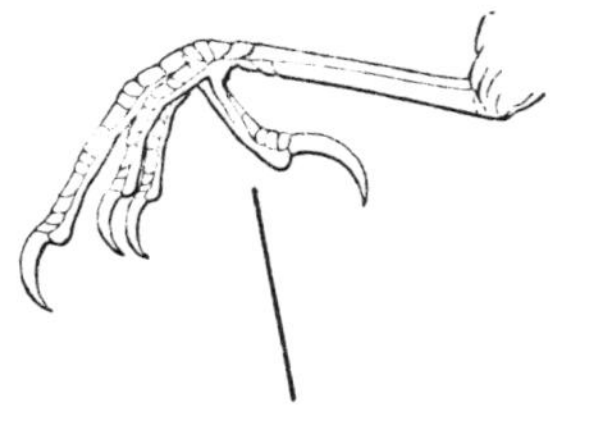

INCUMBENT HALLUX

PLATED OR RETICULATE TARSUS
e.g., PLOVER

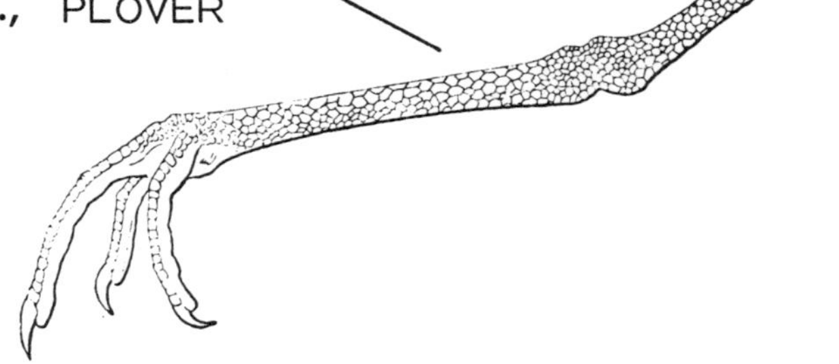

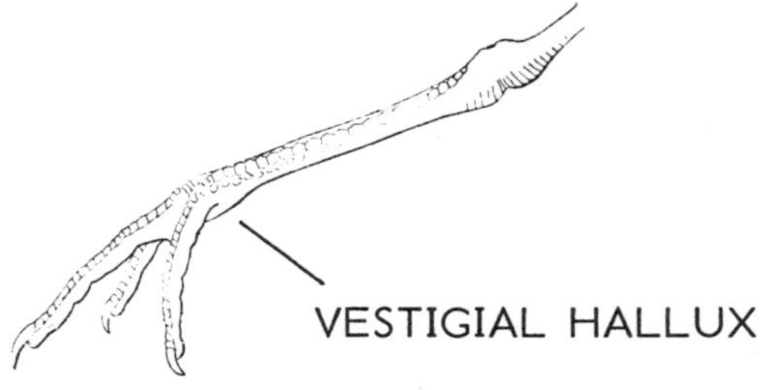

VESTIGIAL HALLUX

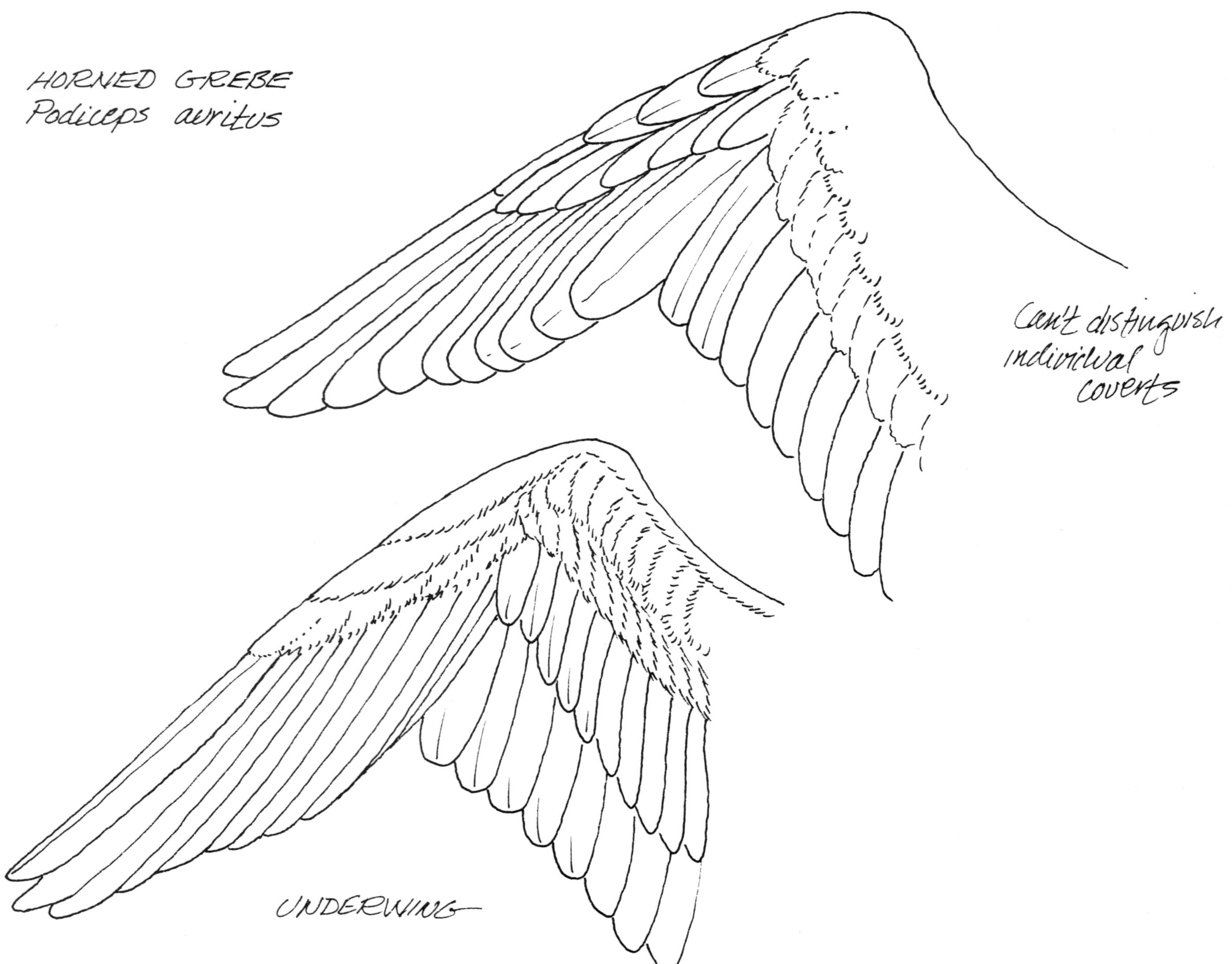
HORNED GREBE
Podiceps auritus
Can't distinguish
individual
coverts
UNDERWING

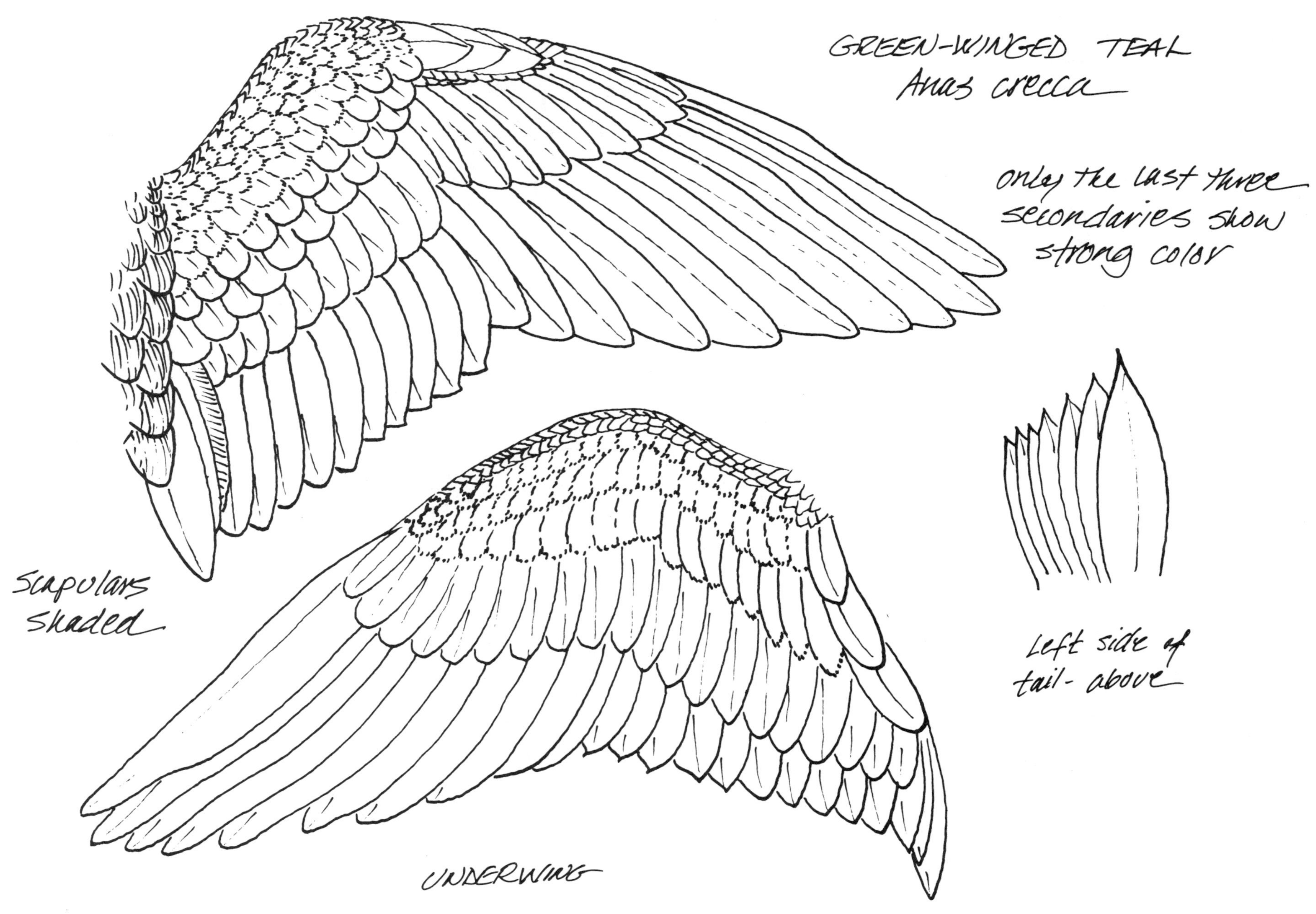
GREEN-WINGED TEAL
Anas crecca
Only the last three
secondaries show
strong color
Scapulars
shaded
Left side of
tail- above
UNDERWING

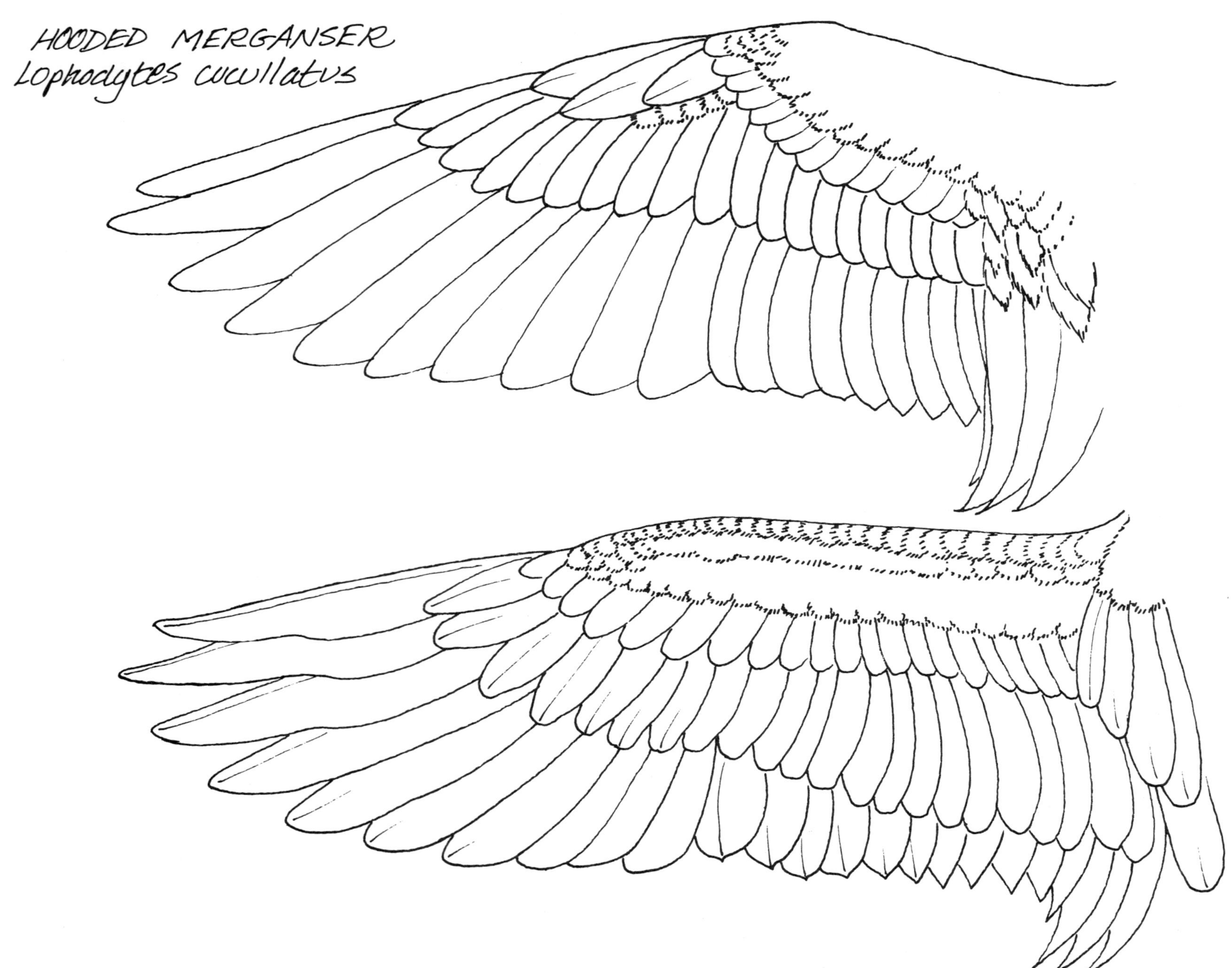
HOODED MERGANSER
Lophodytes cucullatus

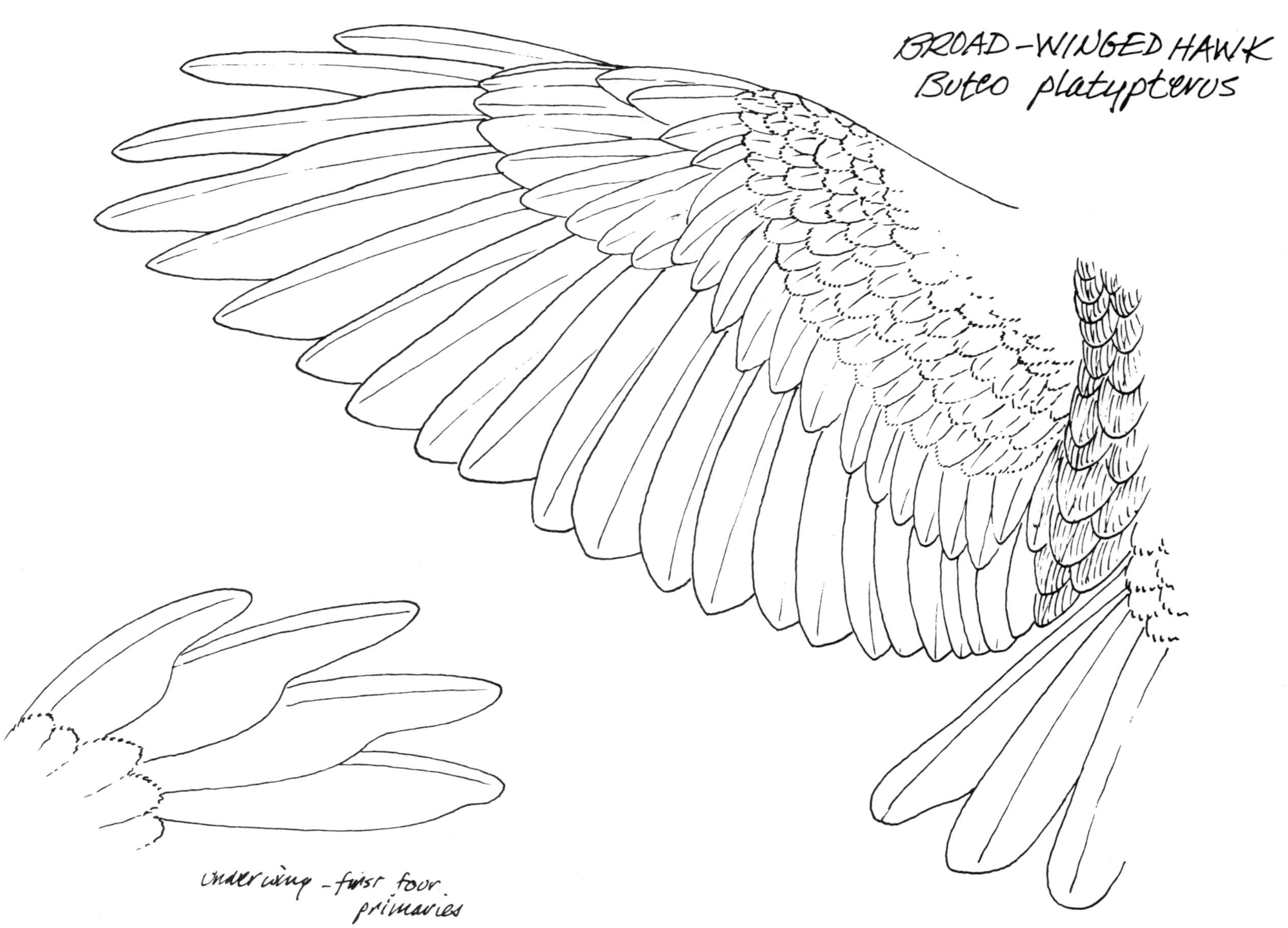

underwing - first four primaries

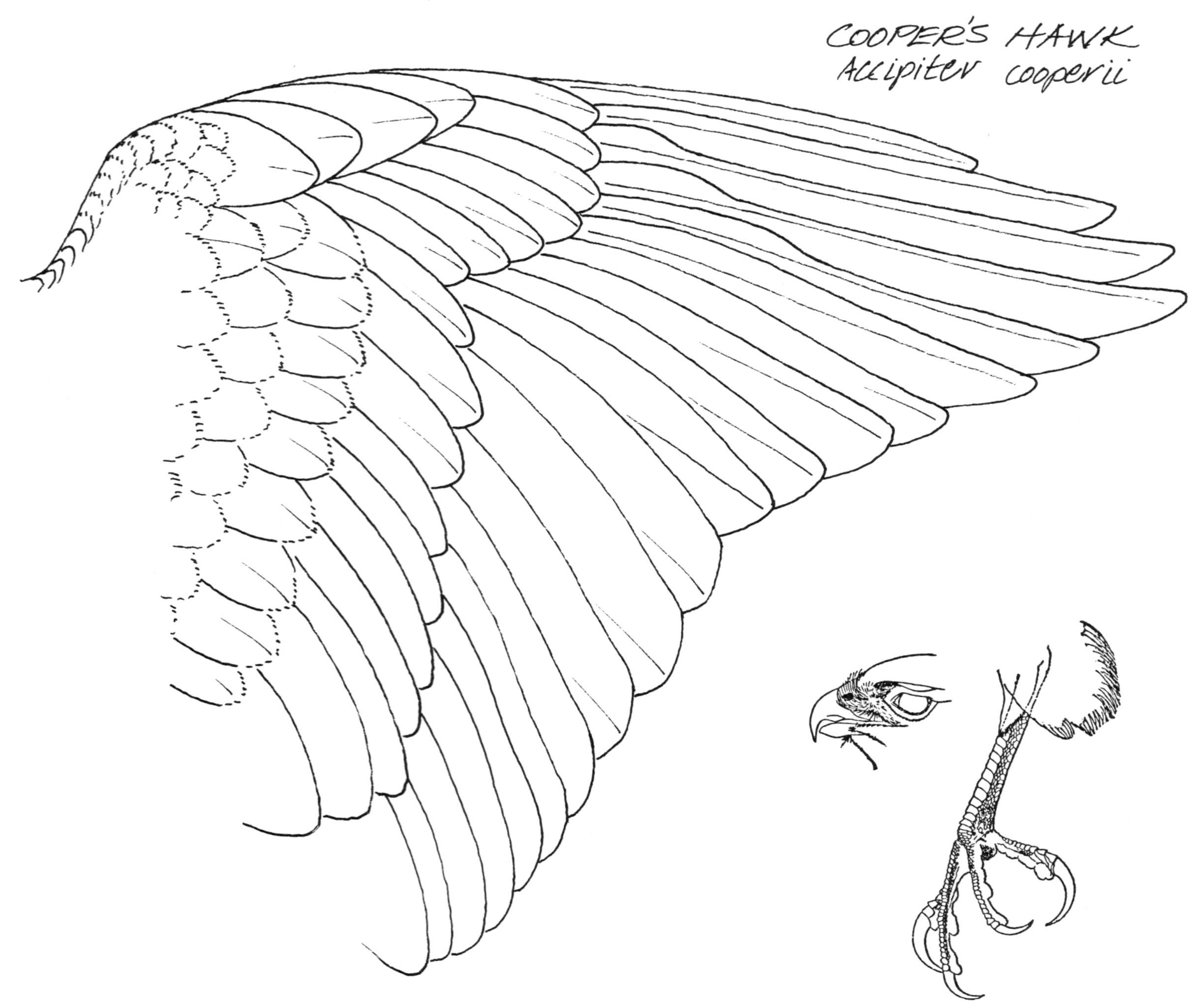
COOPER'S HAWK
Accipiter cooperii

COOPER'S HAWK

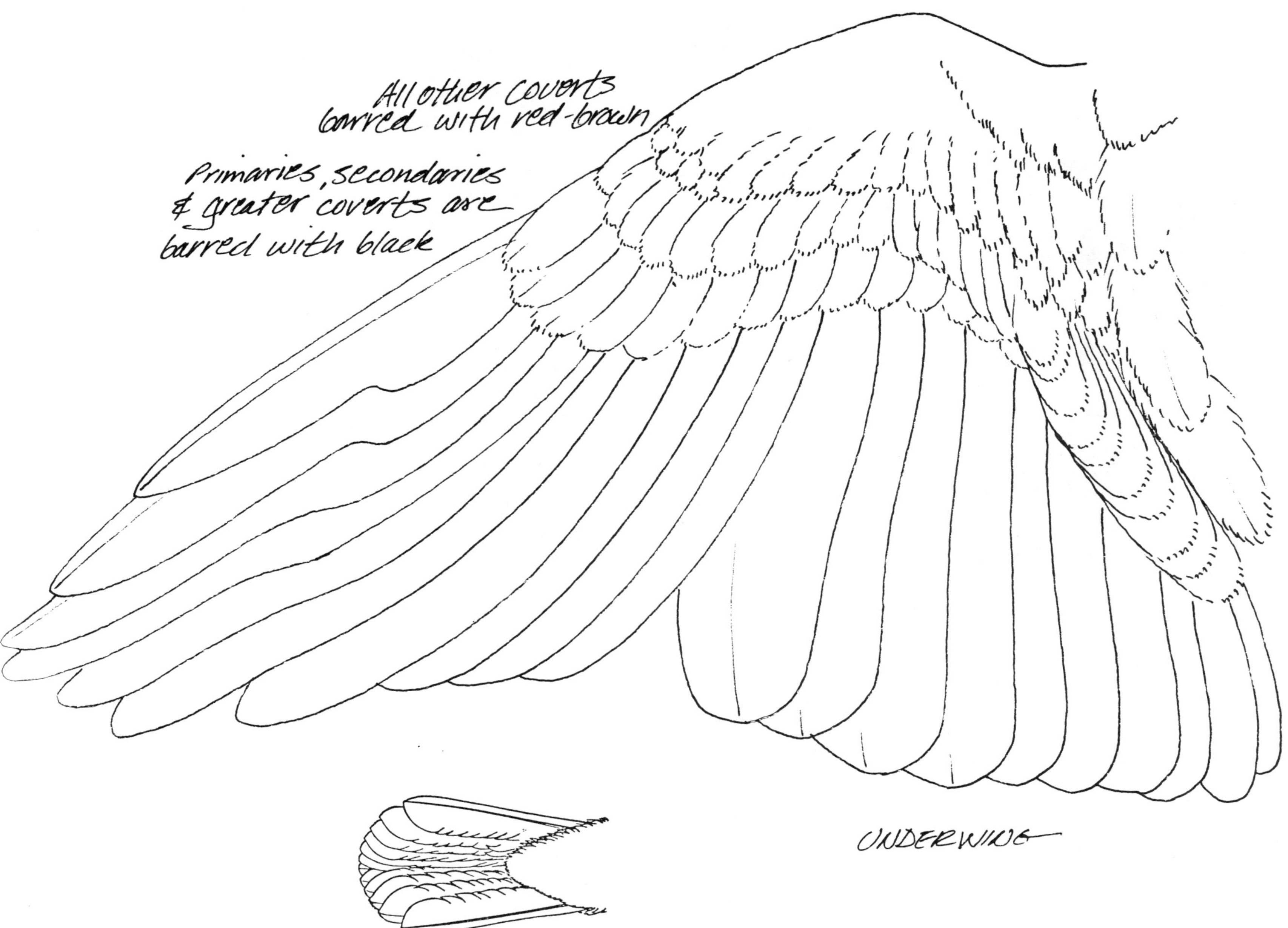

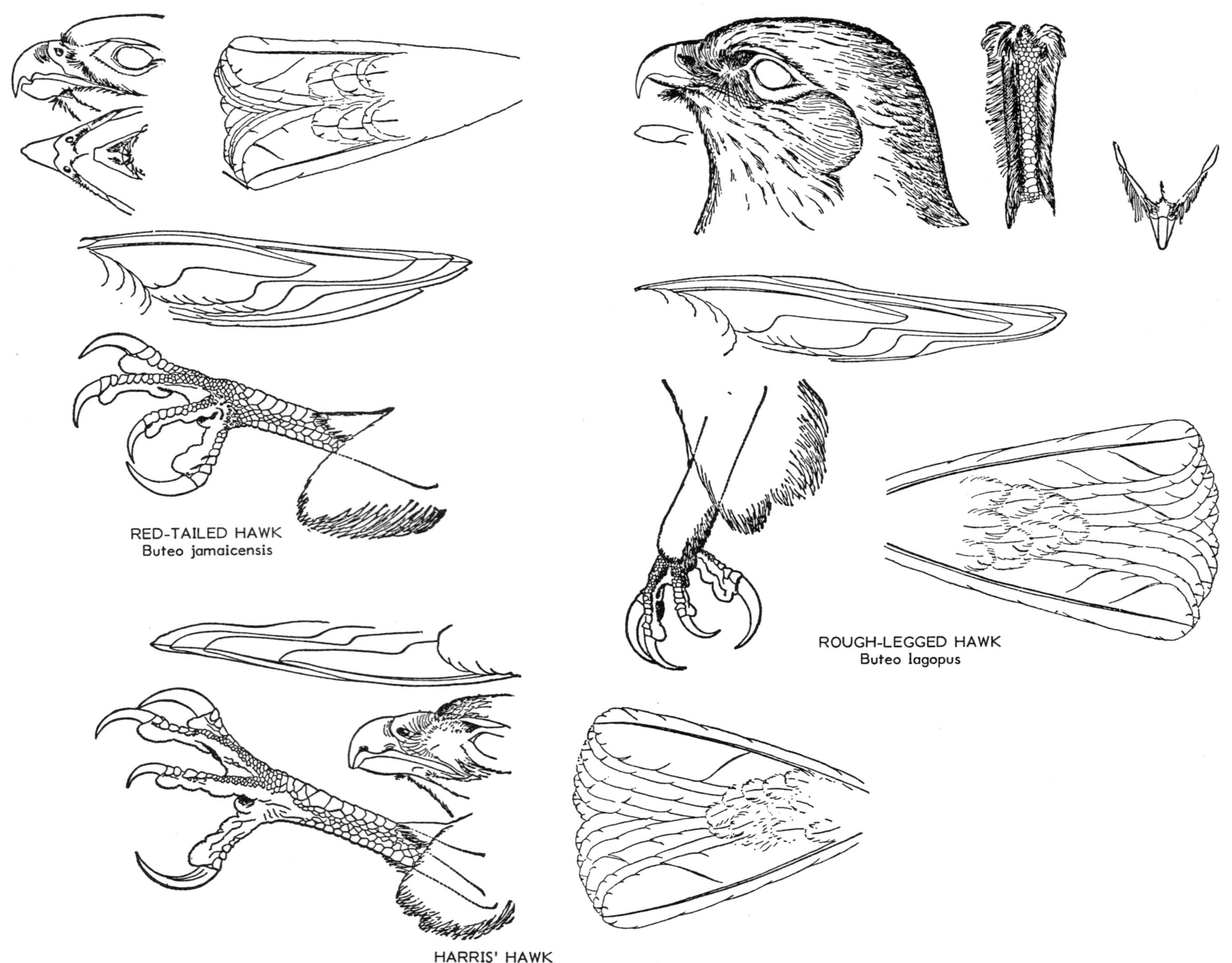
RED-TAILED HAWK
Buteo jamaicensis
ROUGH-LEGGED HAWK
Buteo lagopus
HARRIS' HAWK
Parabuteo unicinctus

AMERICAN KESTREL
Falco sparverius

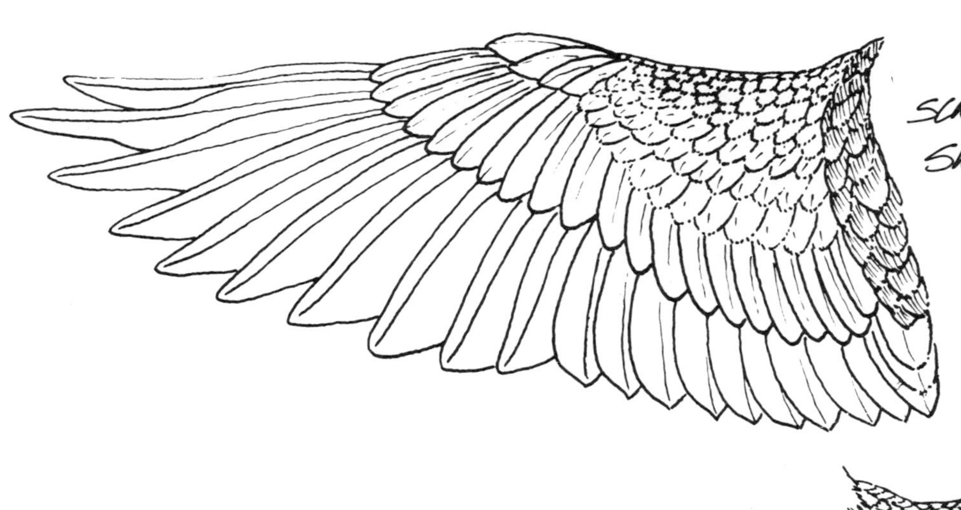

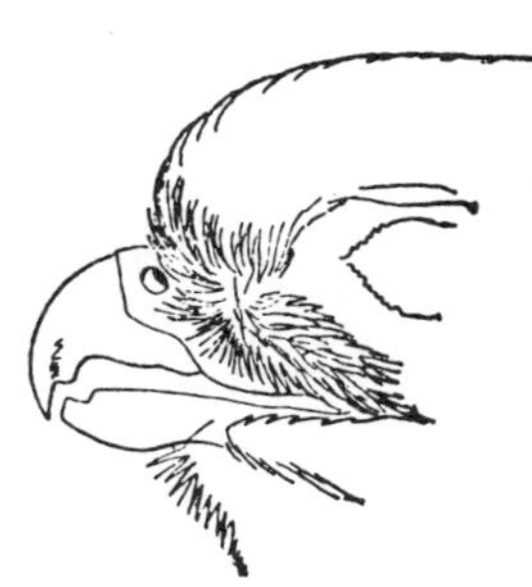

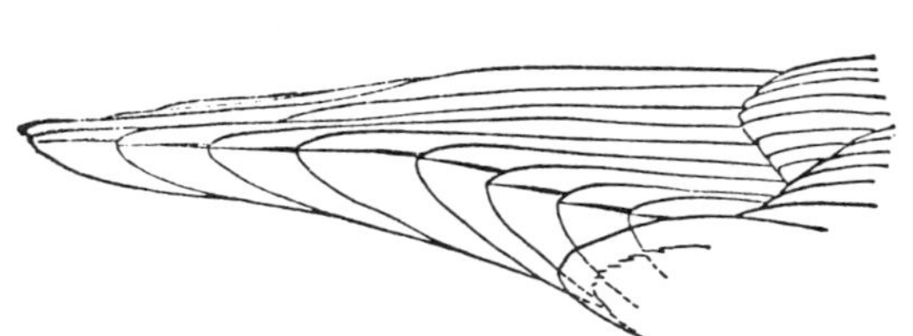

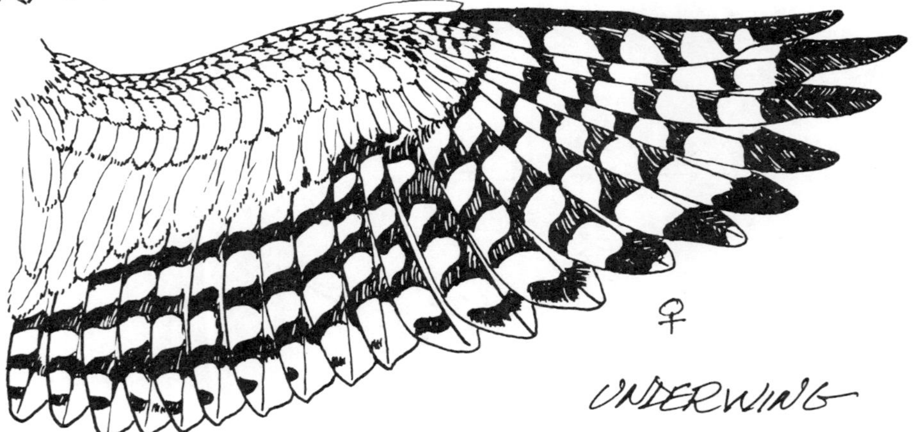

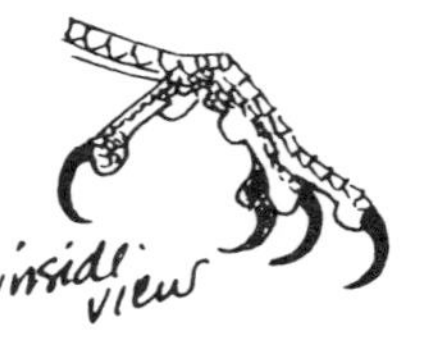

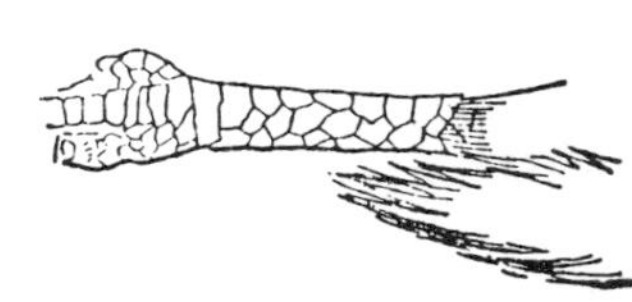

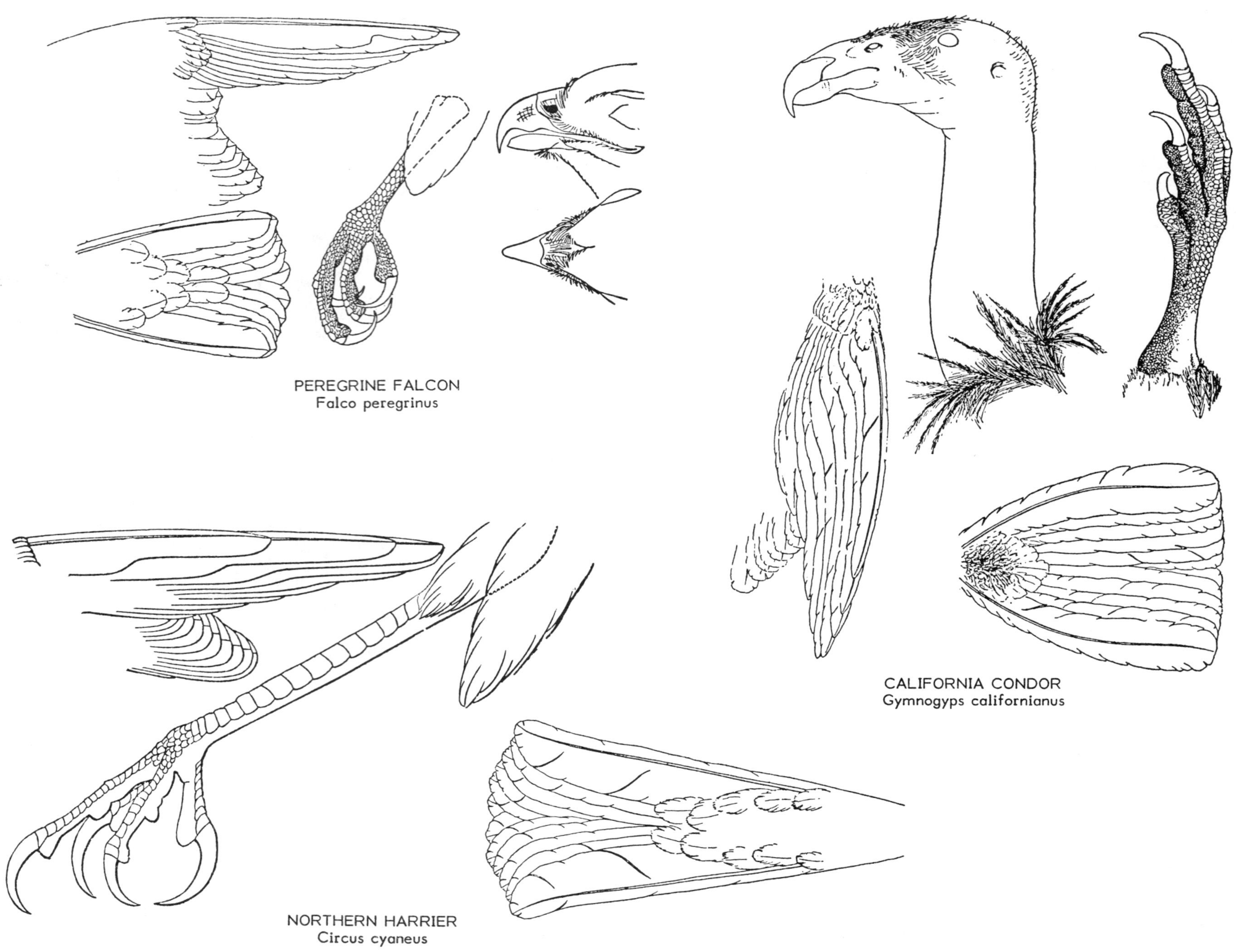
PEREGRINE FALCON
Falco peregrinus
CALIFORNIA CONDOR
Gymnogyps californianus
NORTHERN HARRIER
Circus cyaneus

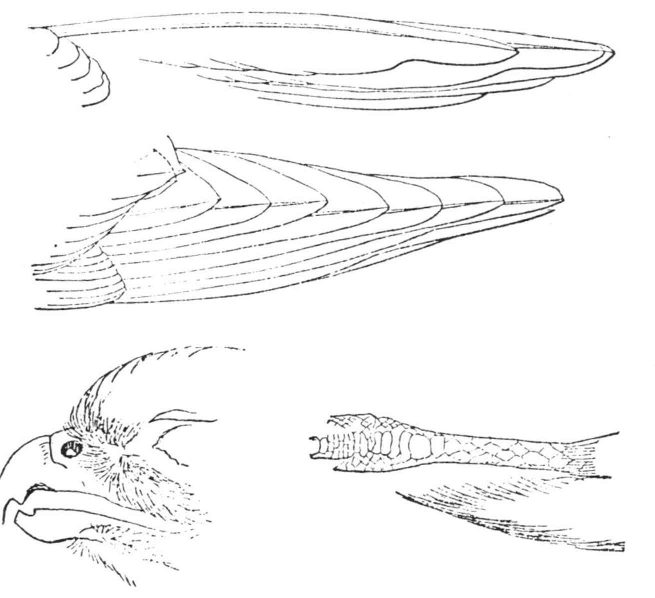

MERLIN
Falco columbarius

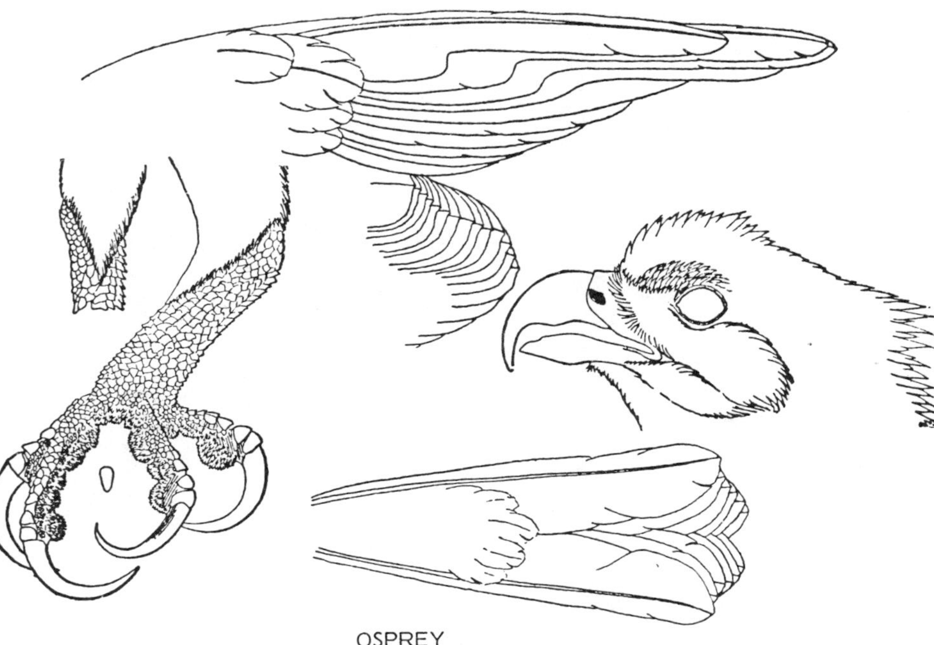

OSPREY
Pandion haliaetus

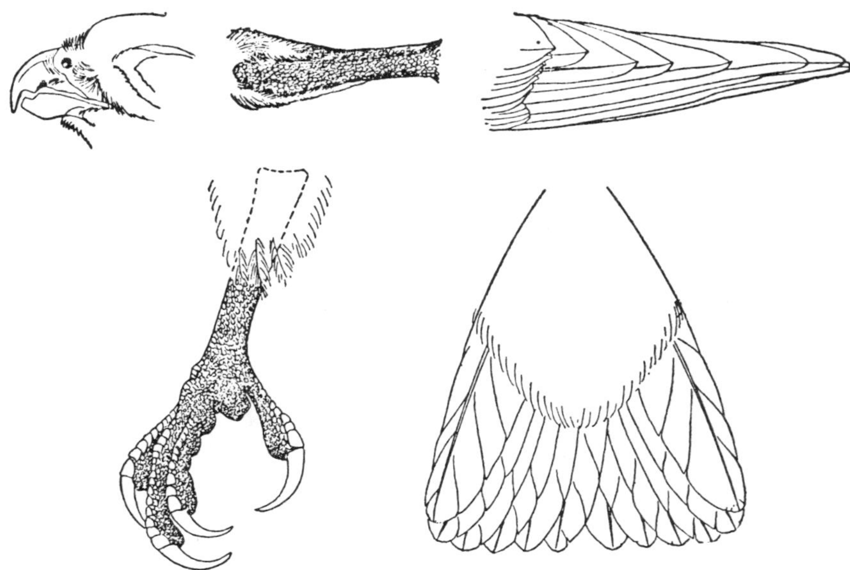

PRAIRIE FALCON
Falco mexicanus

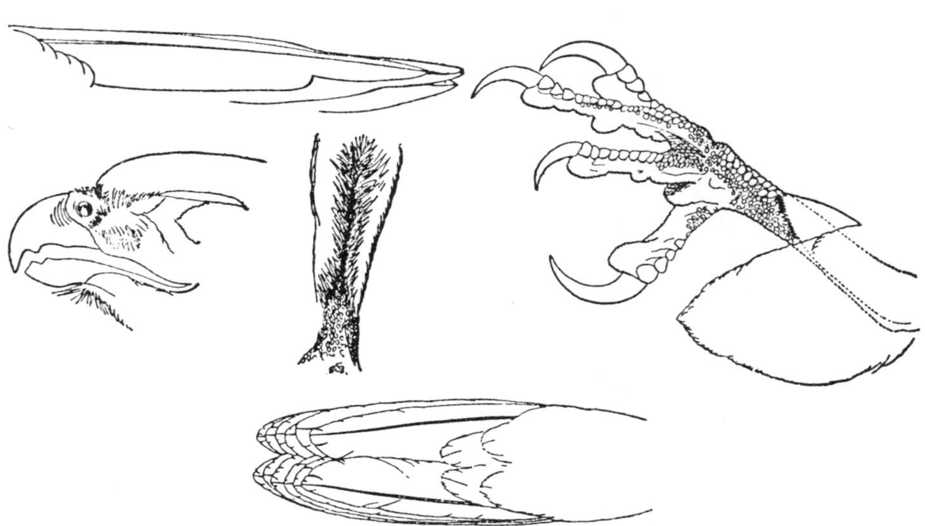

GYRFALCON
Falco rusticolus

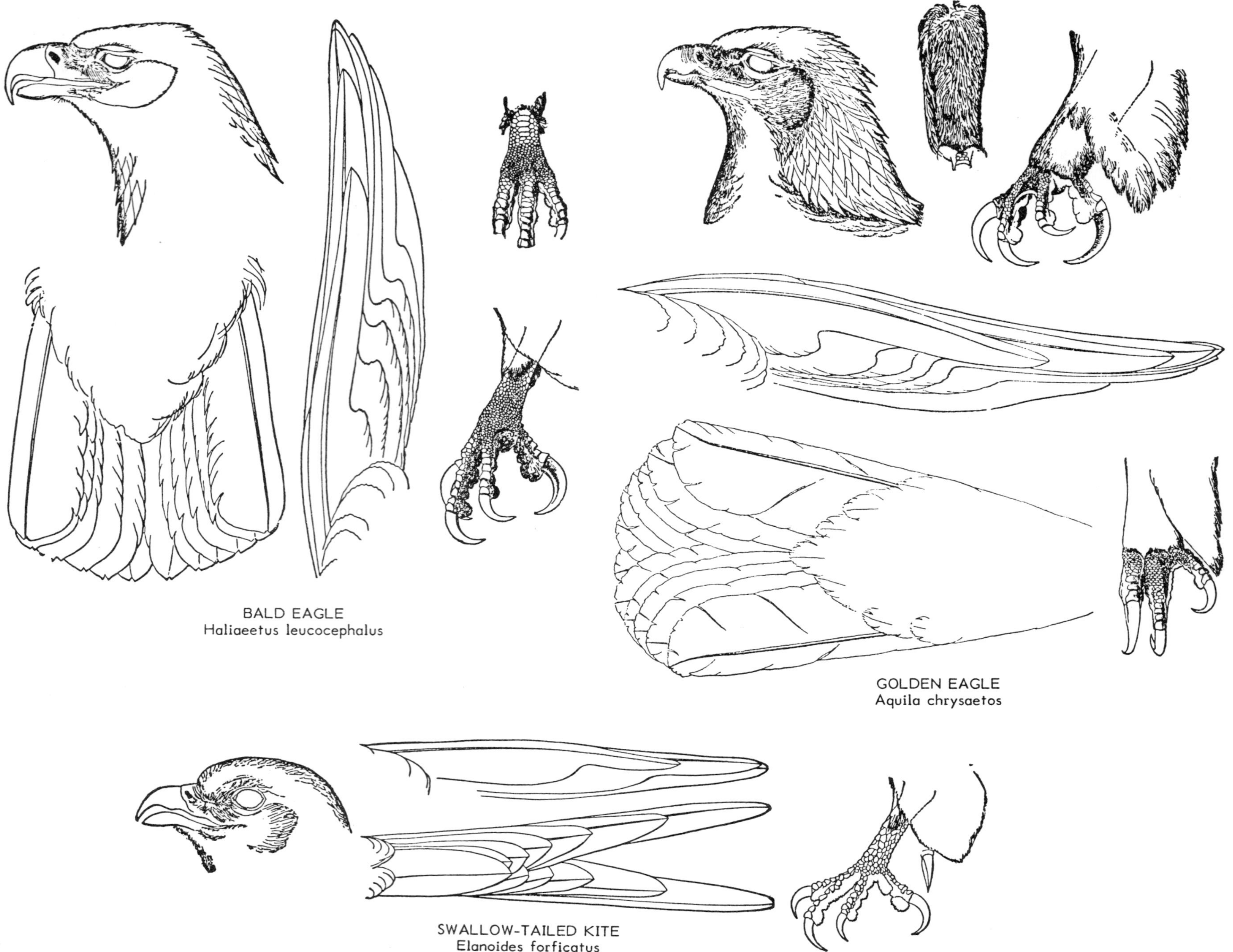
BALD EAGLE
Haliaeetus leucocephalus
GOLDEN EAGLE
Aquila chrysaetos
SWALLOW-TAILED KITE
Elanoides forficatus

RUFFED GROUSE
Bonasa umbellus

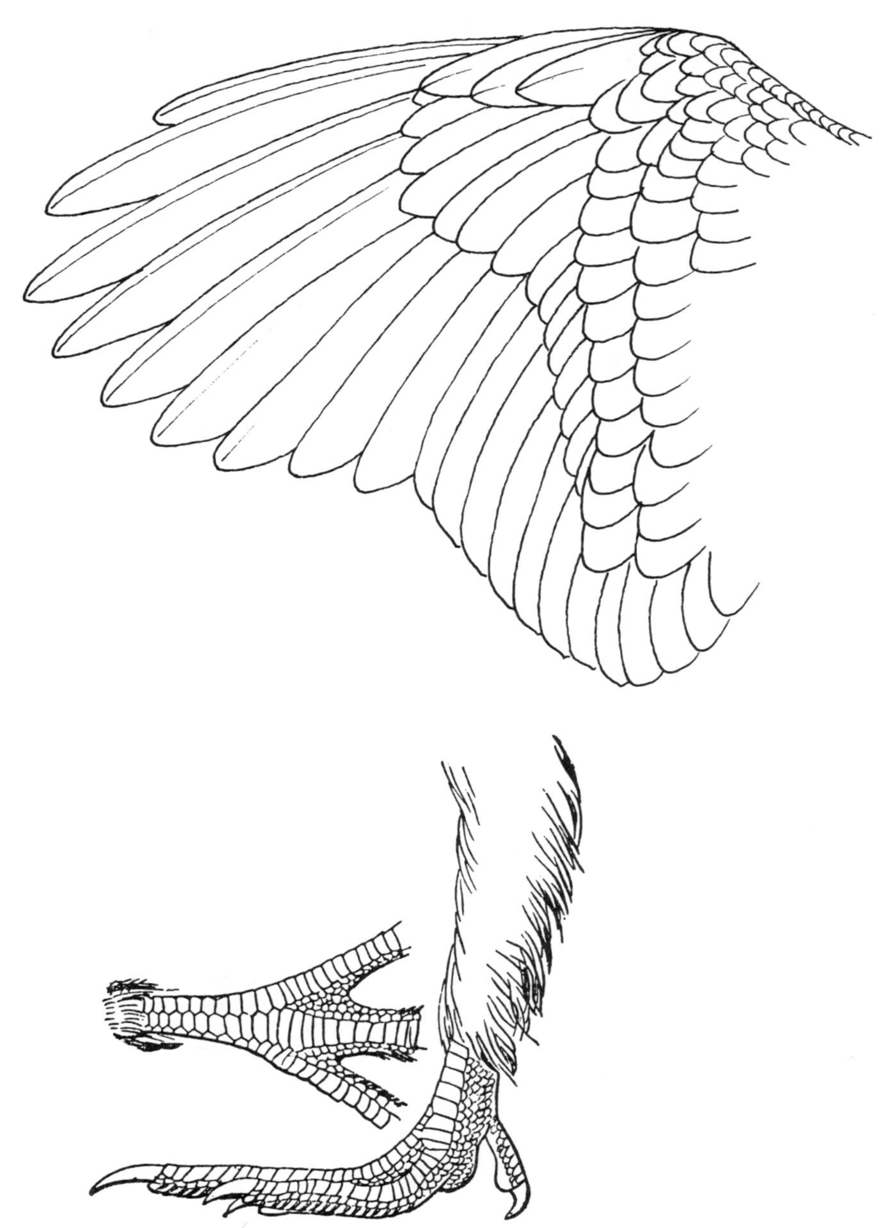

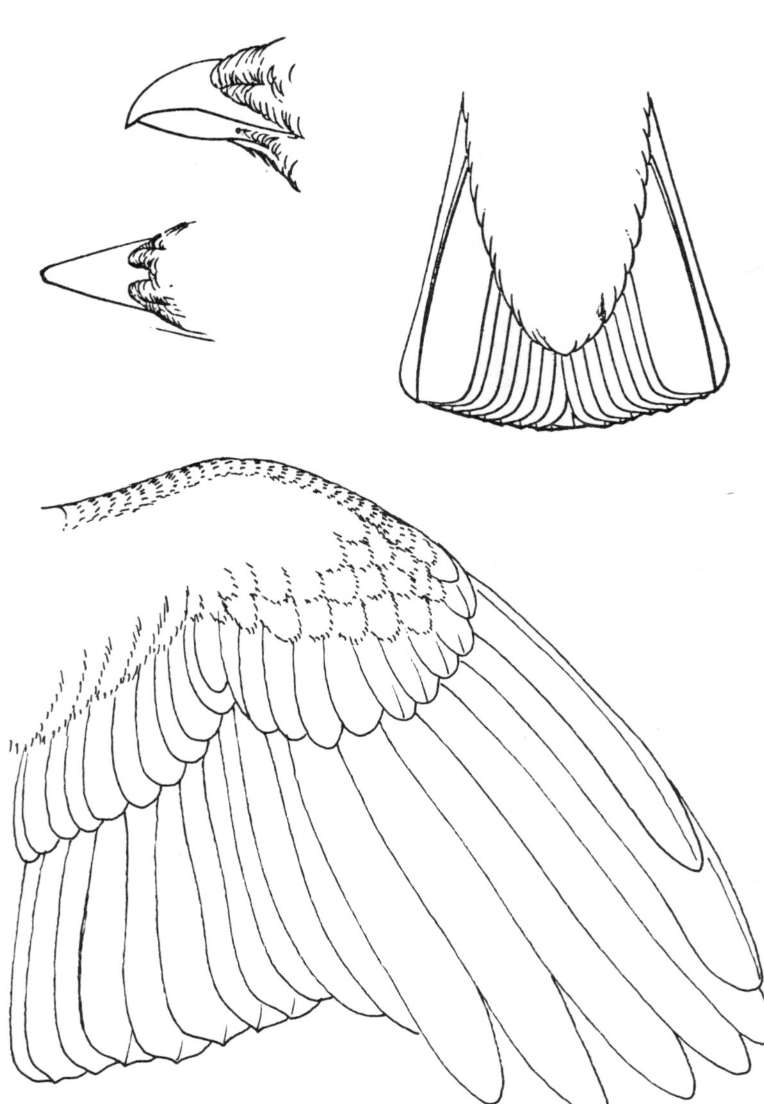

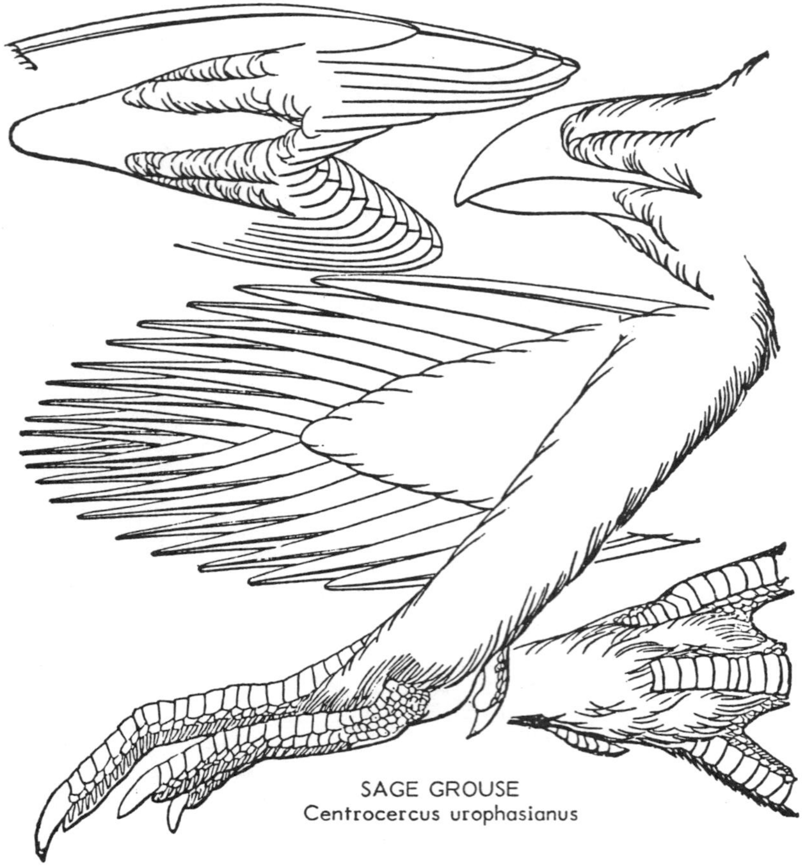

SAGE GROUSE
Centrocercus urophasianus

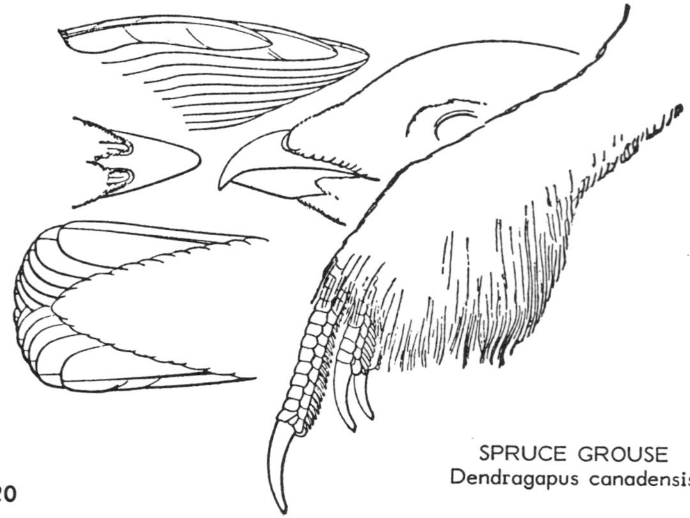

SPRUCE GROUSE
Dendragapus canadensis

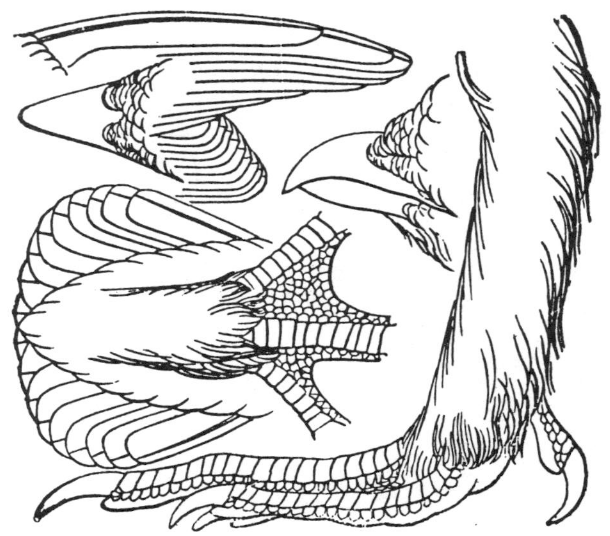

GREATER PRAIRIE CHICKEN
Tympanuchus cupido

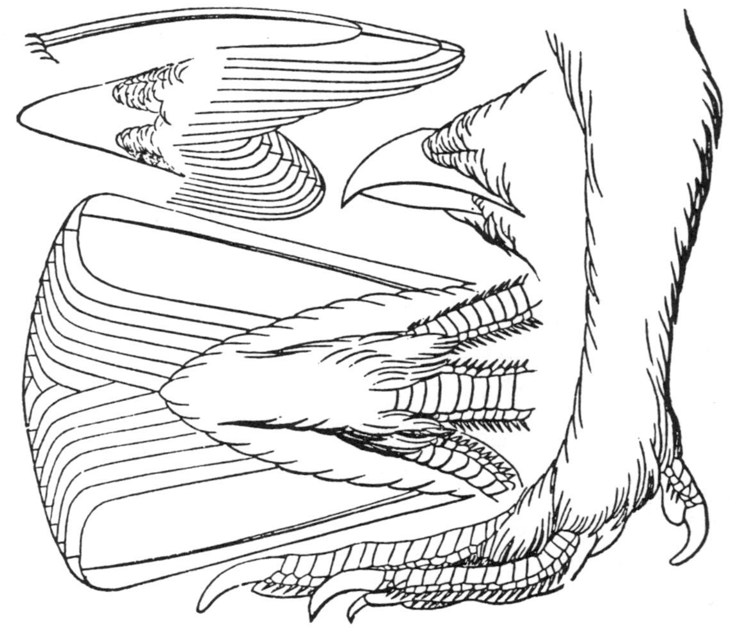

BLUE GROUSE
Dendragapus obscurus

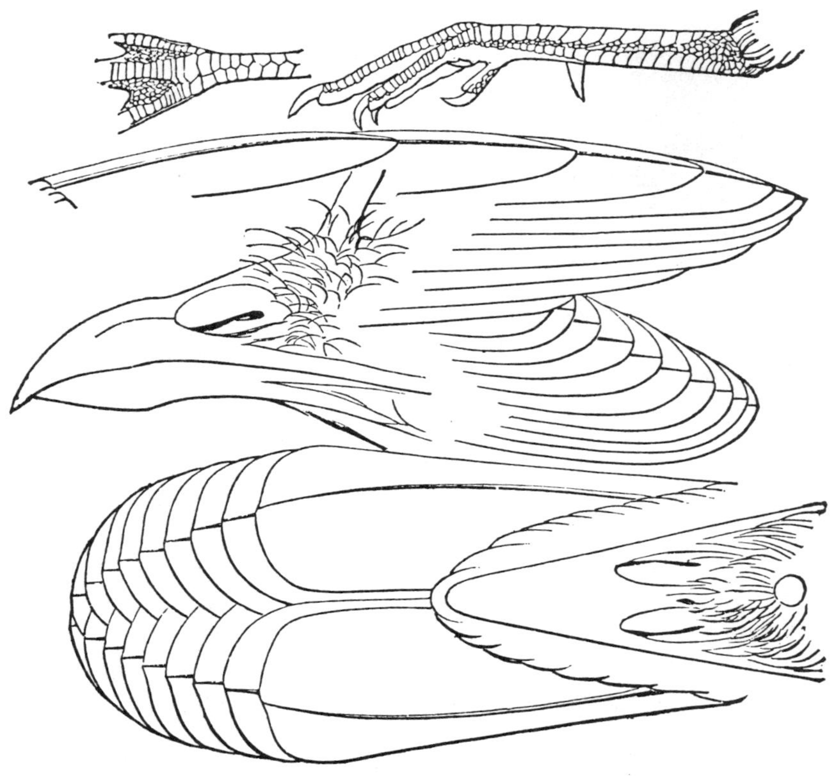

TURKEY
Meleagris gallopavo

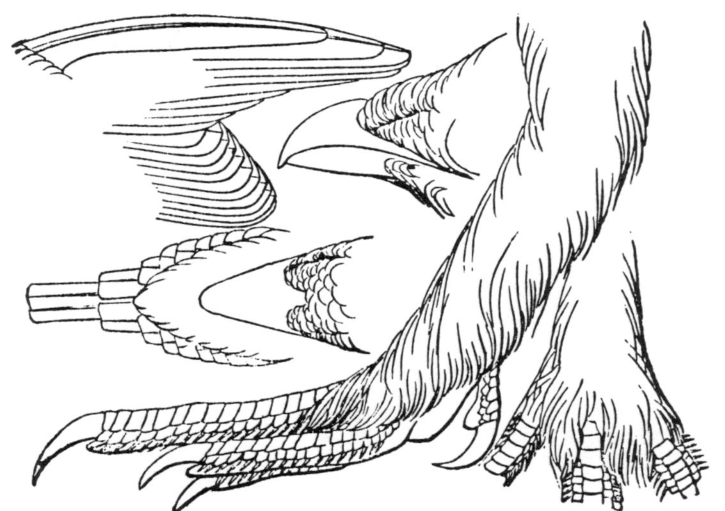

SHARP-TAILED GROUSE
Tympanuchus phasianellus

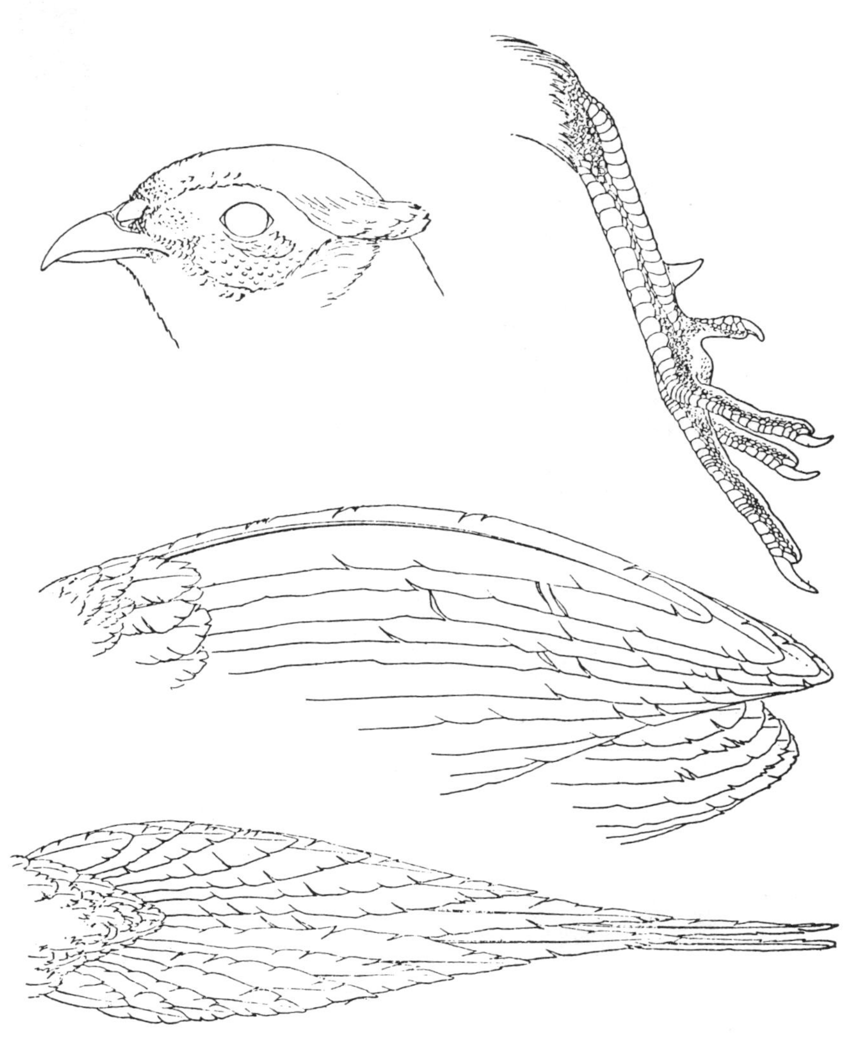

RING-NECKED PHESANT
Phasianus colchicus

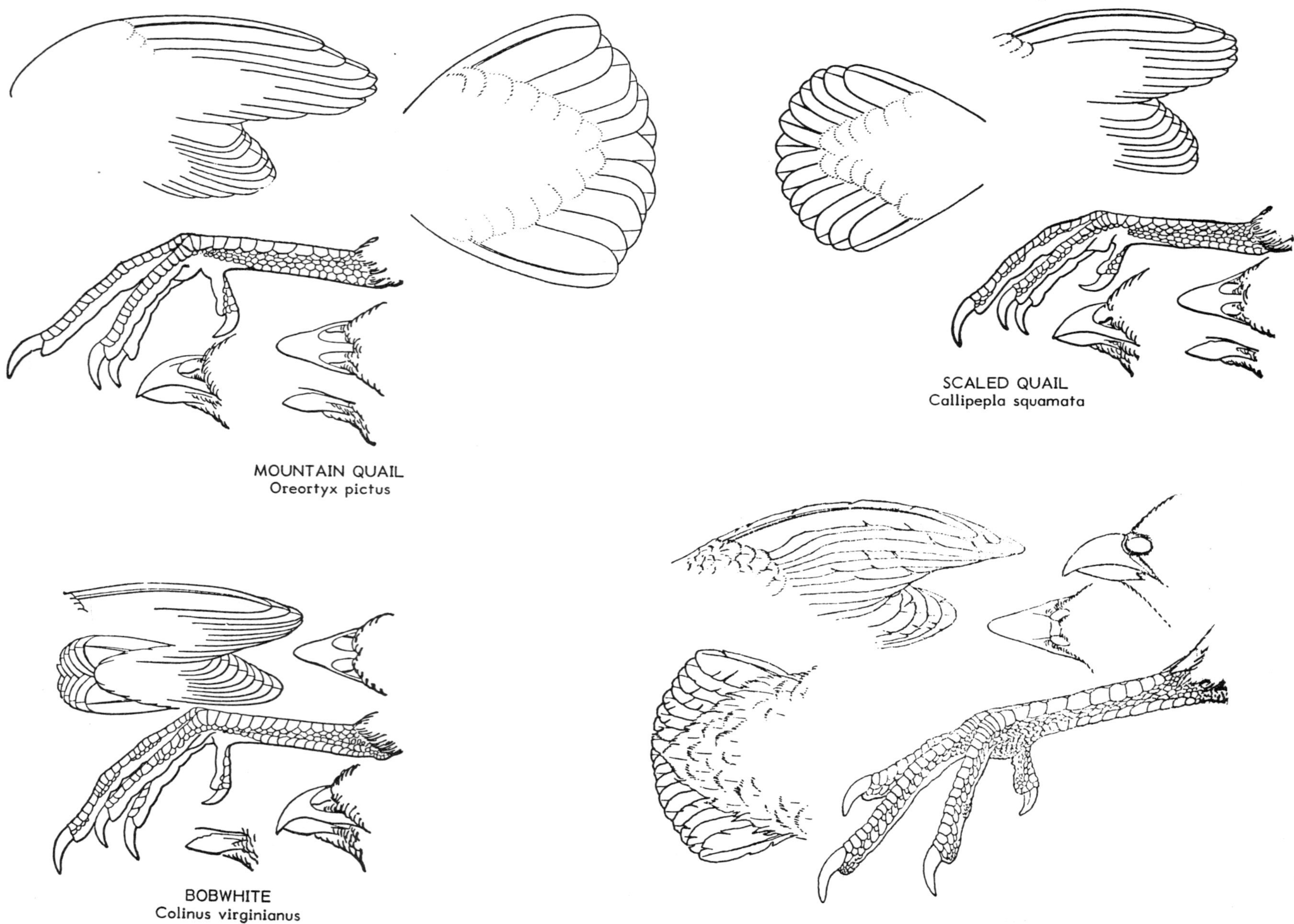
MOUNTAIN QUAIL
Oreortyx pictus
SCALED QUAIL
Callipepla squamata
BOBWHITE
Colinus virginianus
GRAY PARTRIDGE
Perdix perdix

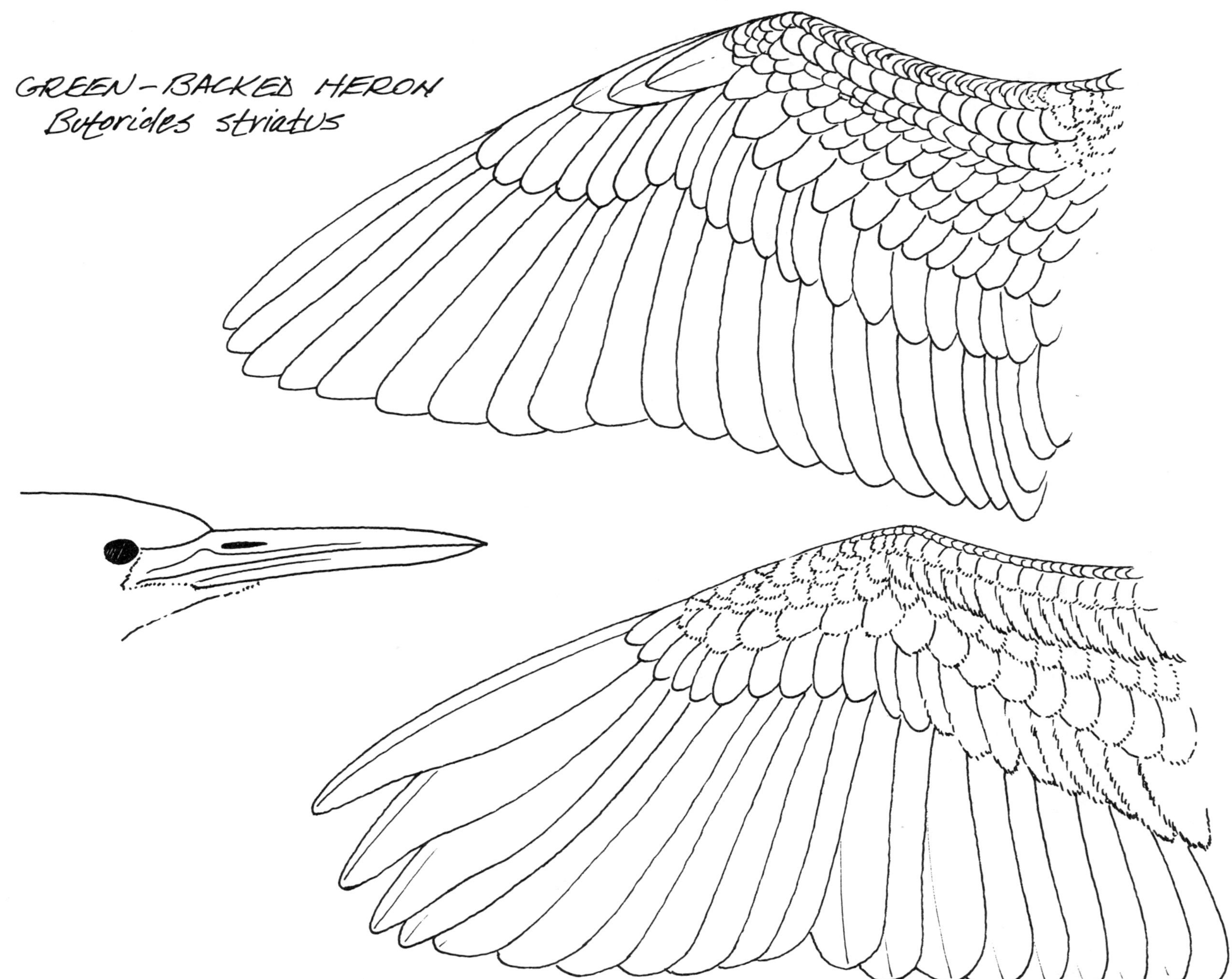
GREEN-BACKED HERON
Butorides striatus

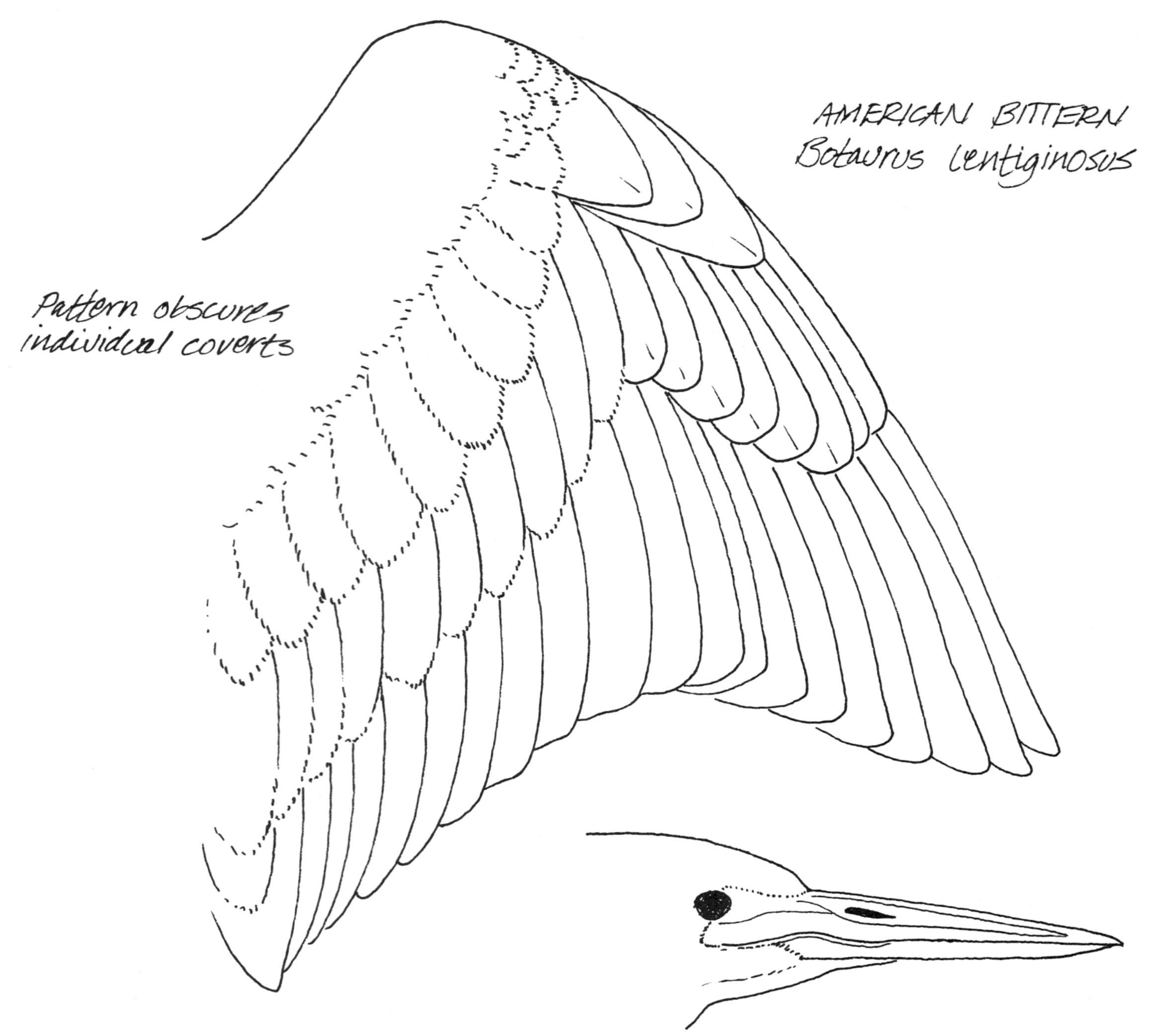
AMERICAN BITTERN
Botaurus lentiginosus
Pattern obscures
individual coverts

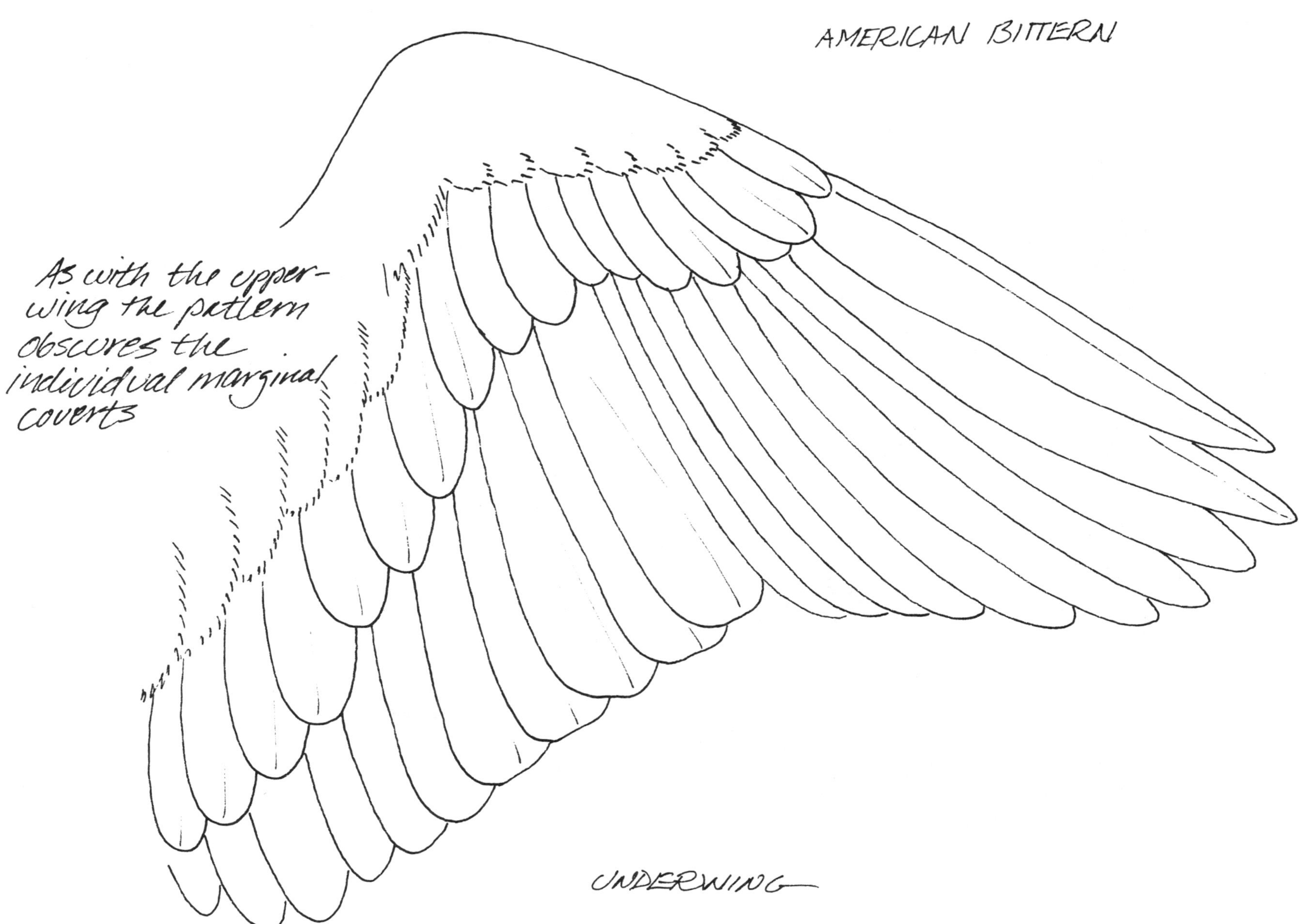
AMERICAN BITTERN
As with the upper-
wing the pattern
obscures the
individual marginal
coverts
UNDERWING

AMERICAN COOT

Fulica americana

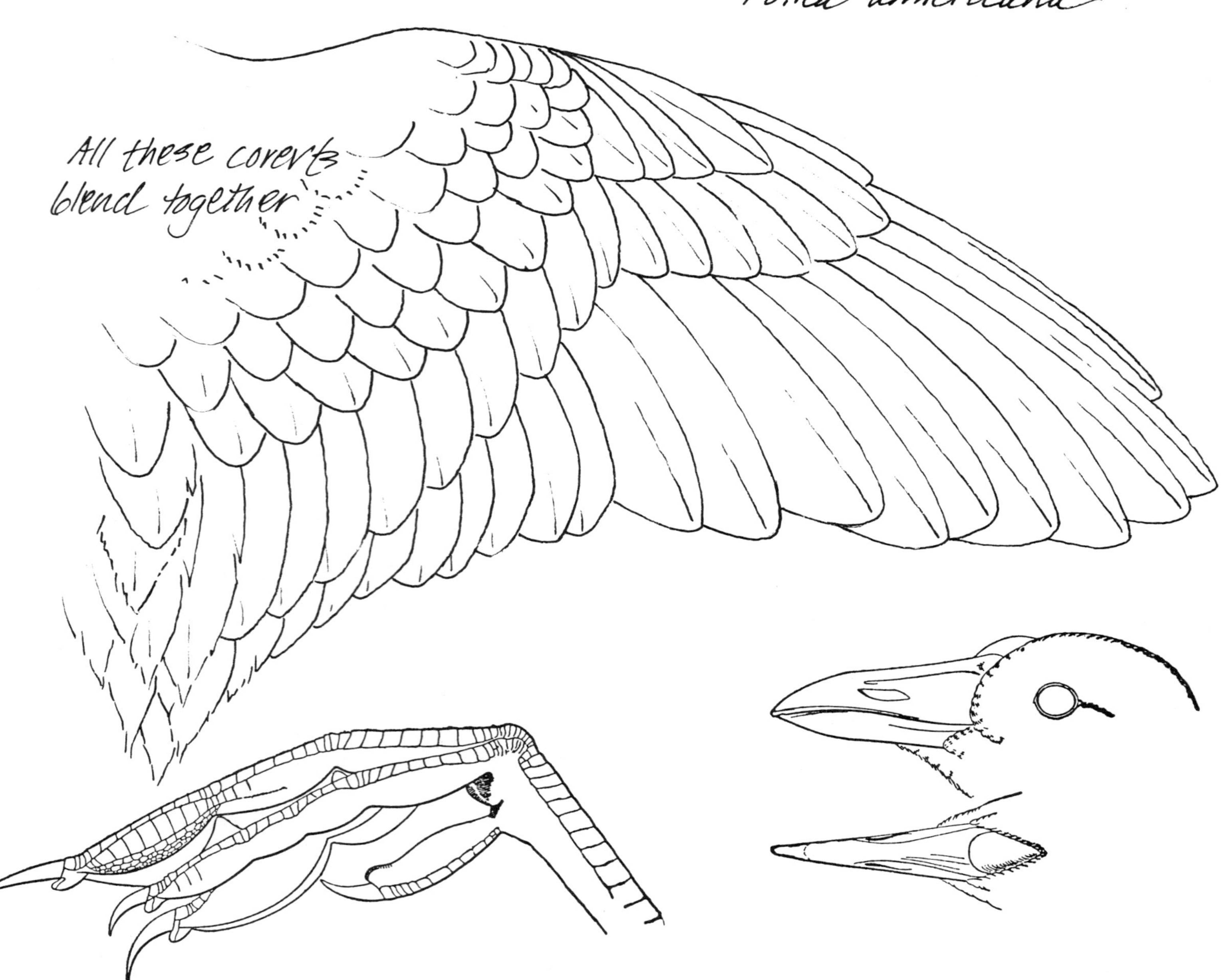

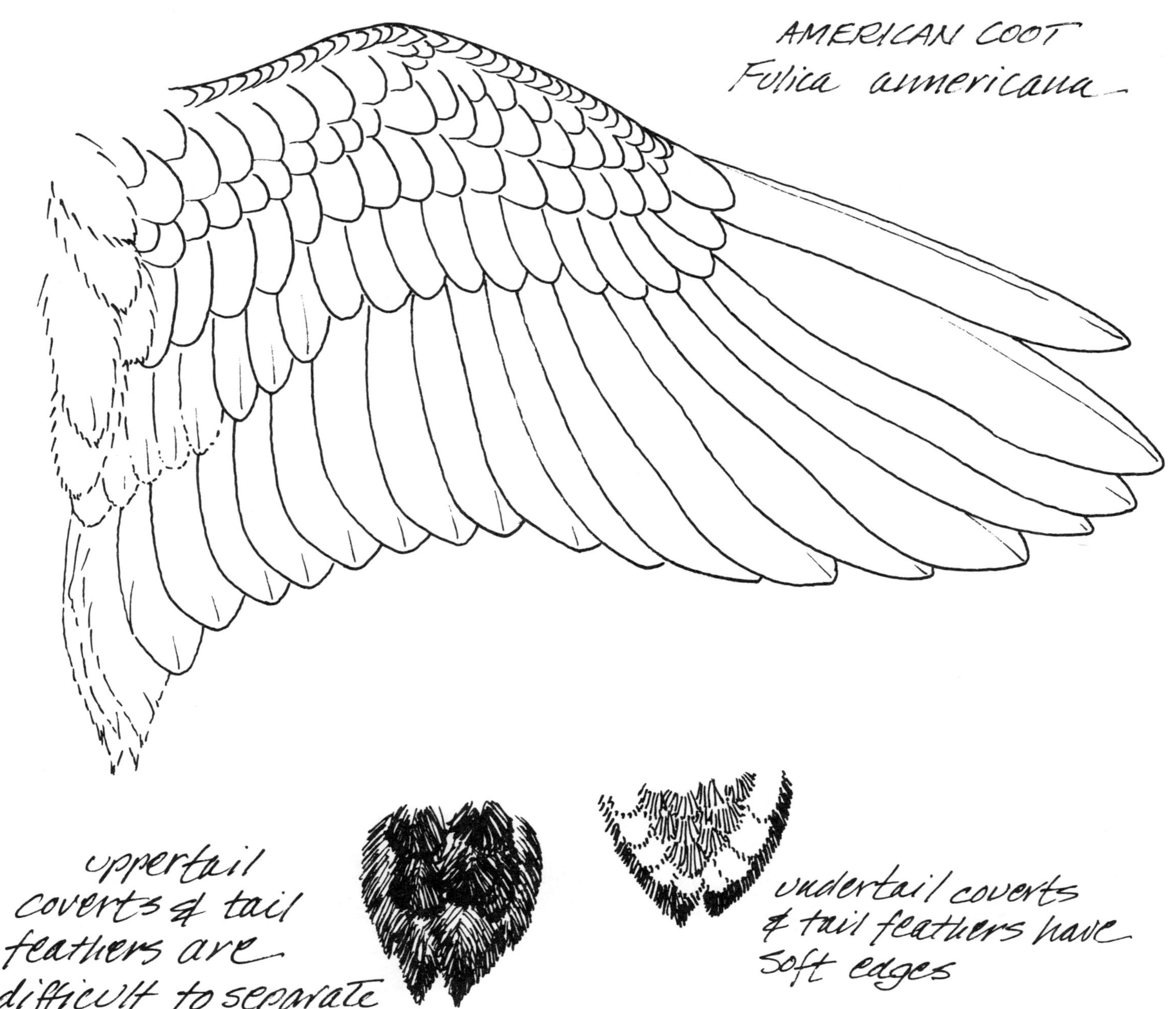
AMERICAN COOT
Fulica americana
uppertail coverts & tail feathers are difficult to separate
undertail coverts & tail feathers have soft edges

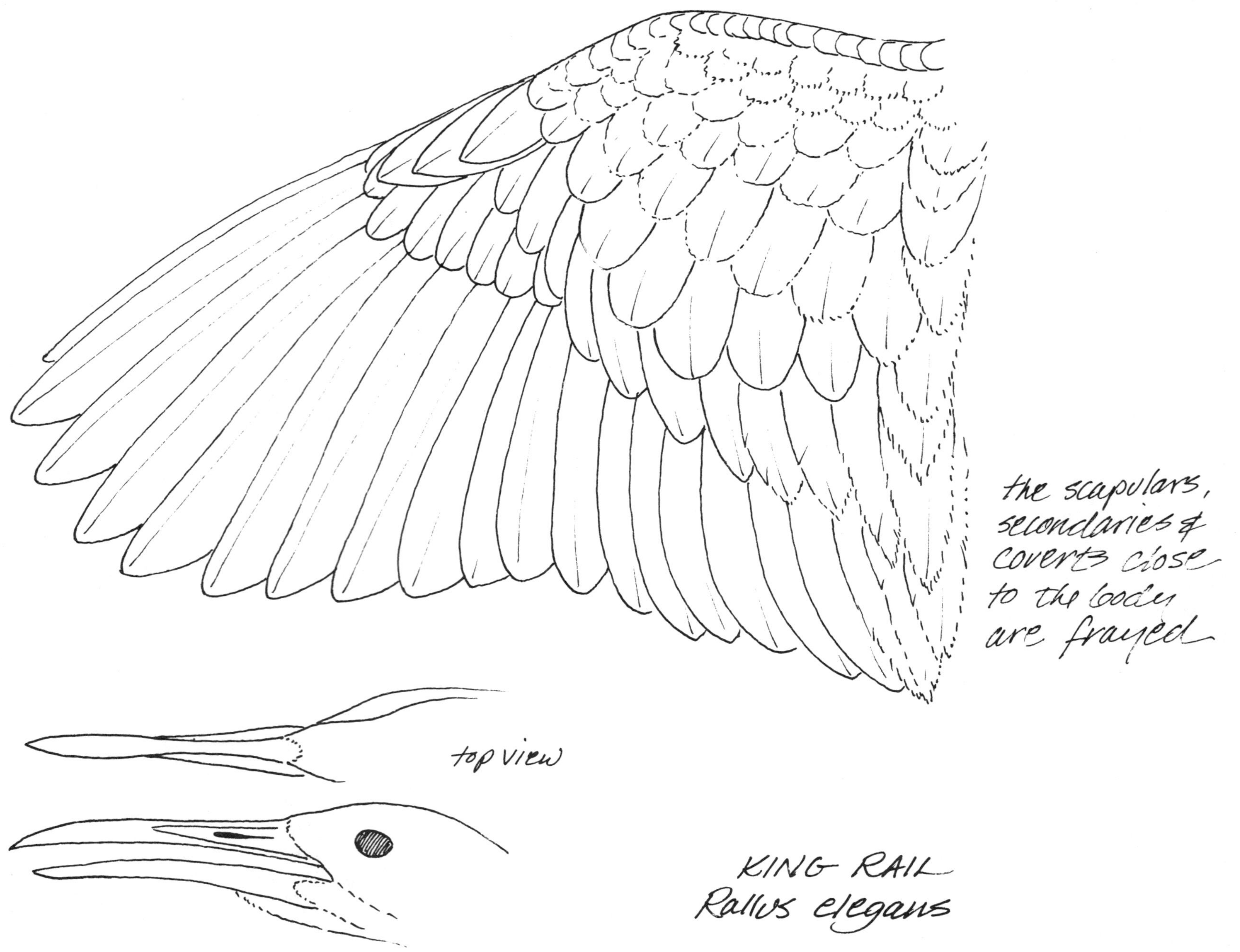

KING RAIL
Rallus elegans

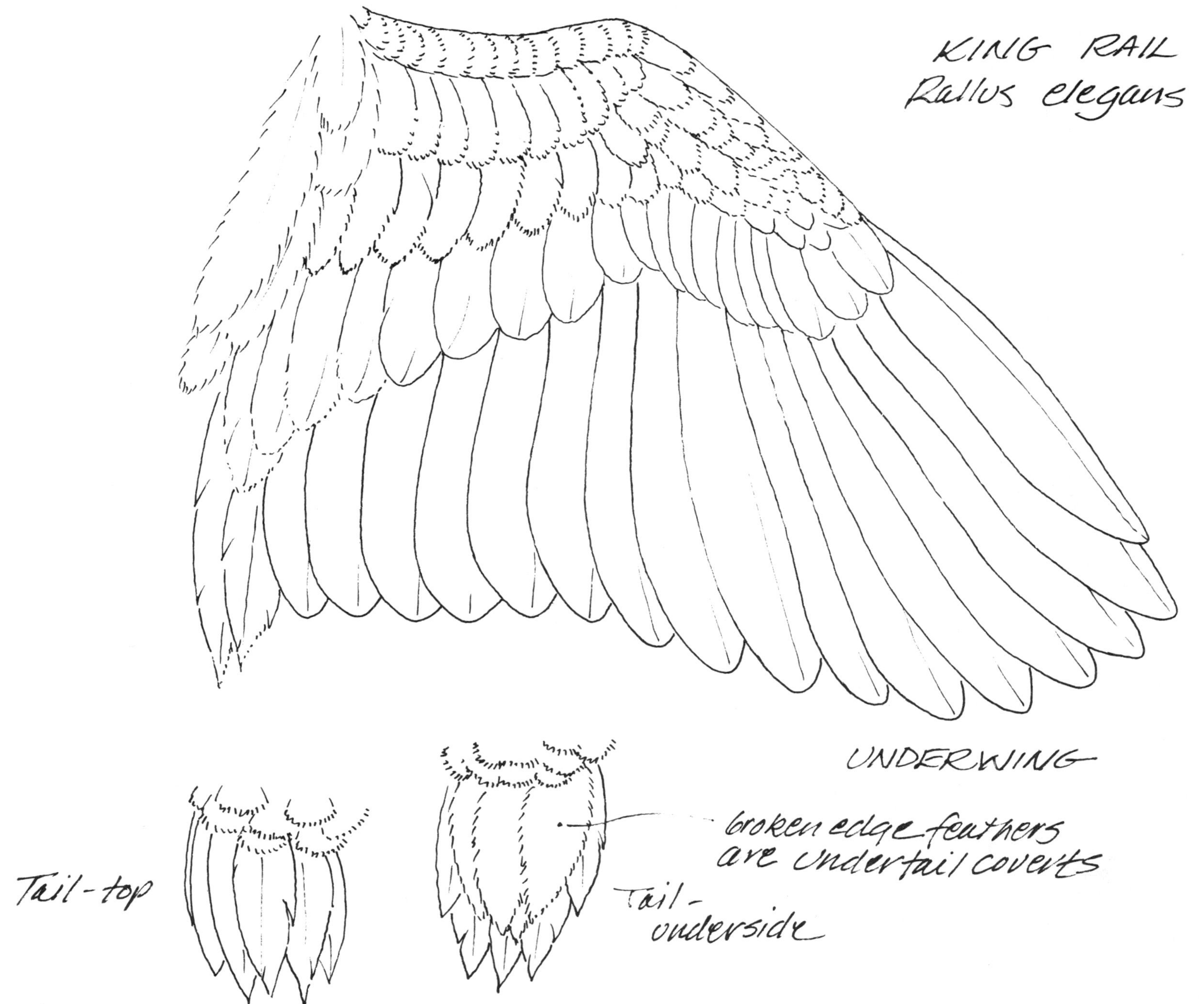
KING RAIL
Rallus elegans
UNDERWING
broken edge feathers
are undertail coverts
Tail-top
Tail-
underside

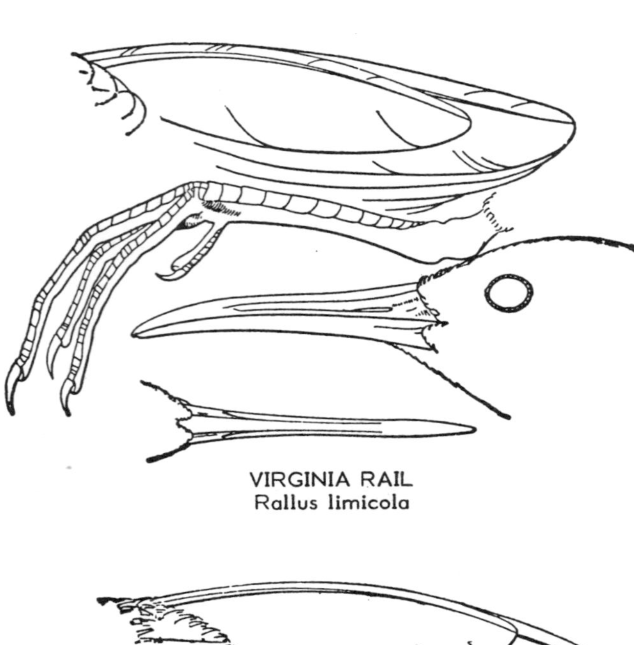

VIRGINIA RAIL
Rallus limicola

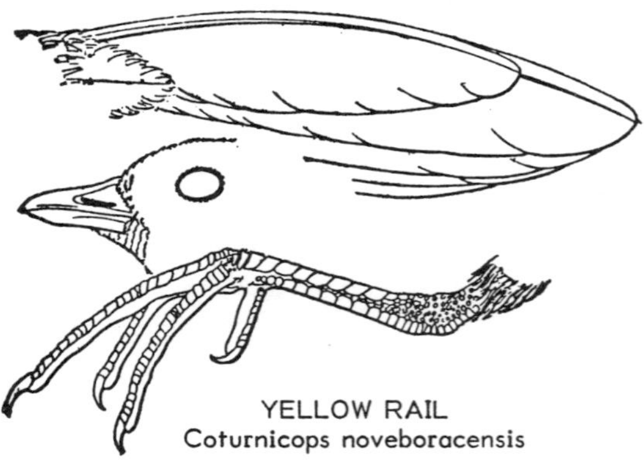

YELLOW RAIL
Coturnicops noveboracensis

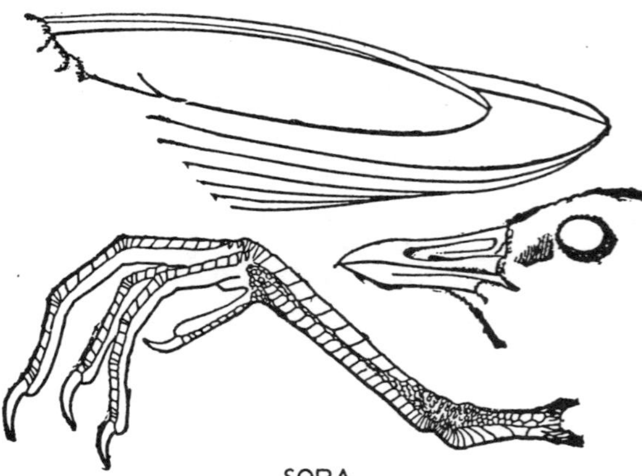

SORA
Porzana carolina

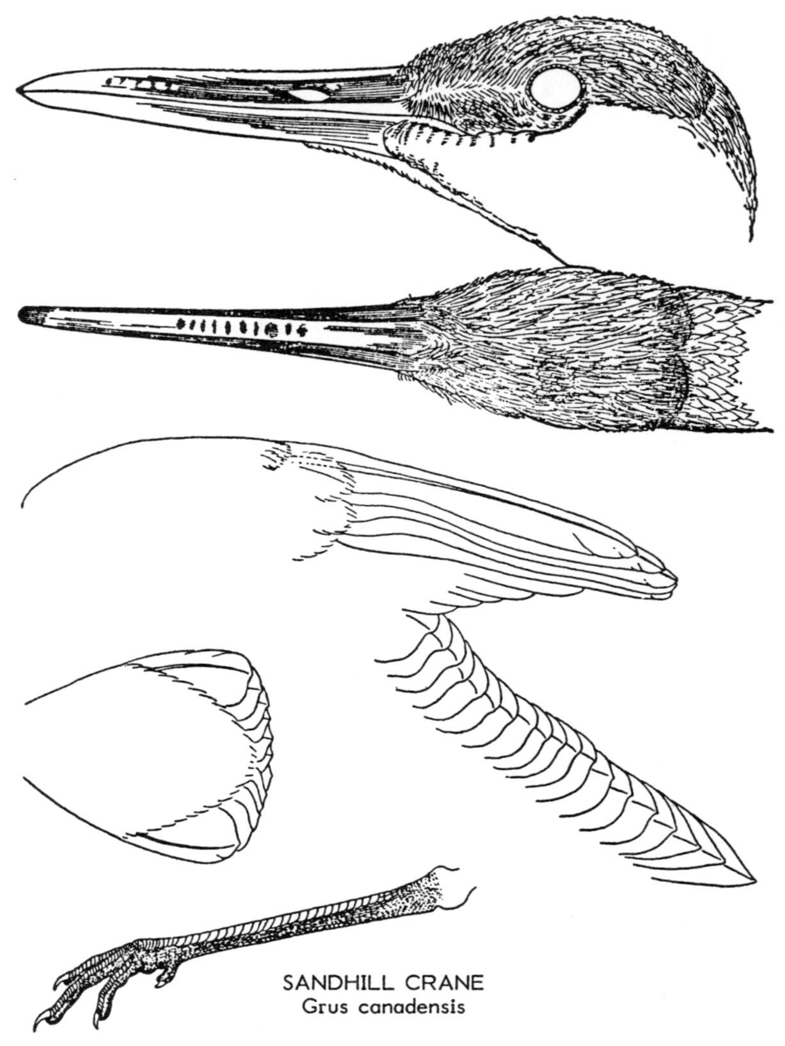

SANDHILL CRANE
Grus canadensis

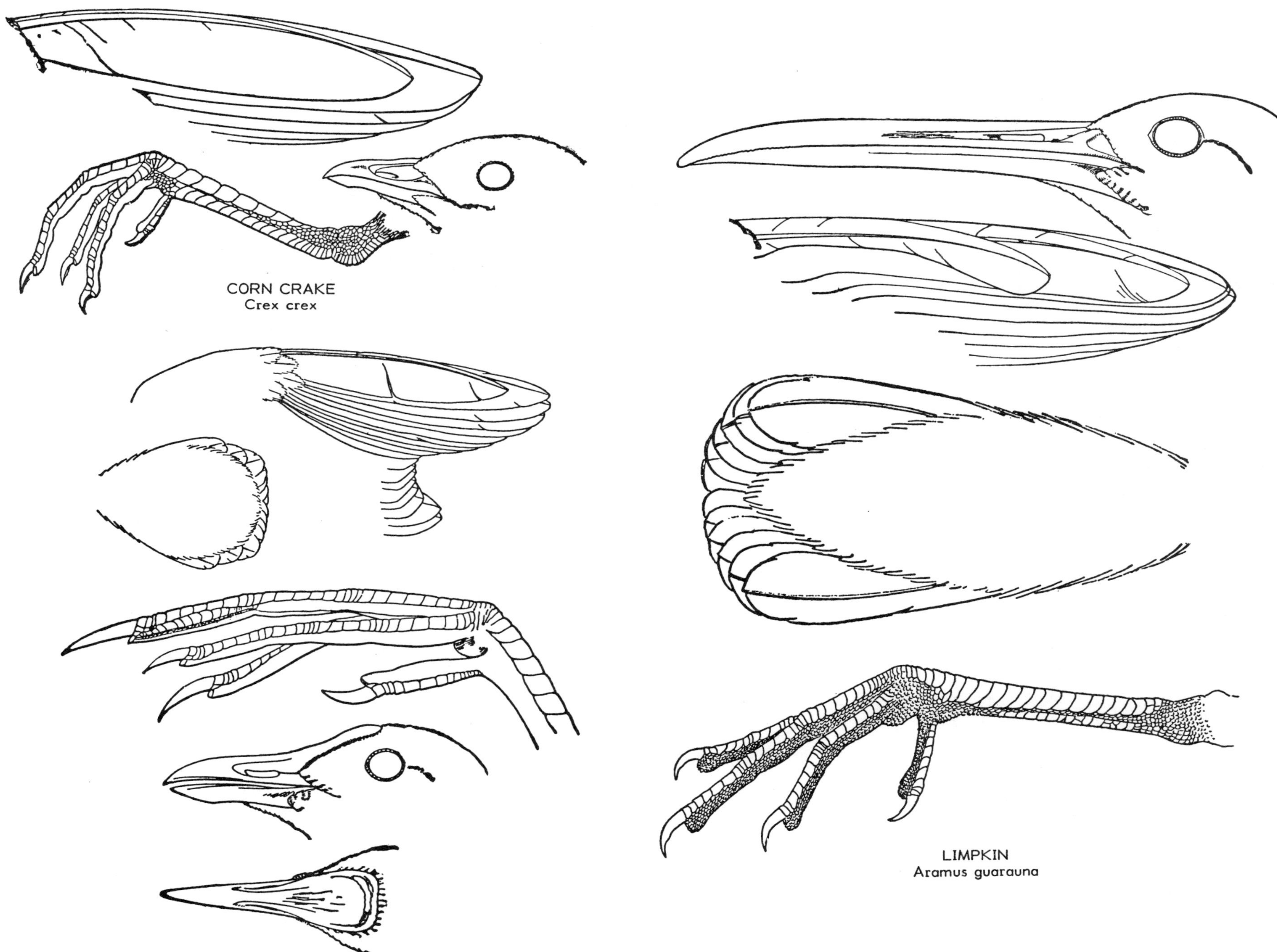
CORN CRAKE
Crex crex
COMMON GALLINULE
Gallinula chloropus
LIMPKIN
Aramus guarauna

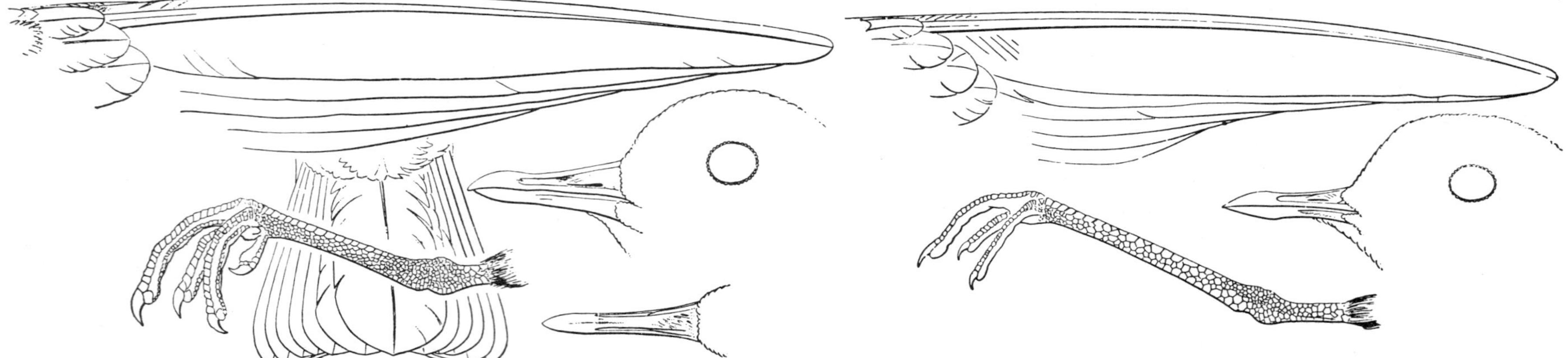

SURFBIRD
Aphriza virgata

MOUNTAIN PLOVER
Charadrius montana

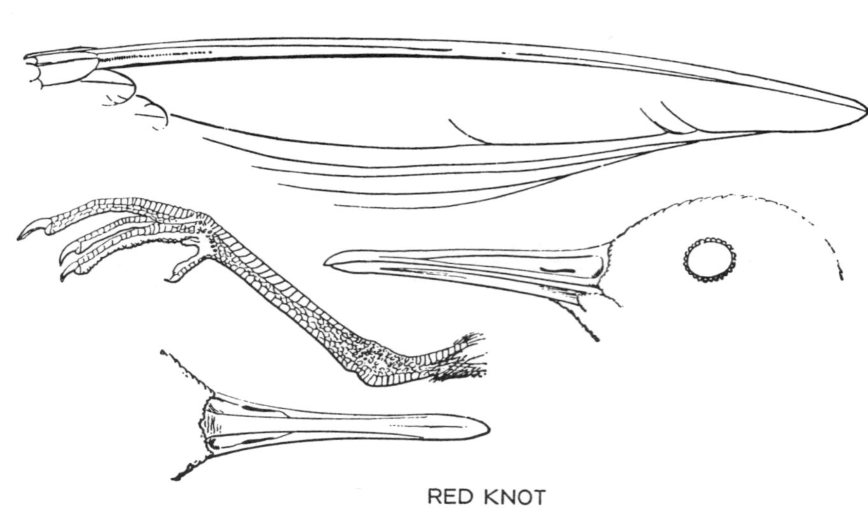

RED KNOT
Calidris canutus

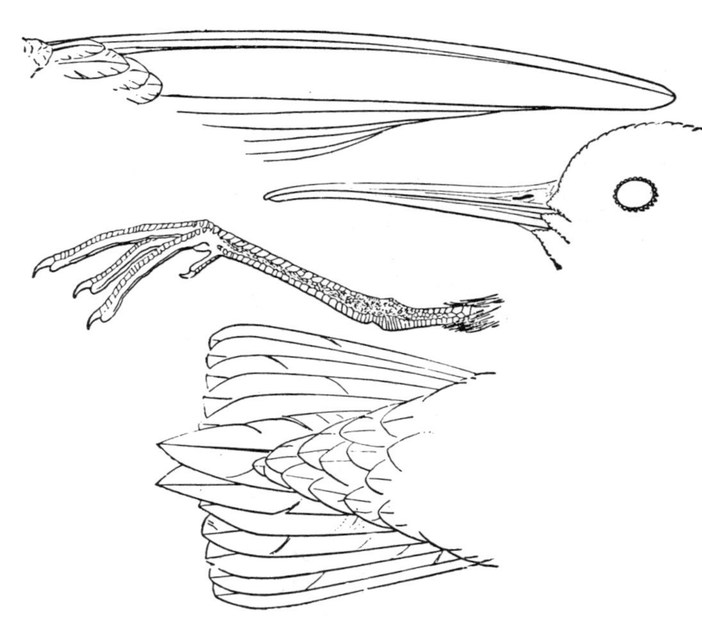

DUNLIN
Calidris alpina

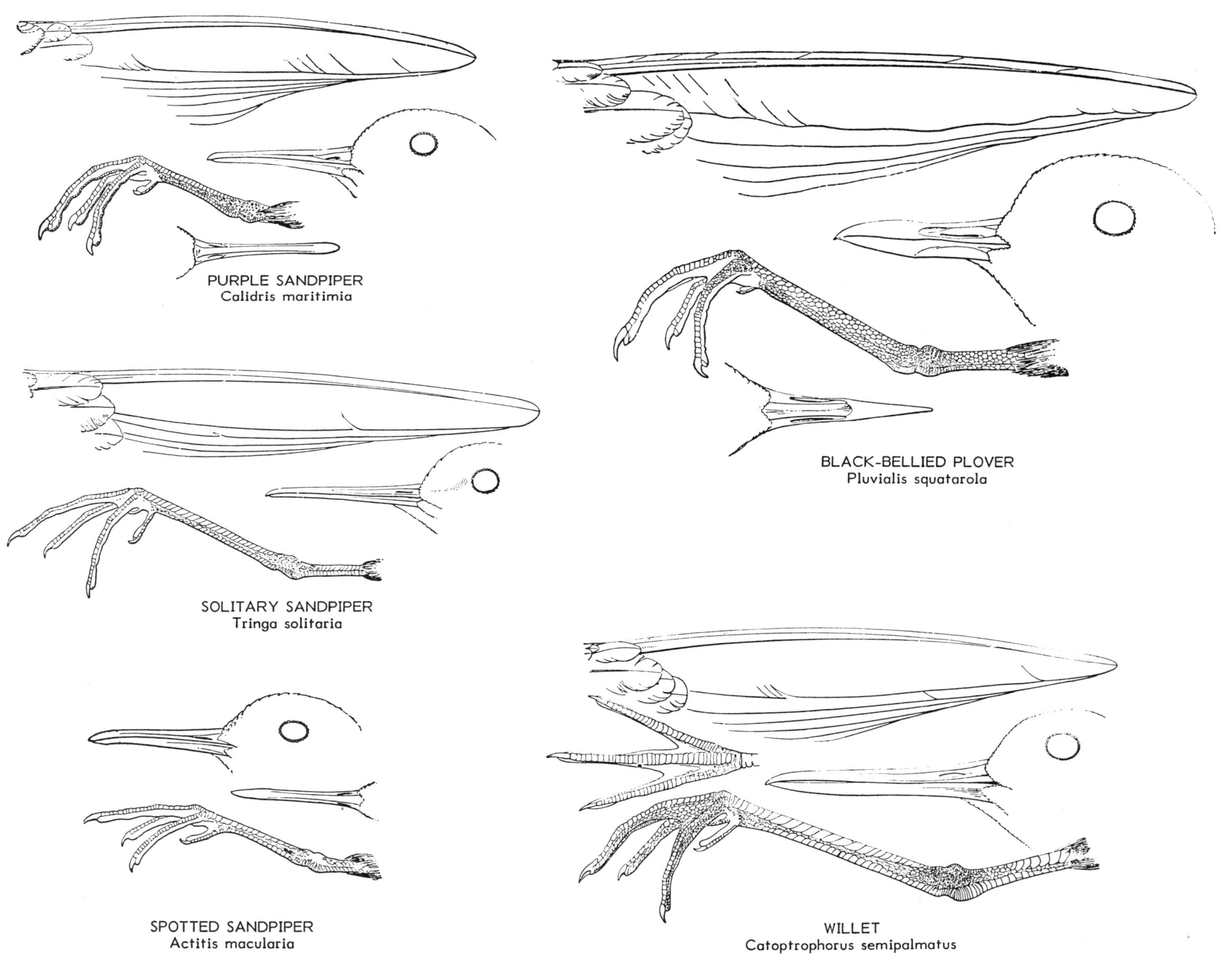
PURPLE SANDPIPER
Calidris maritimia
BLACK-BELLIED PLOVER
Pluvialis squatarola
SOLITARY SANDPIPER
Tringa solitaria
SPOTTED SANDPIPER
Actitis macularia
WILLET
Catoptrophorus semipalmatus

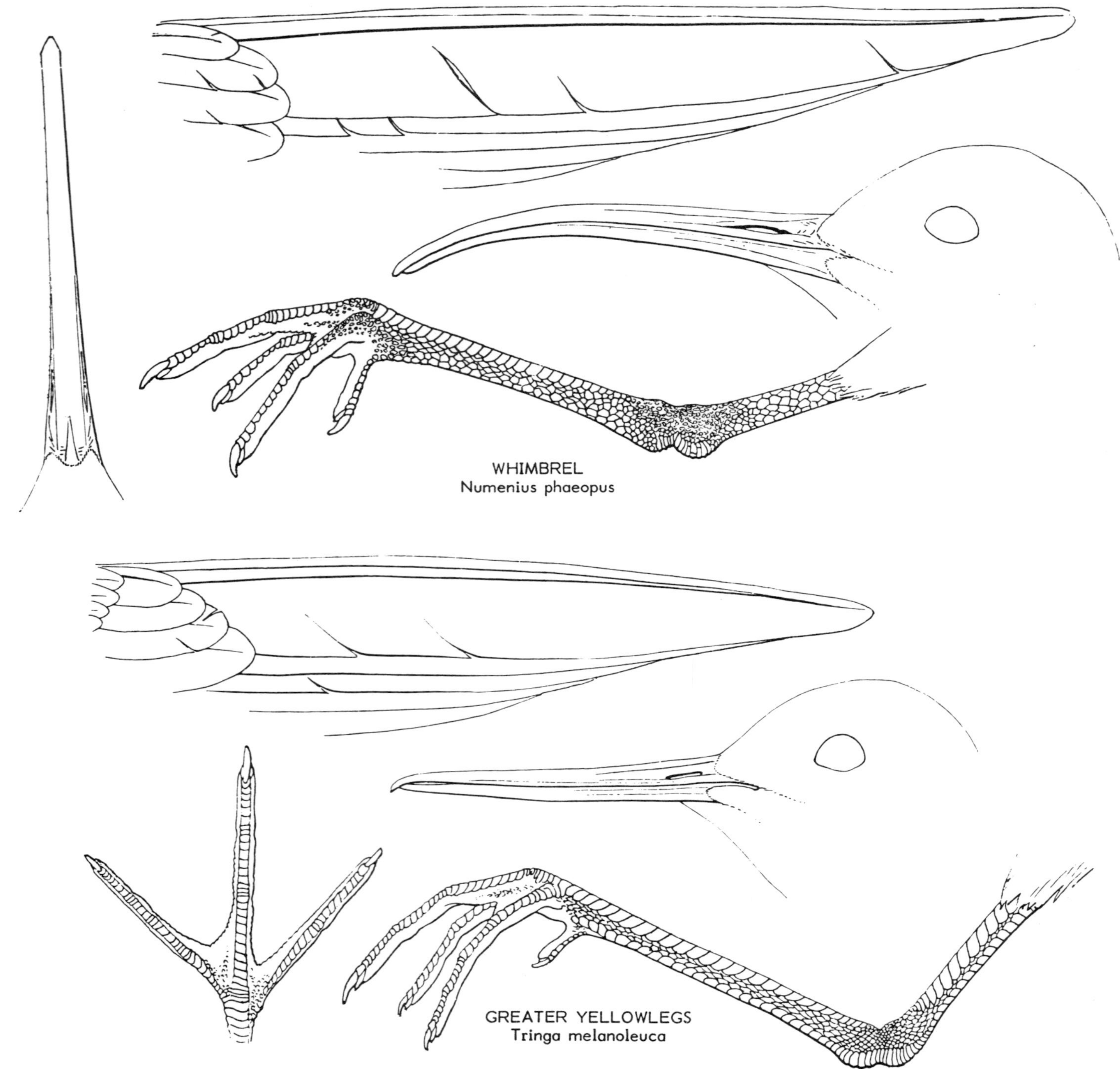

WHIMBREL
Numenius phaeopus

GREATER YELLOWLEGS
Tringa melanoleuca

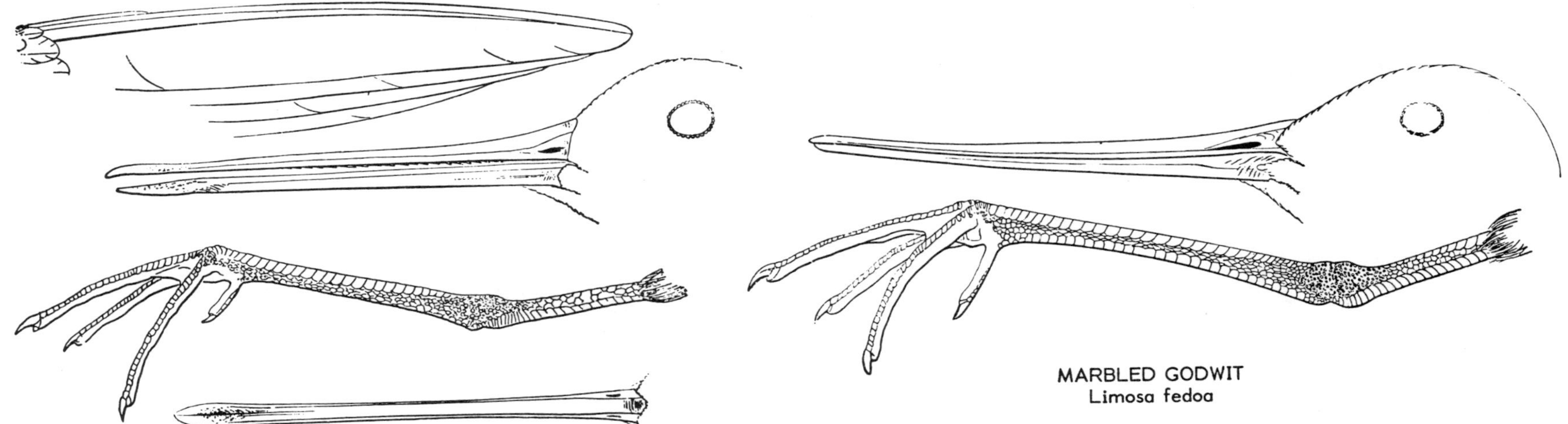

MARBLED GODWIT
Limosa fedoa

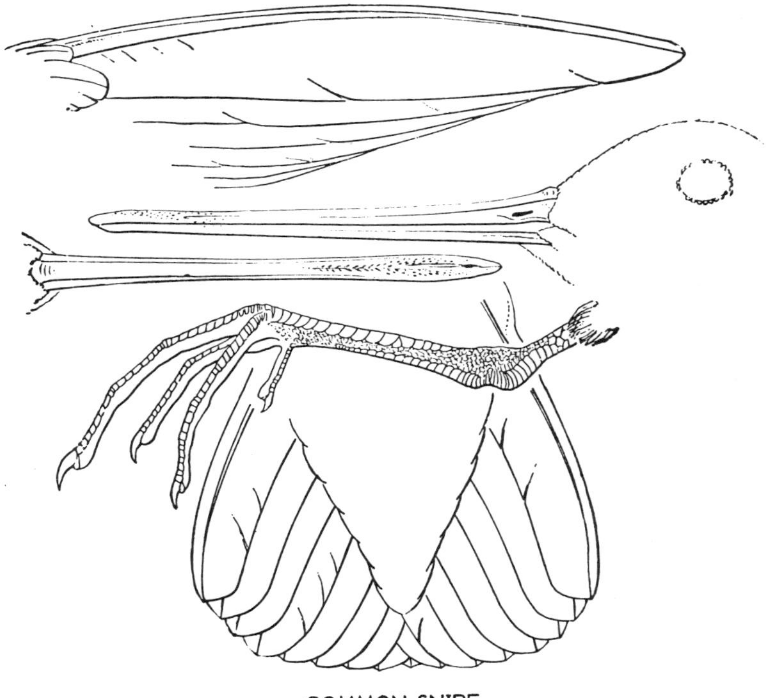

SHORT-BILLED DOWITCHER
Limnodromus griseus

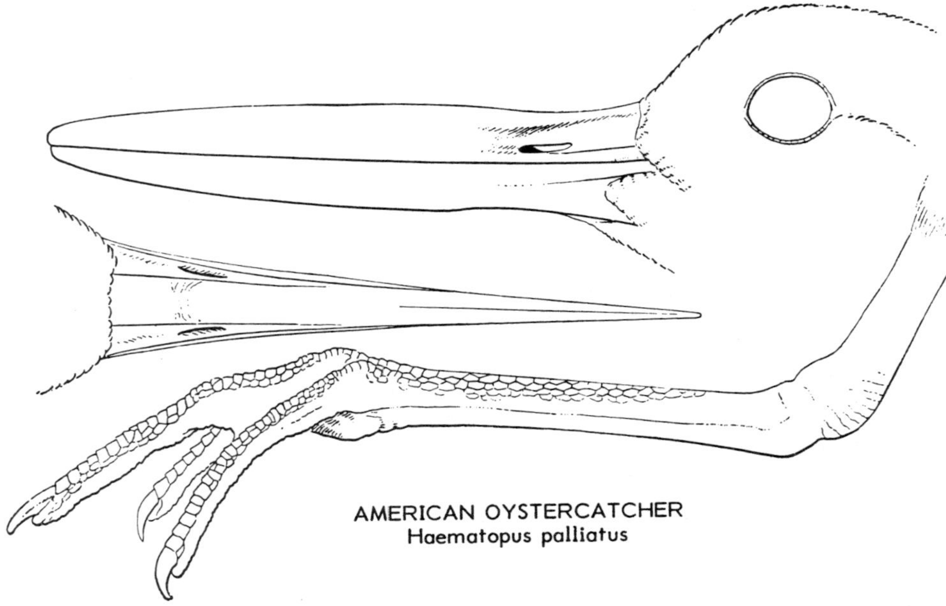

AMERICAN OYSTERCATCHER
Haematopus palliatus

COMMON SNIPE
Gallinago gallinago

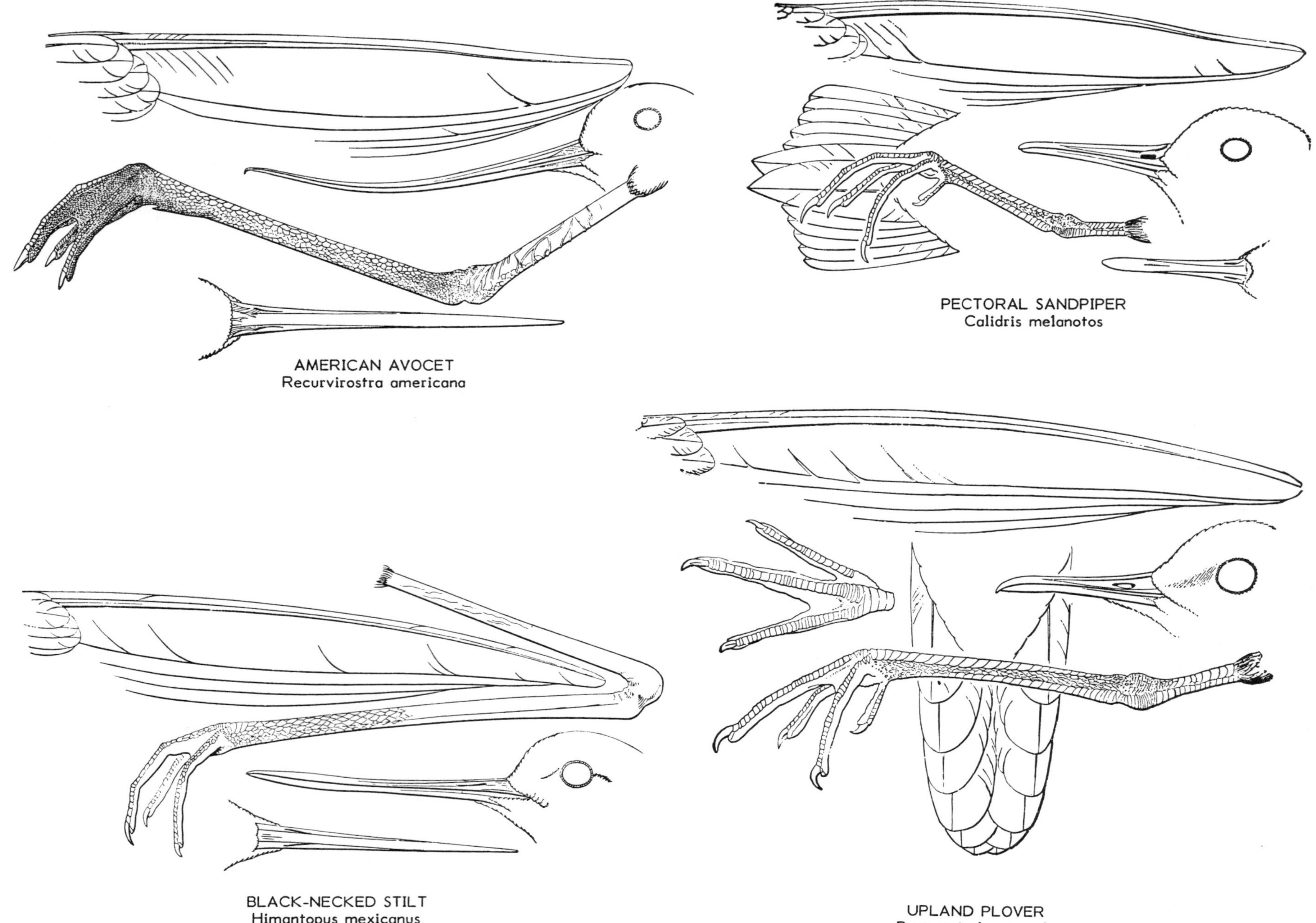
AMERICAN AVOCET
Recurvirostra americana
PECTORAL SANDPIPER
Calidris melanotos
BLACK-NECKED STILT
Himantopus mexicanus
UPLAND PLOVER
Bartramia longicauda

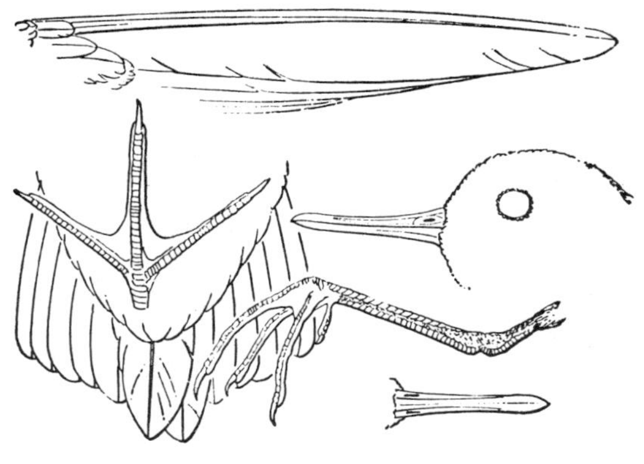
SEMIPALMATED SANDPIPER
Calidris pusilla

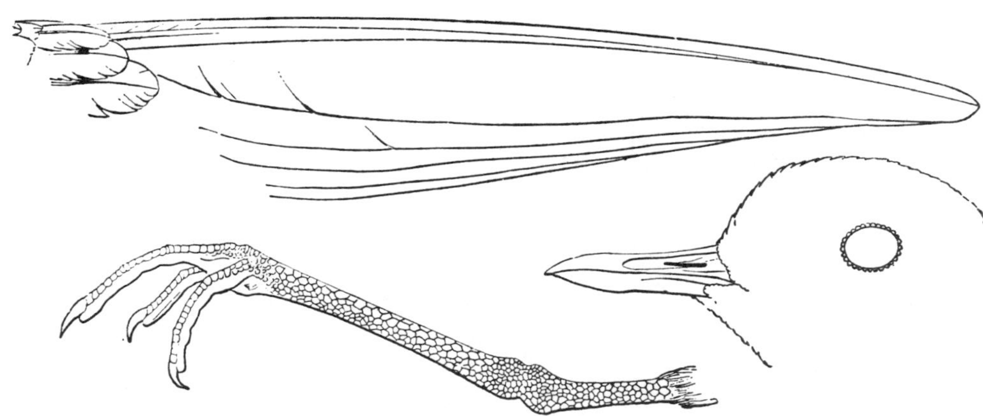
LESSER GOLDEN PLOVER
Pluvialis dominica

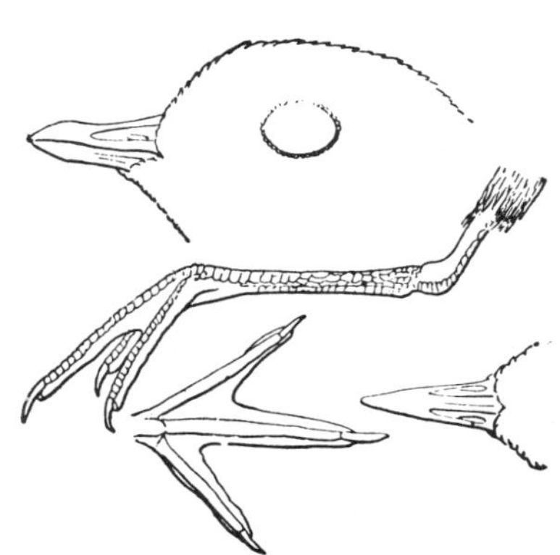
SEMIPALMATED PLOVER
Charadrius semipalmatus

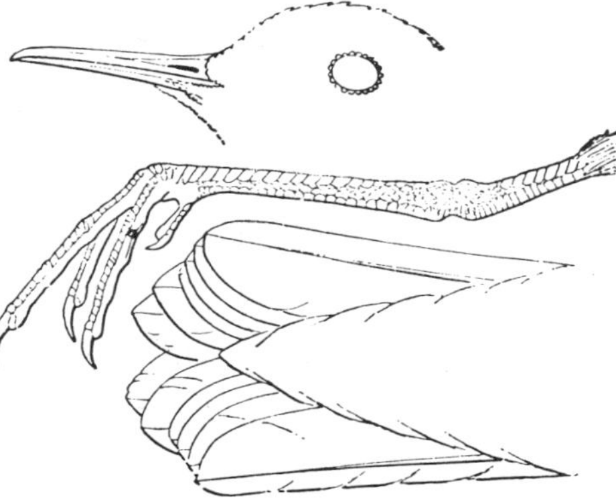
BUFF-BREASTED SANDPIPER
Tryngites subruficollis

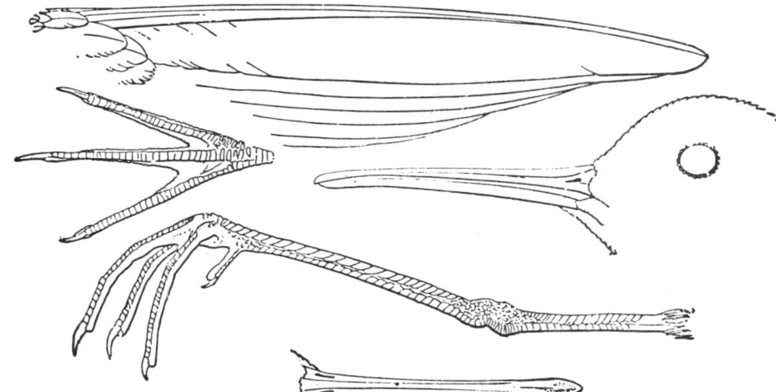
STILT SANDPIPER
Calidris himantopus

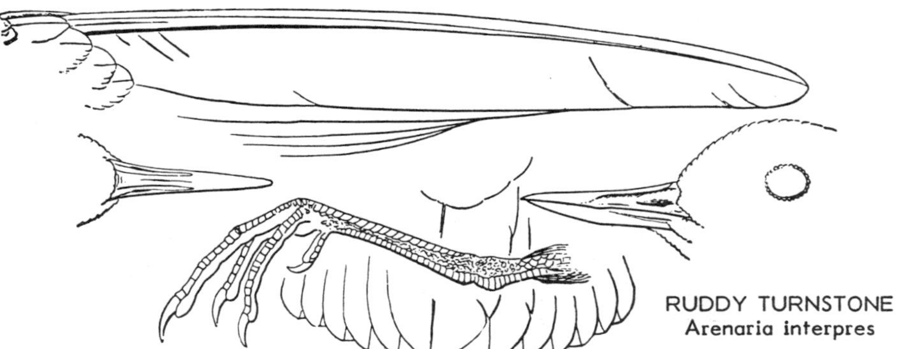
RUDDY TURNSTONE
Arenaria interpres

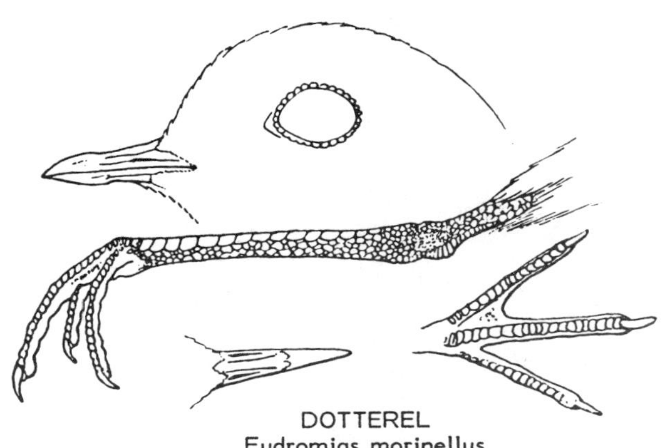
DOTTEREL
Eudromias morinellus

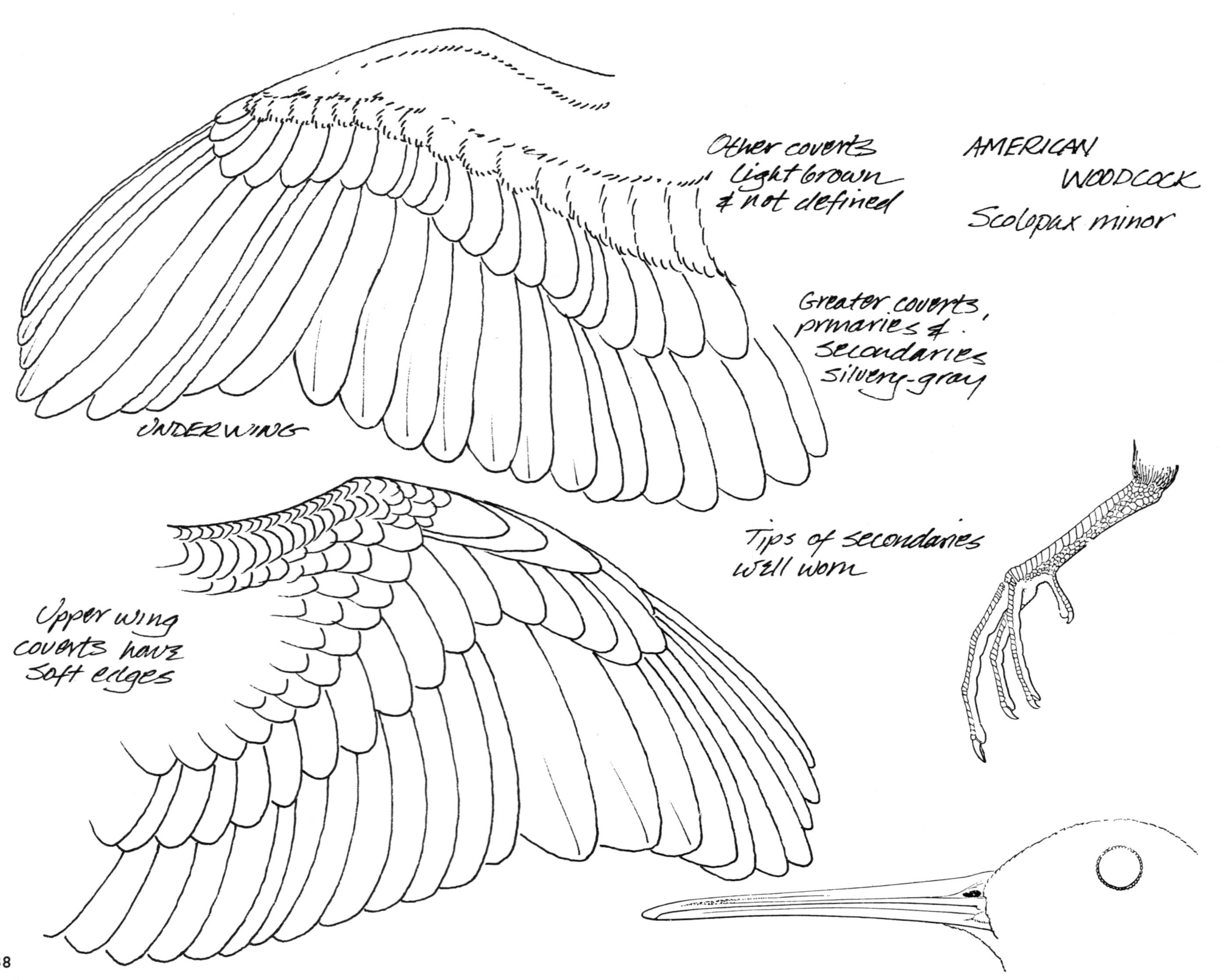
AMERICAN WOODCOCK
Scolopax minor
Other coverts light brown & not defined
Greater coverts, primaries & secondaries silvery-gray
UNDERWING
Tips of secondaries well worn
Upper wing coverts have soft edges

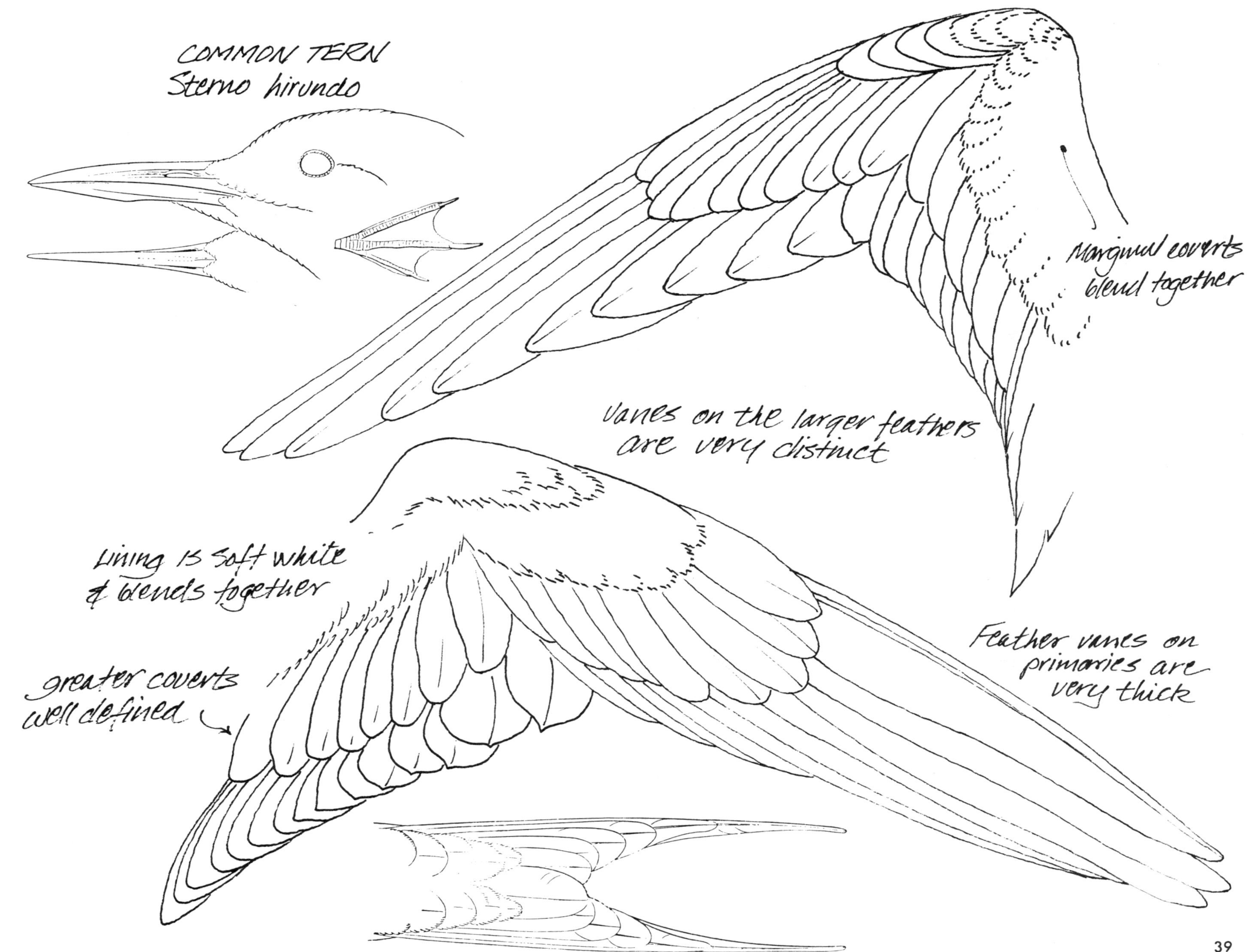
COMMON TERN
Sterna hirundo
Marginal coverts blend together
Vanes on the larger feathers are very distinct
Lining is soft white & blends together
Feather vanes on primaries are very thick
greater coverts well defined

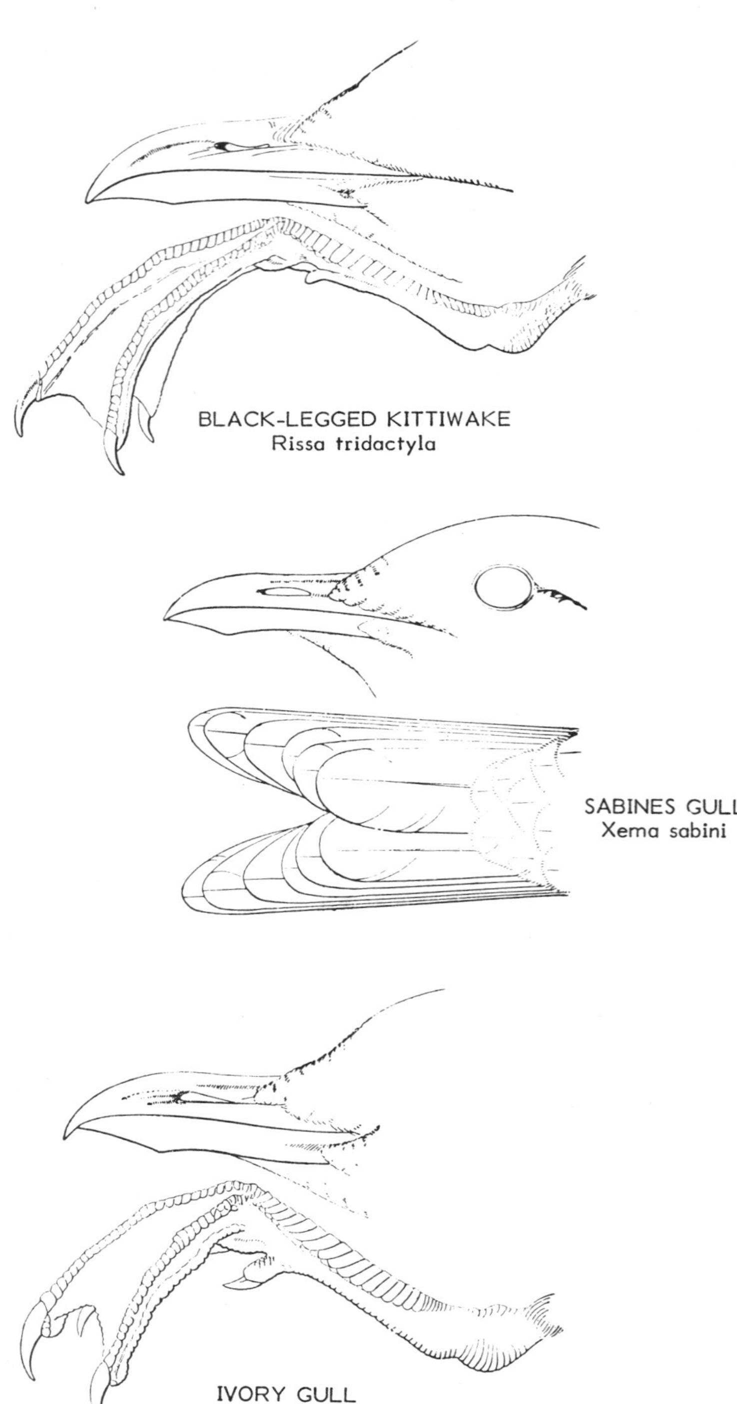

BLACK-LEGGED KITTIWAKE
Rissa tridactyla

SABINES GULL
Xema sabini

IVORY GULL
Pagophila eburnea

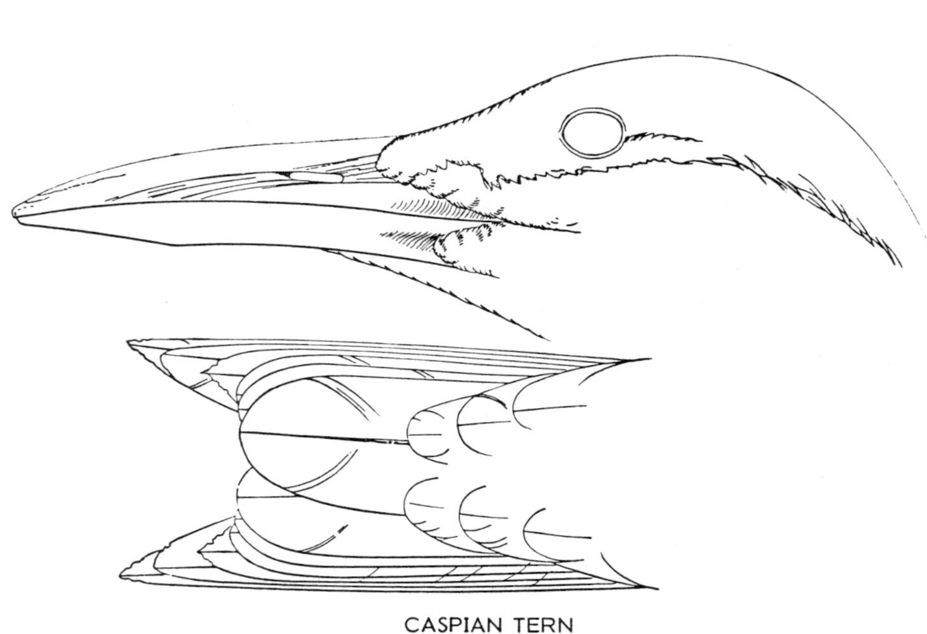

CASPIAN TERN
Sterna caspia

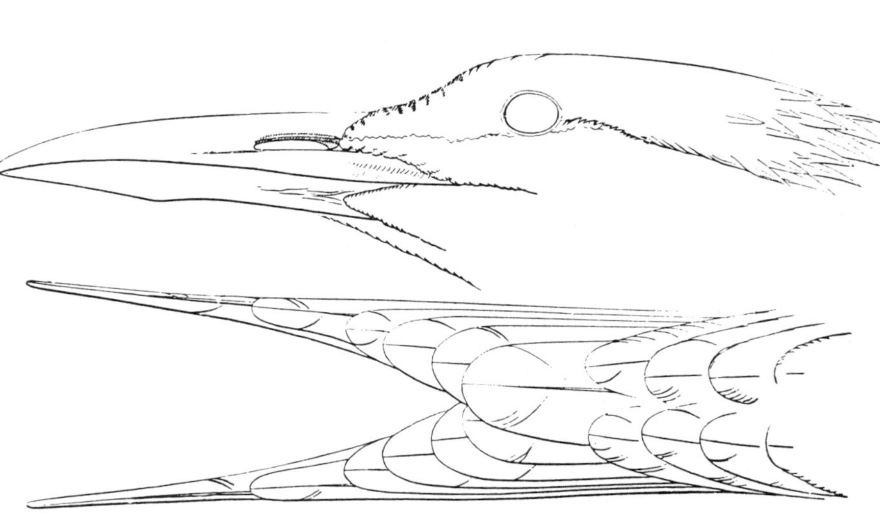

ROYAL TERN
Thalasseus maximus

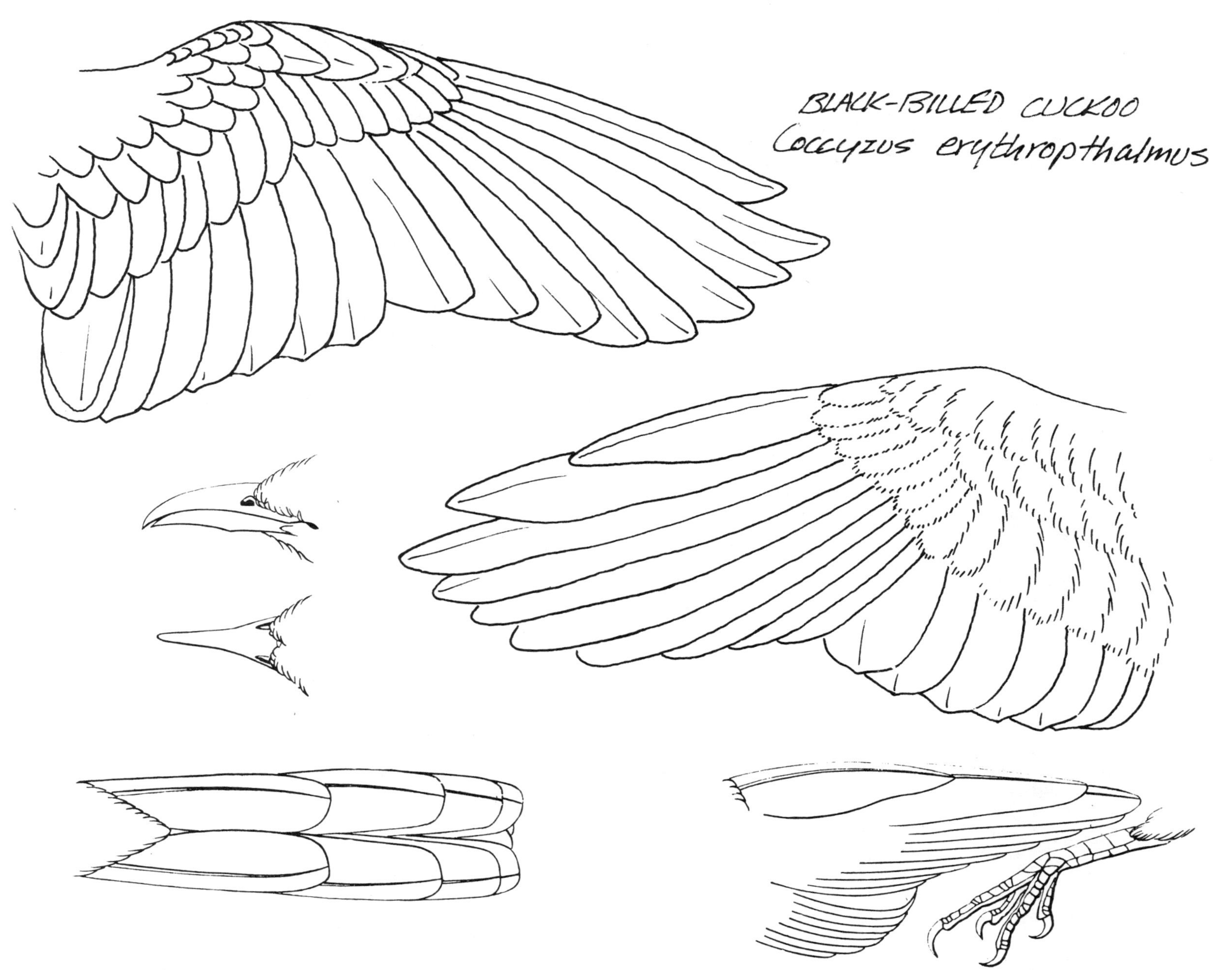
BLACK-BILLED CUCKOO
Coccyzus erythropthalmus

SCREECH OWL
Otus asio

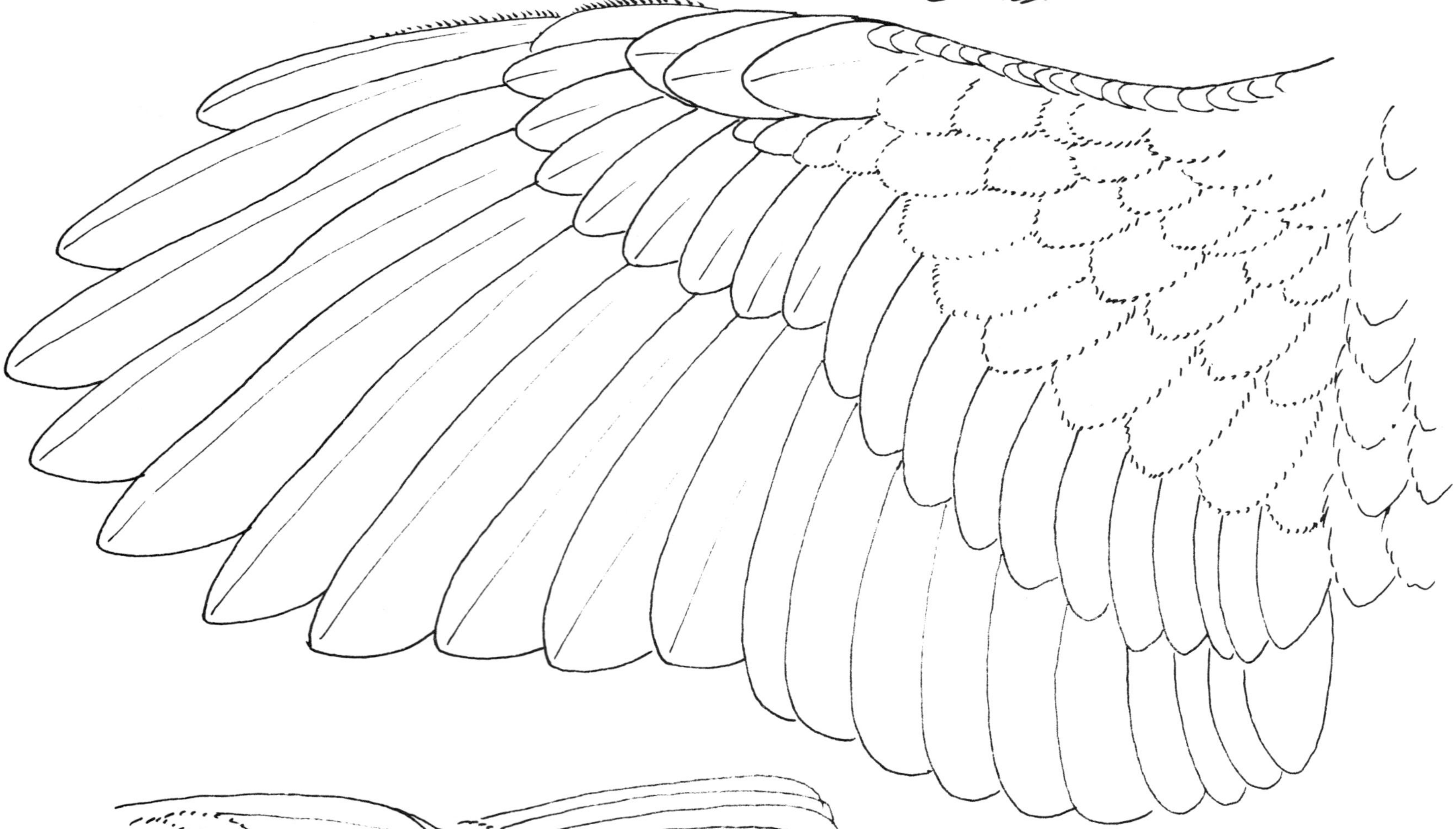

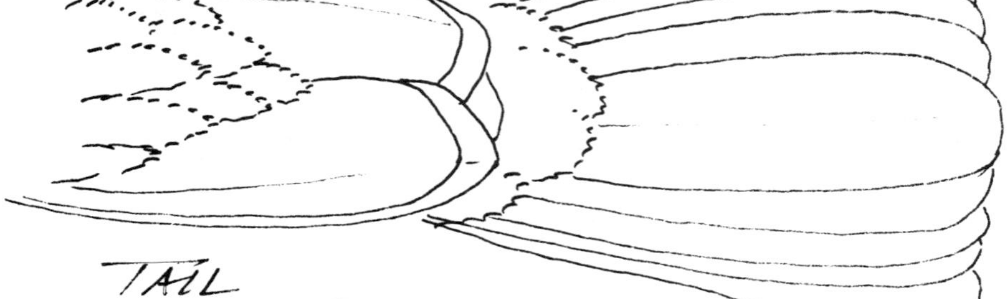

TAIL
UNDERSIDE

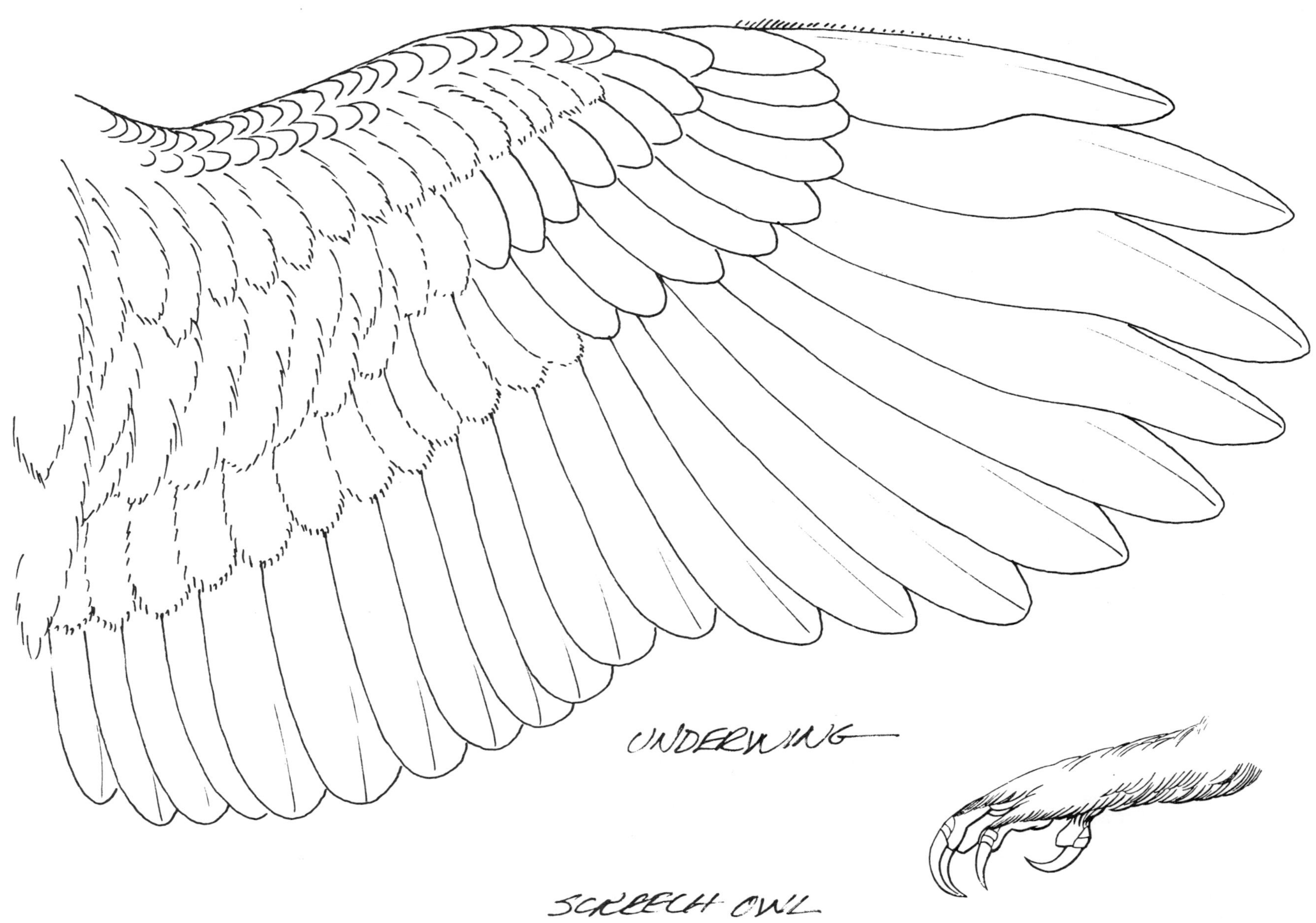
UNDERWING
SCREECH OWL

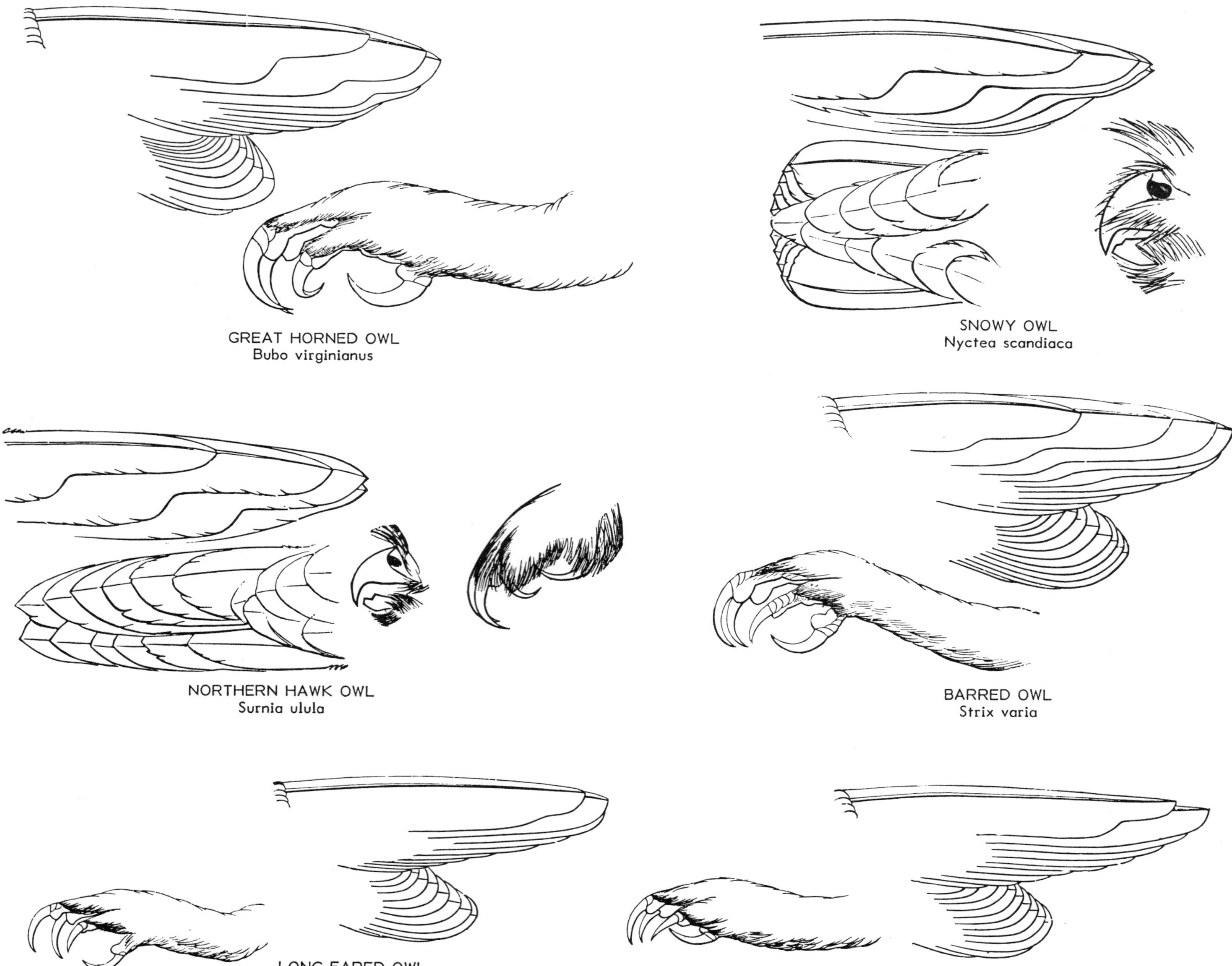

GREAT HORNED OWL
Bubo virginianus

SNOWY OWL
Nyctea scandiaca

NORTHERN HAWK OWL
Surnia ulula

BARRED OWL
Strix varia

LONG-EARED OWL
Asio otus

SHORT-EARED OWL
Asio flammeus

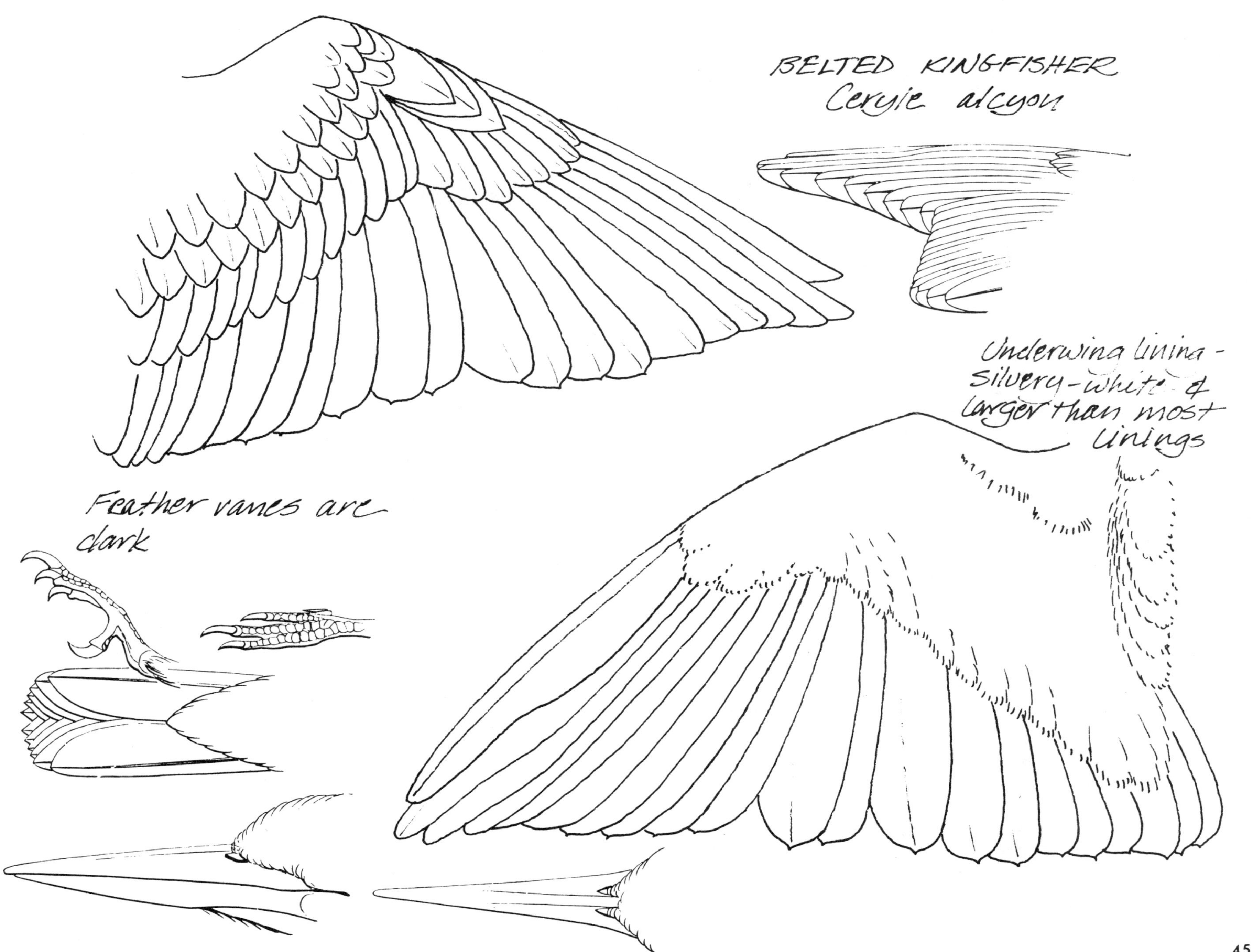
BELTED KINGFISHER
Ceryle alcyon
Underwing lining - silvery-white & larger than most linings
Feather vanes are dark

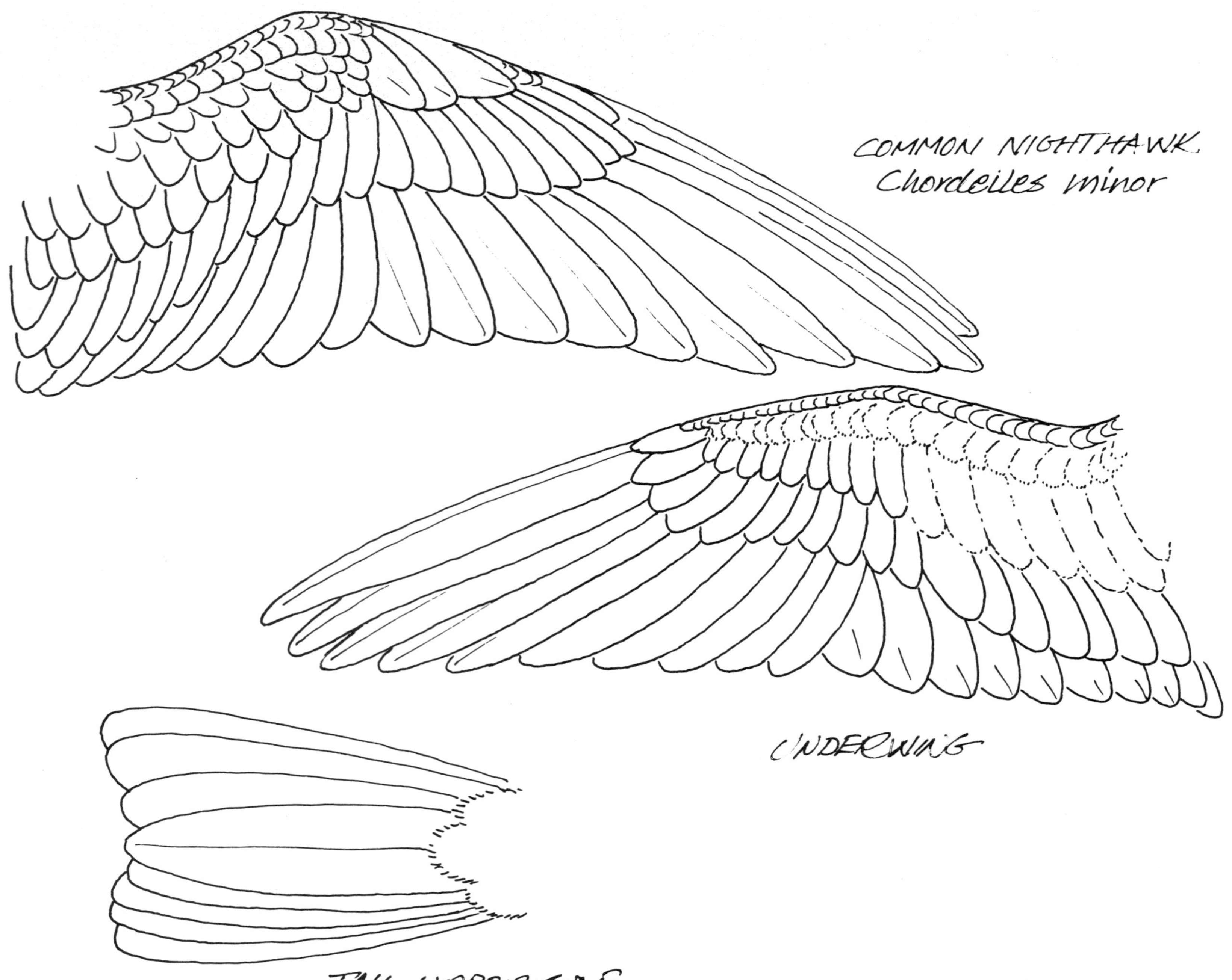
COMMON NIGHTHAWK
Chordeiles minor
UNDERWING
TAIL-UPPER SIDE
scaled to wings

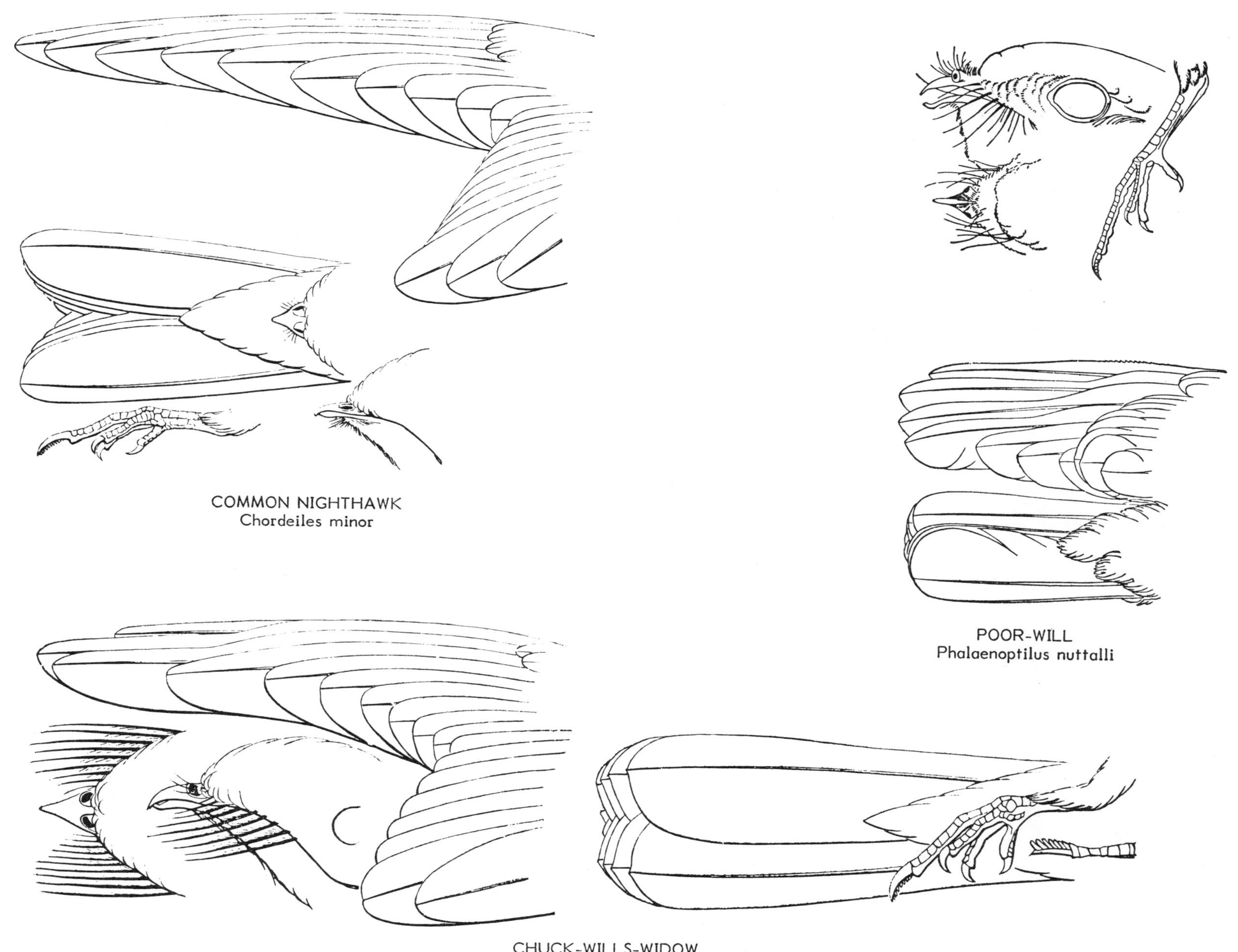

COMMON NIGHTHAWK
Chordeiles minor

POOR-WILL
Phalaenoptilus nuttalli

CHUCK-WILLS-WIDOW
Caprimulgus carolinensis

RUBY-THROATED HUMMING-BIRD, Archilochus colubris

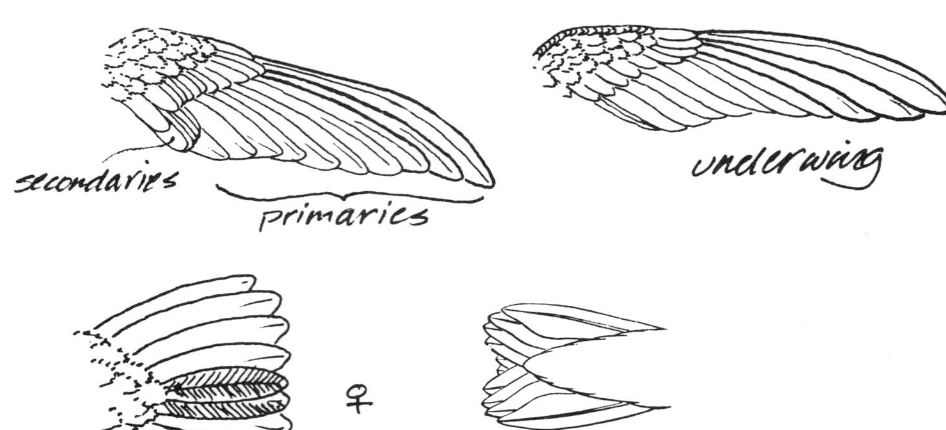

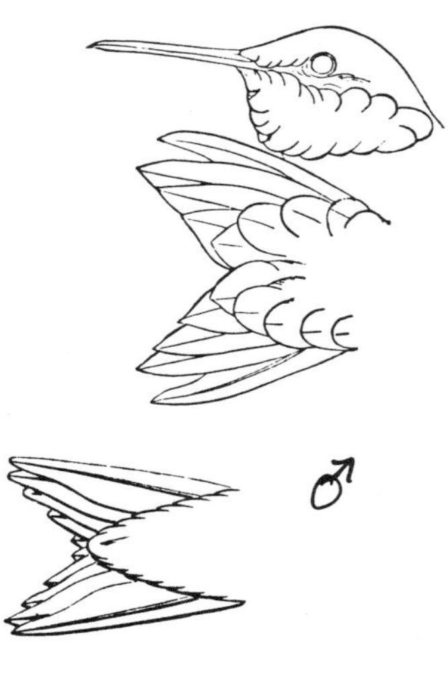

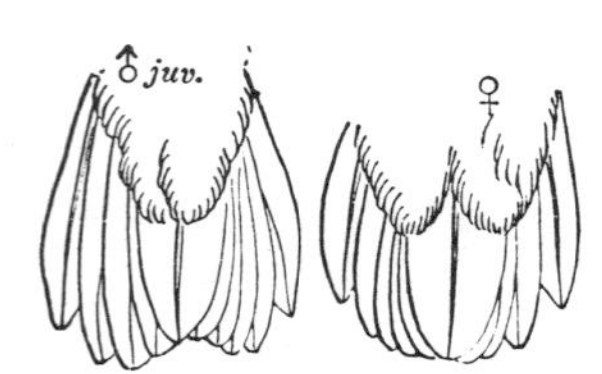

BLACK-CHINNED HUMMINGBIRD
Archilochus alexandri

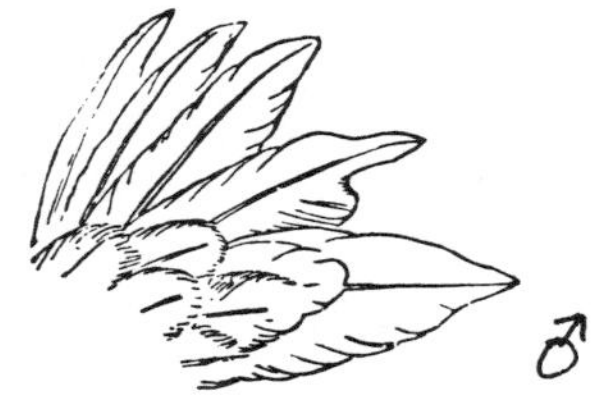

RUFOUS HUMMINGBIRD
Selasphorus rufus

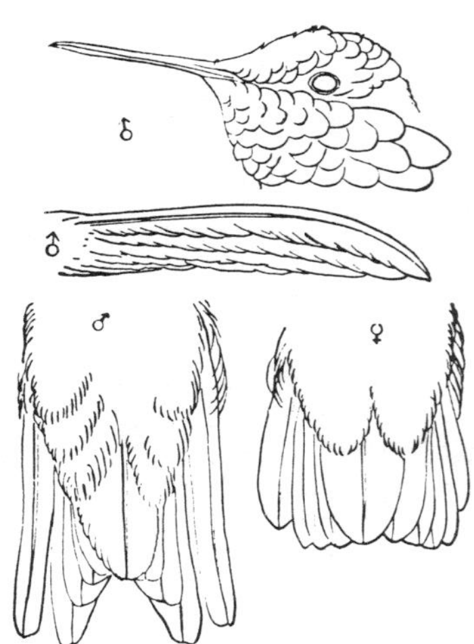

ANNA'S HUMMINGBIRD
Calypte anna

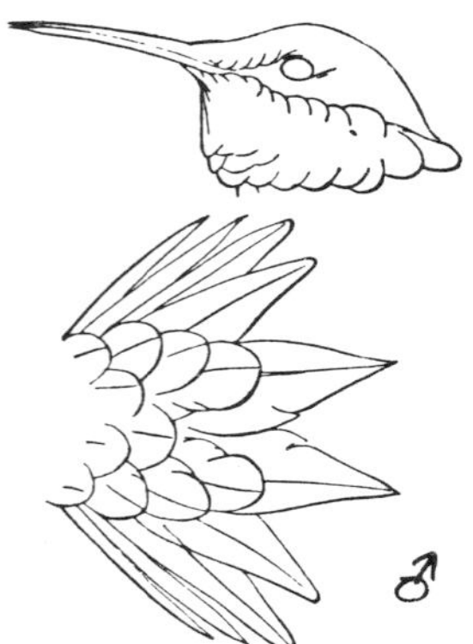

ALLENS HUMMINGBIRD
Selasphorus sasin

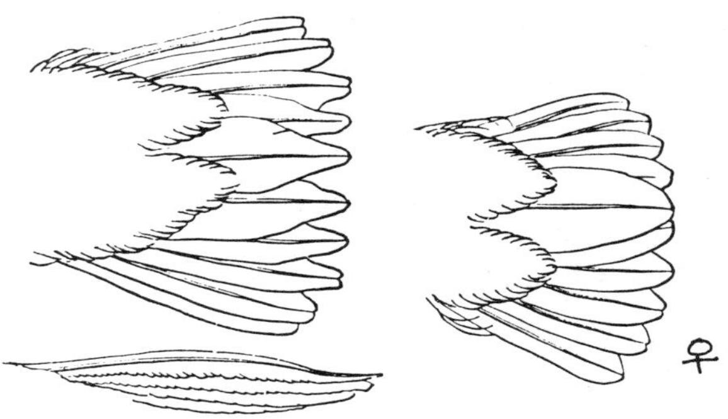

BROAD-TAILED HUMMINGBIRD
Selasphorus platycercus

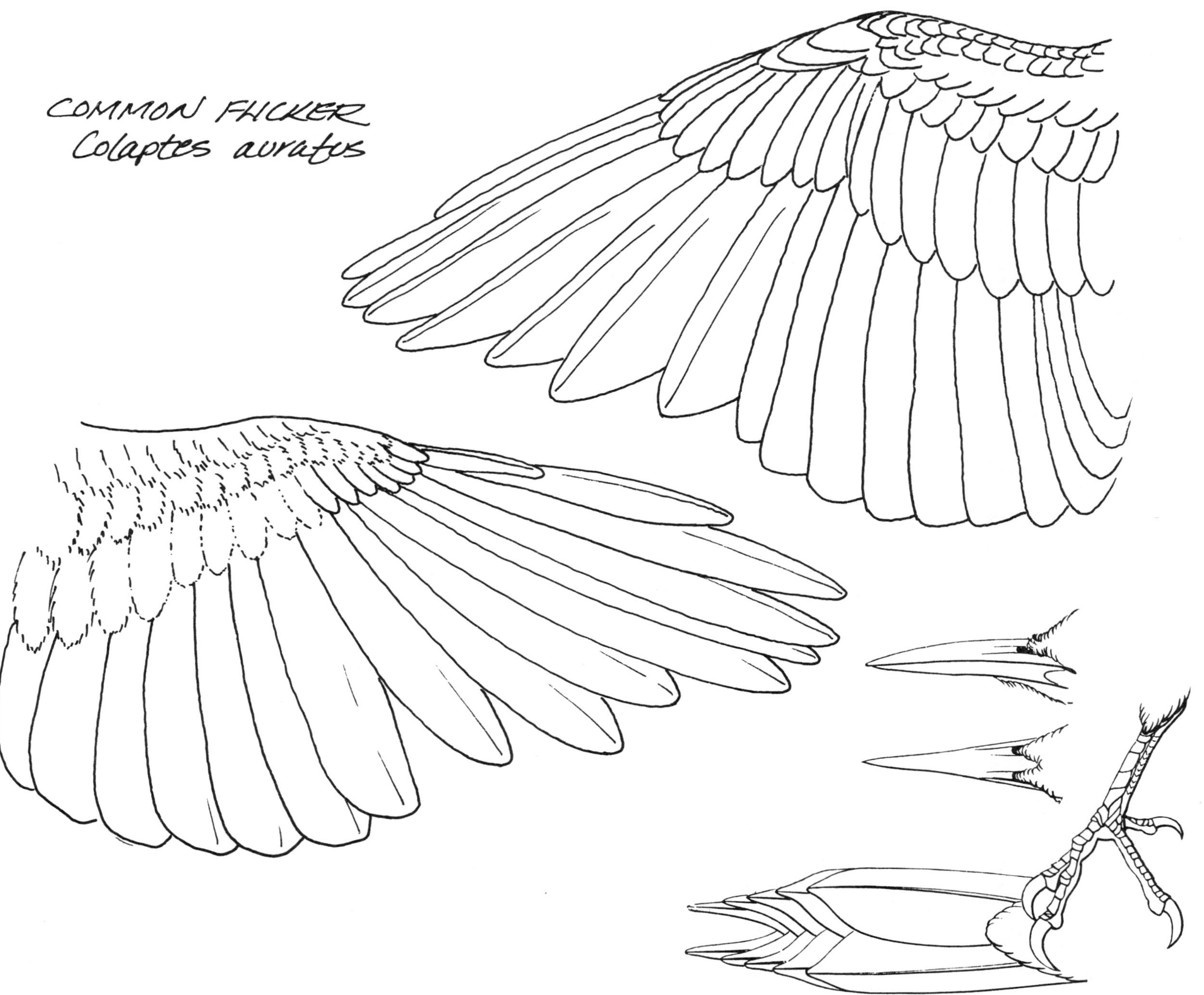
COMMON FLICKER
Colaptes auratus

DOWNY WOODPECKER
Dendrocopos pubescens

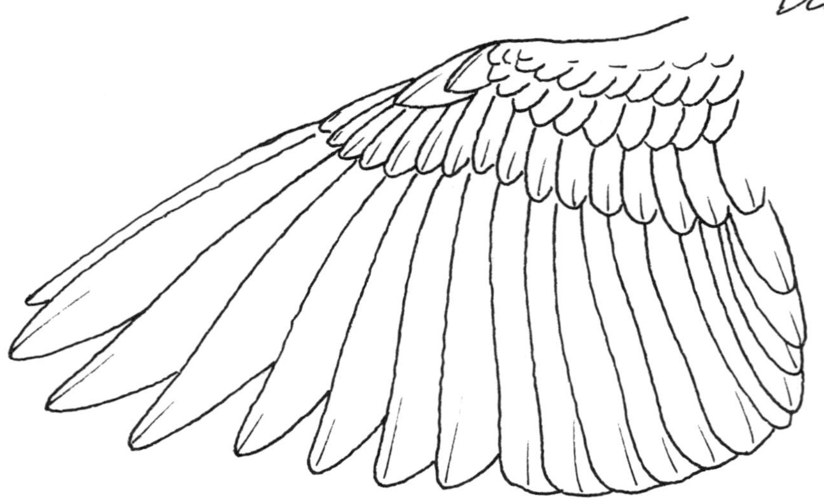

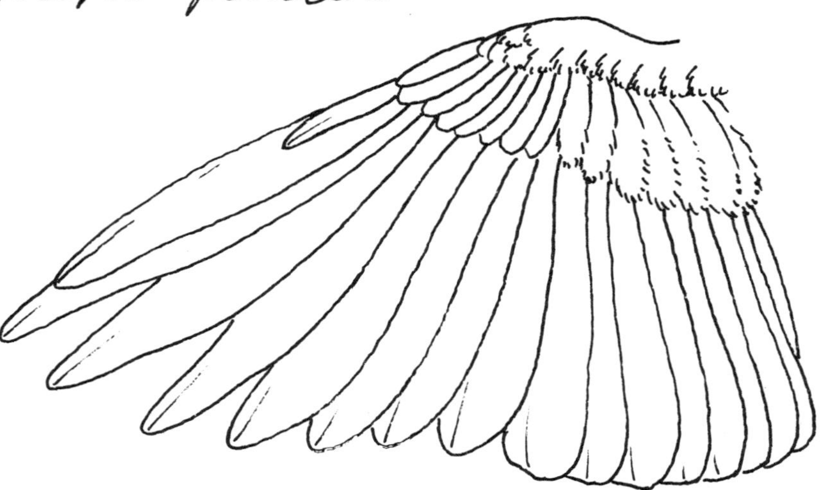

UNDERWING

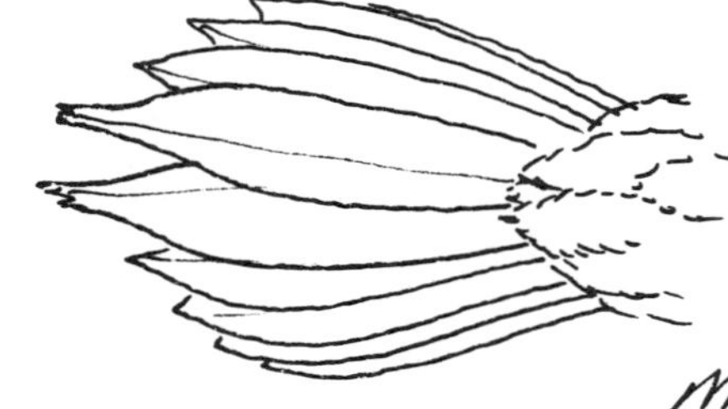

upper tail
tail feather tips
may be ragged

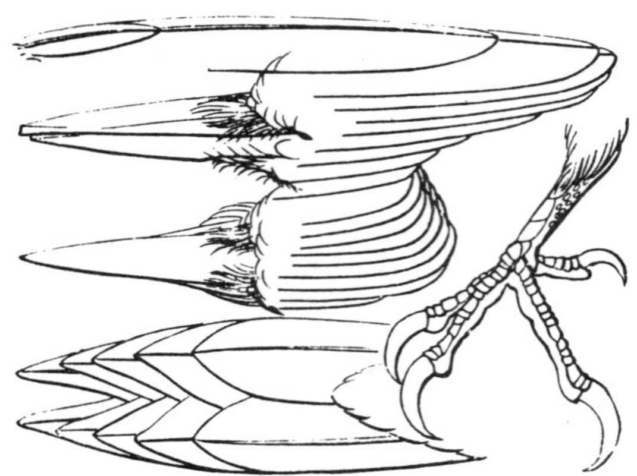

HAIRY WOODPECKER
Picoides villosus

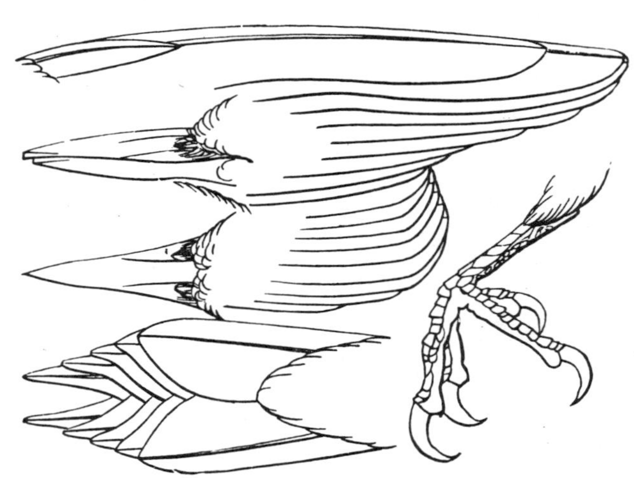

RED-HEADED WOODPECKER
Melanerpes erythrocephalus

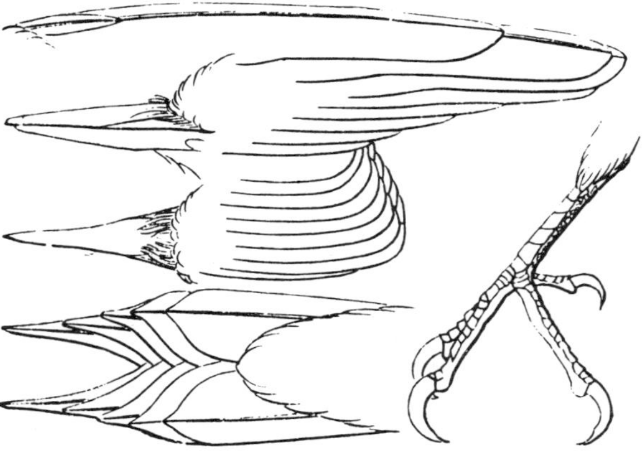

YELLOW-BELLIED SAPSUCKER
Sphyrapicus varius

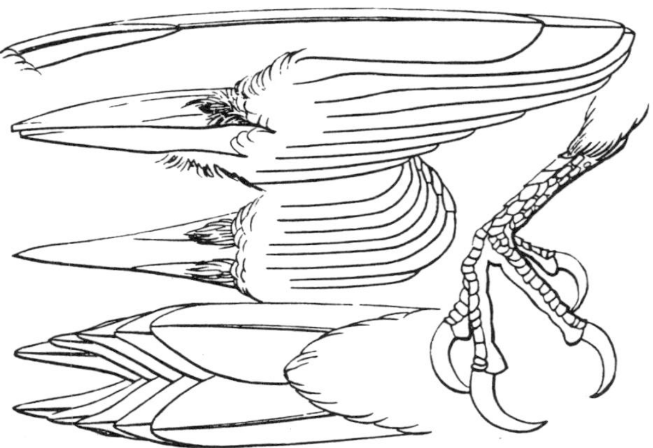

RED-BELLIED WOODPECKER
Melanerpes carolinus

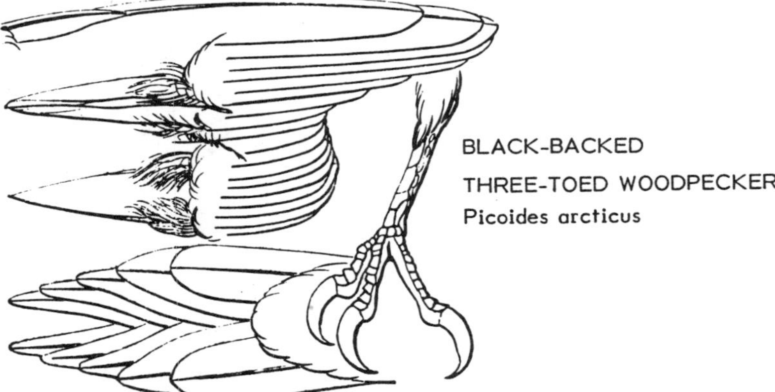

BLACK-BACKED
THREE-TOED WOODPECKER
Picoides arcticus

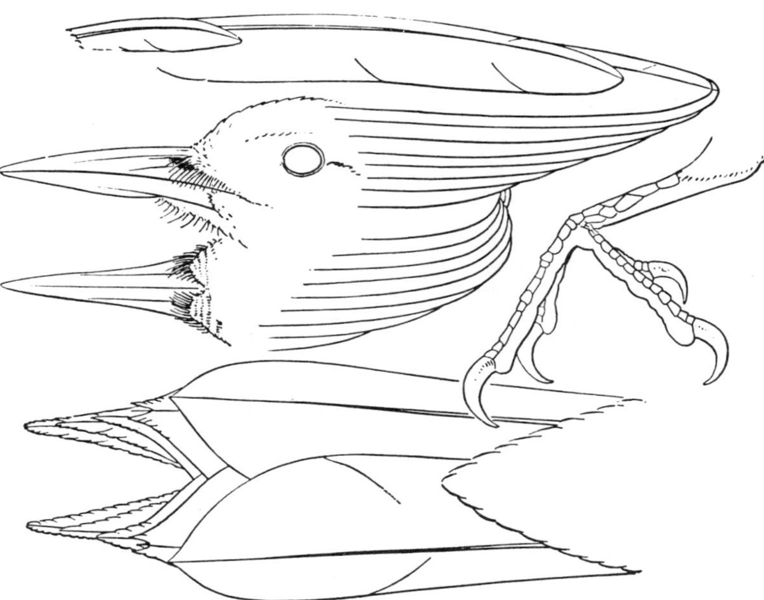

LEWIS' WOODPECKER
Melanerpes lewis

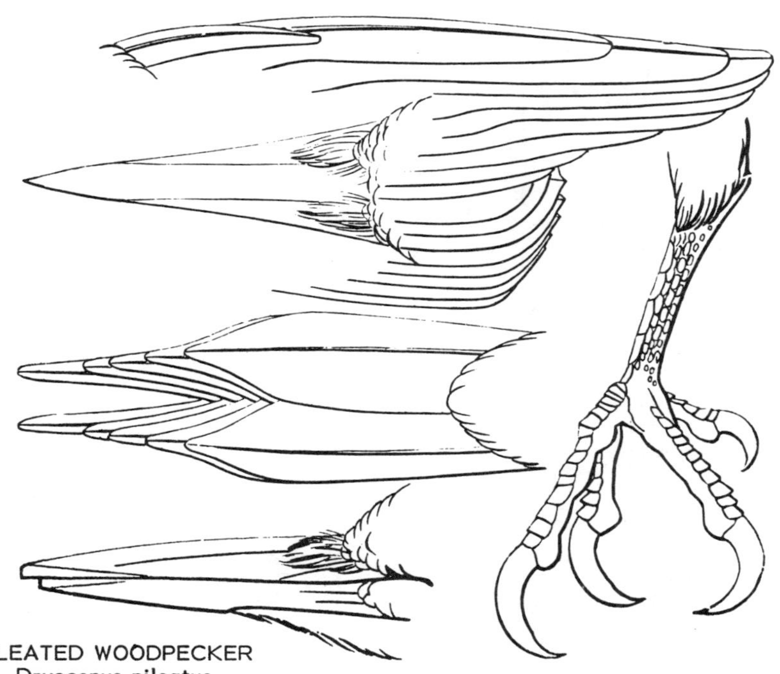

PILEATED WOODPECKER
Dryocopus pileatus

WILLOW FLYCATCHER
Empidonax traillii

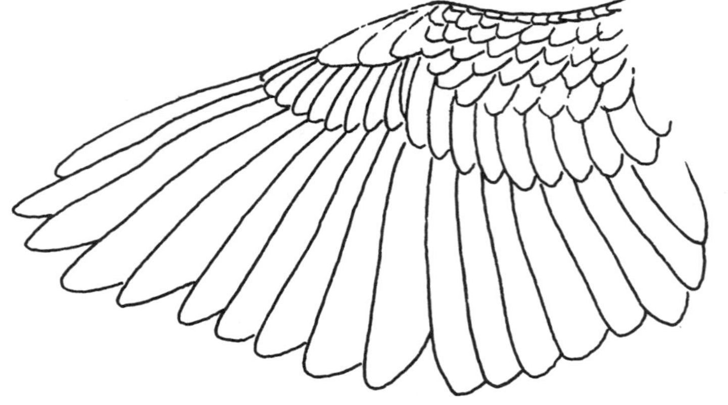

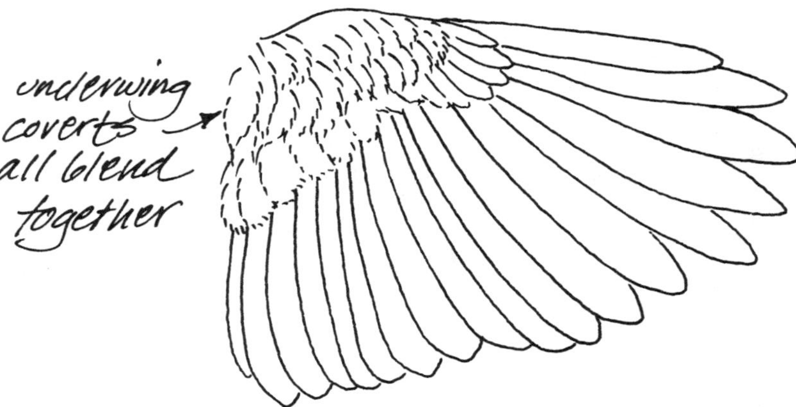

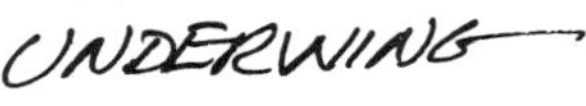

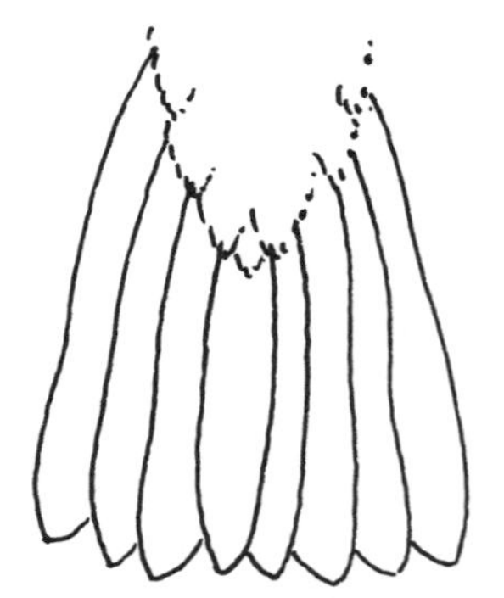

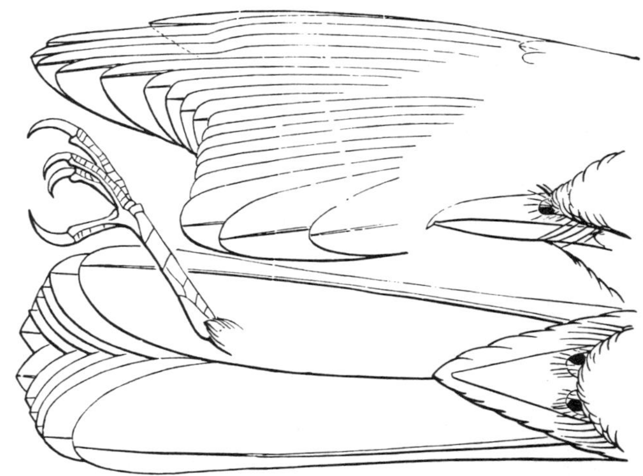

GREAT-CRESTED FLYCATCHER
Myiarchus crinitus

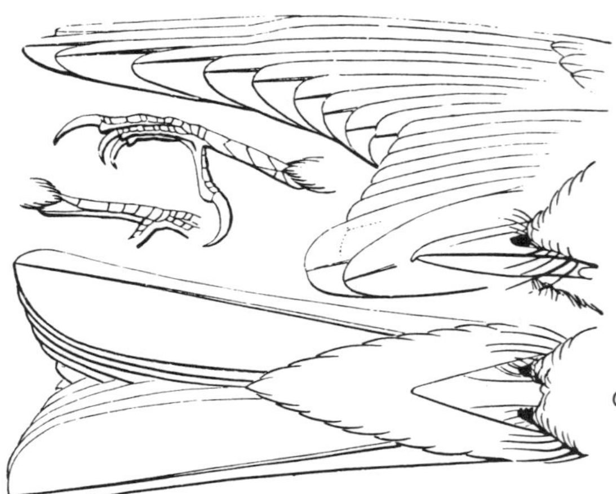

OLIVE-SIDED FLYCATCHER
Nuttallornis borealis

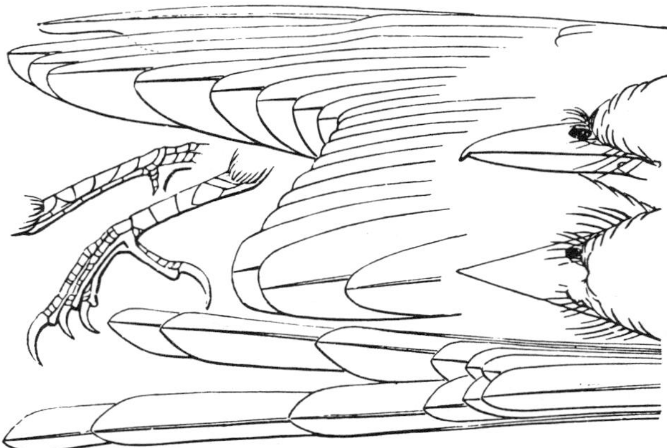

SCISSOR-TAILED FLYCATCHER
Tyrannus forficatus

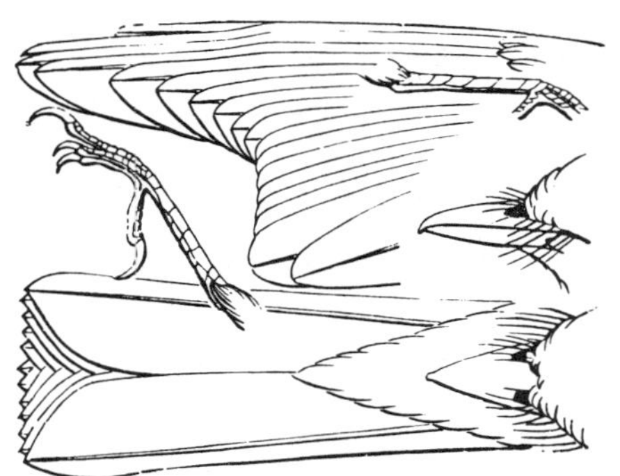

ACADIAN FLYCATCHER
Empidonax virescens

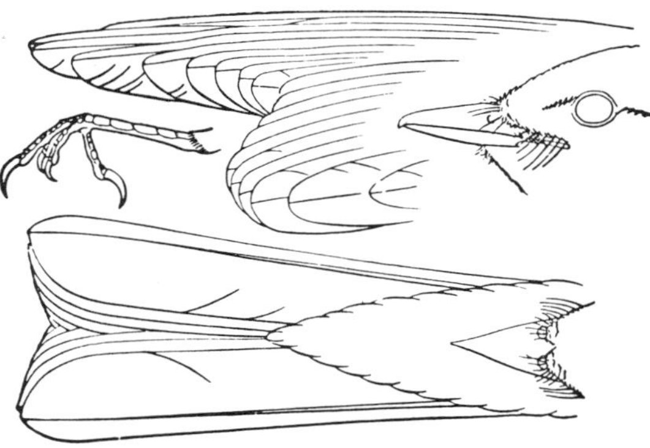

EASTERN WOOD PEWEE
Contopus virens

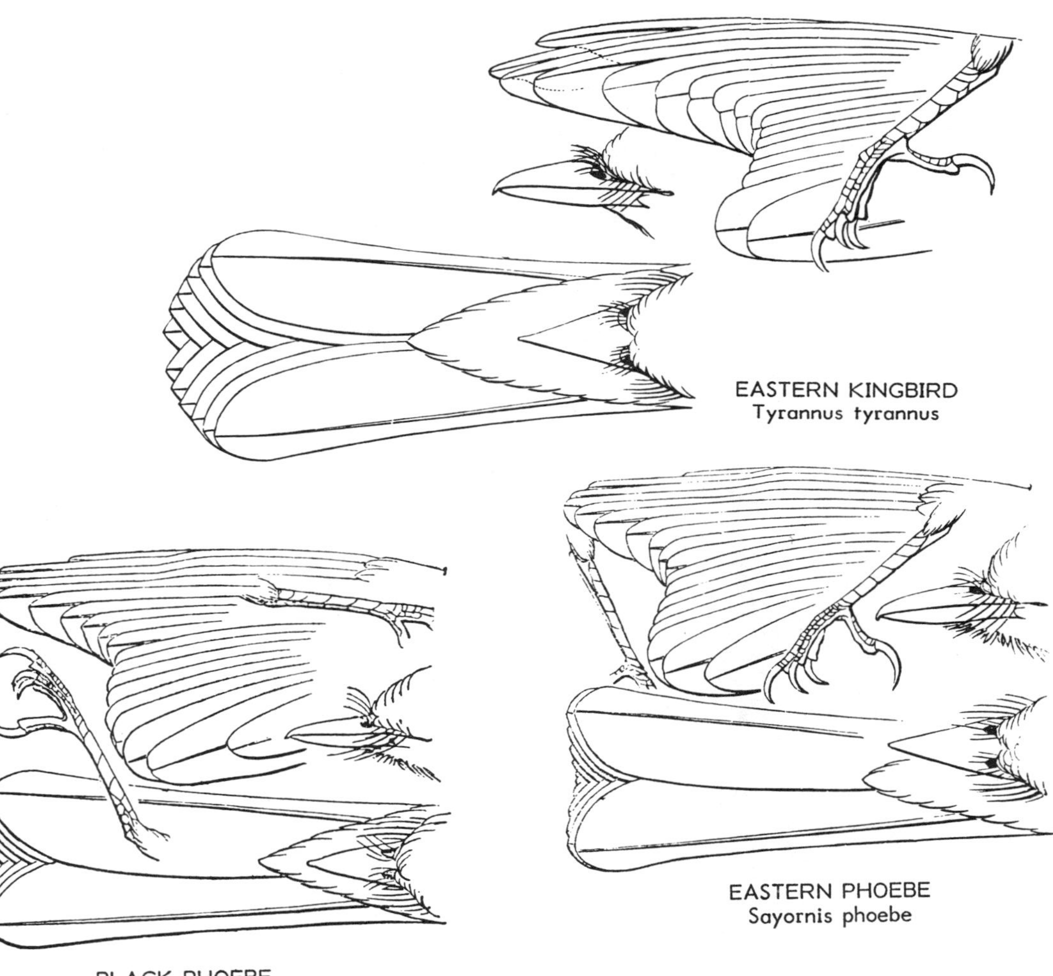

EASTERN KINGBIRD
Tyrannus tyrannus

BLACK PHOEBE
Sayornis nigricans

EASTERN PHOEBE
Sayornis phoebe

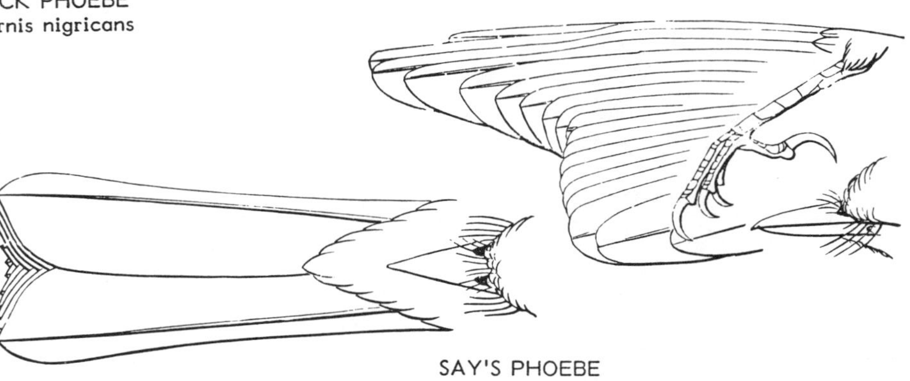

SAY'S PHOEBE
Sayornis saya

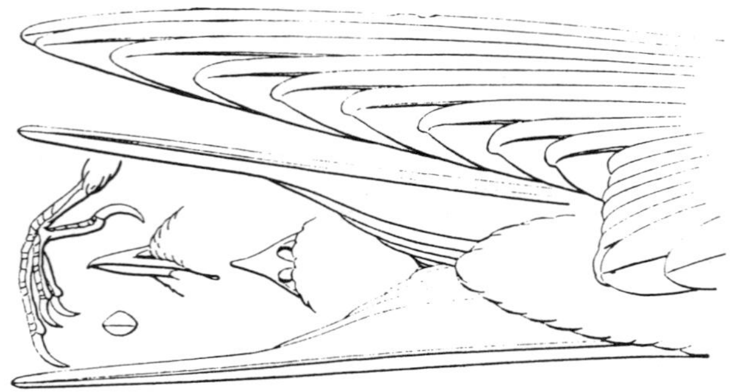

BARN SWALLOW
Hirundo rustica

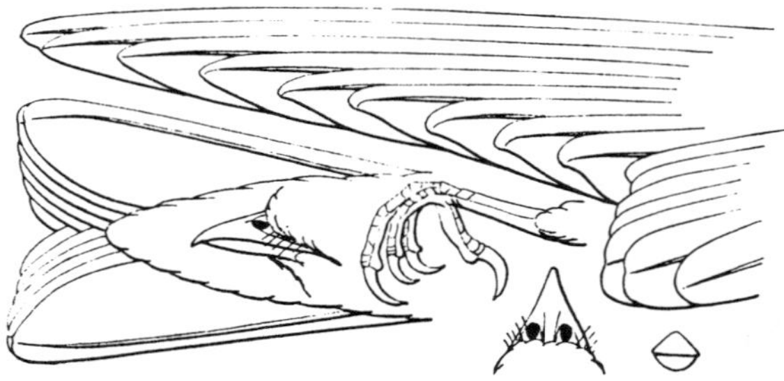

CLIFF SWALLOW
Petrochelidon pyrrhonota

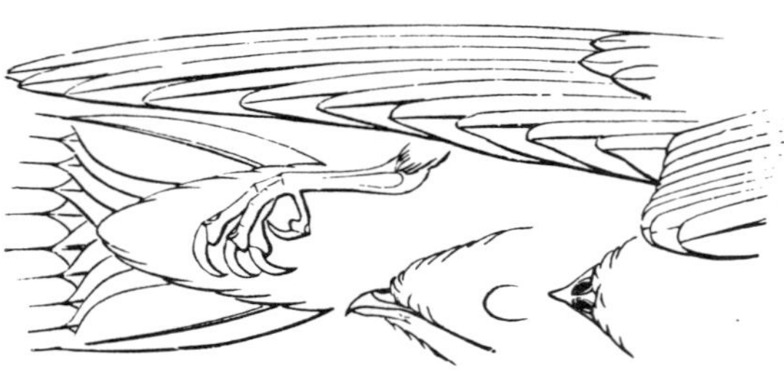

CHIMNEY SWIFT
Chaetura pelagica

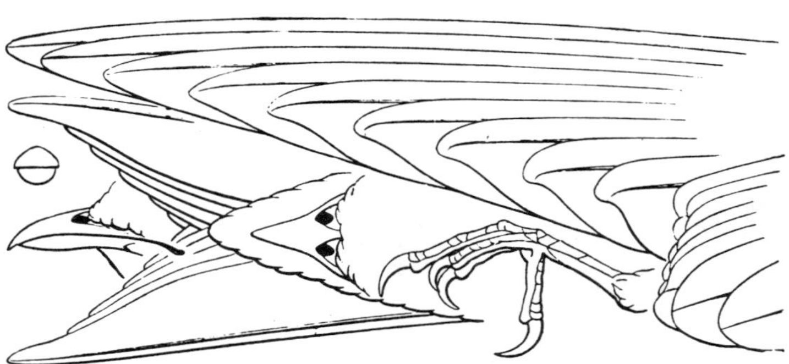

PURPLE MARTIN
Progne subis

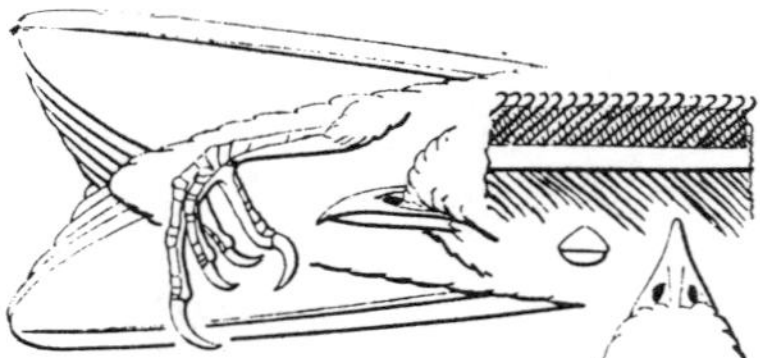

ROUGH-WINGED SWALLOW
Stelgidopteryx ruficollis

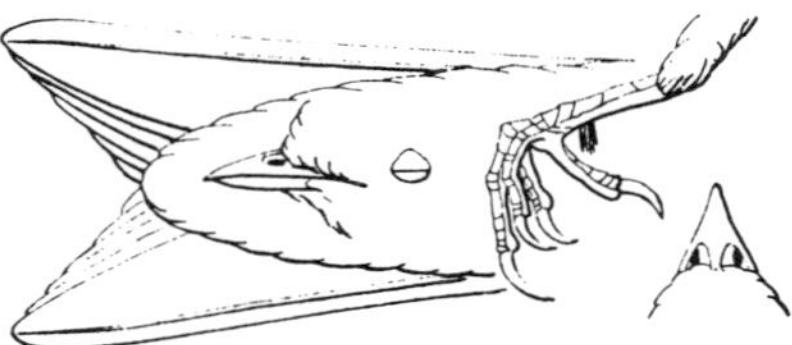

BANK SWALLOW
Riparia riparia

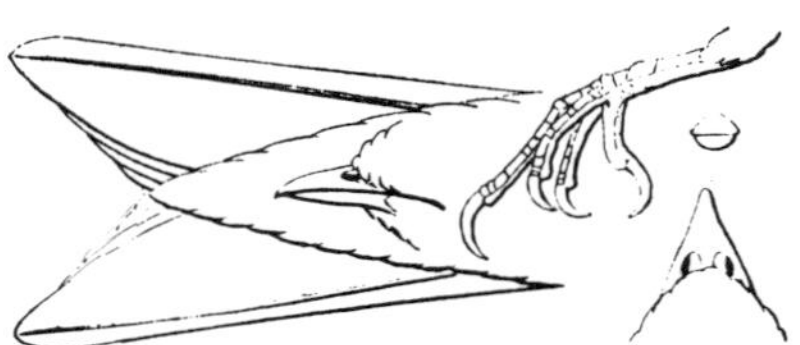

TREE SWALLOW
Iridoprocene bicolor

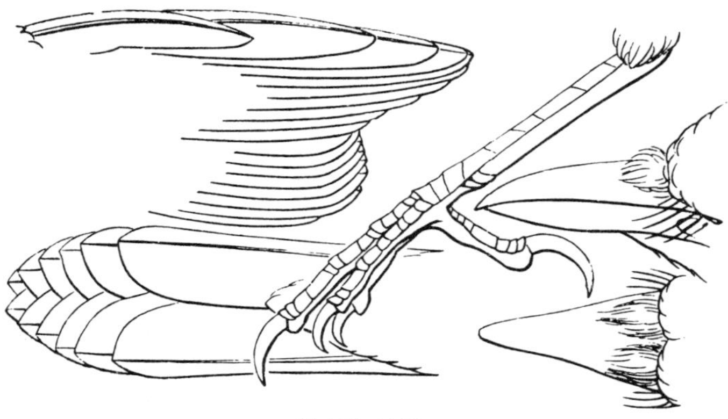
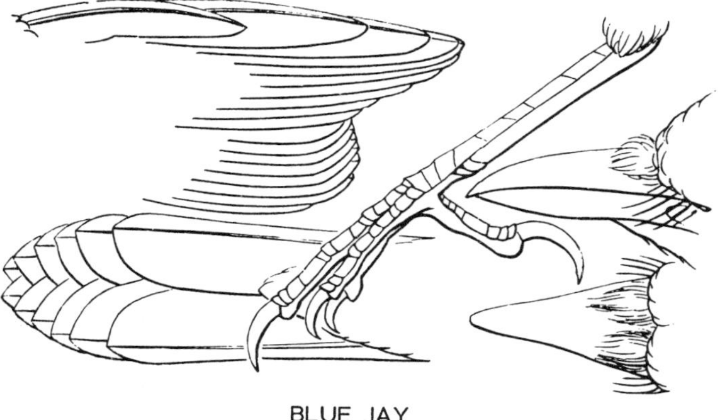

BLUE JAY
Cyanocitta cristata

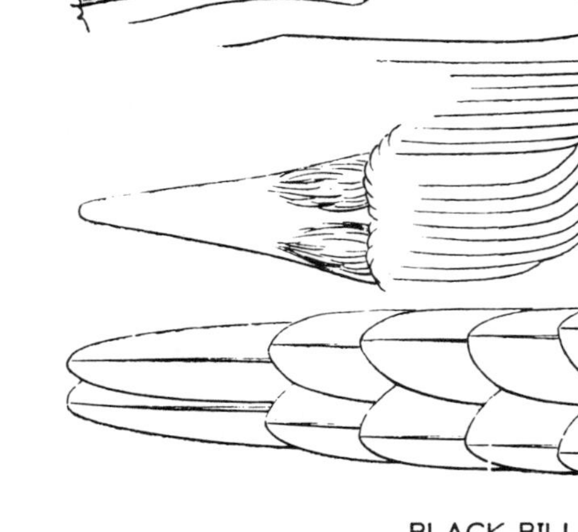
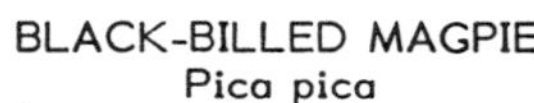

BLACK-BILLED MAGPIE
Pica pica

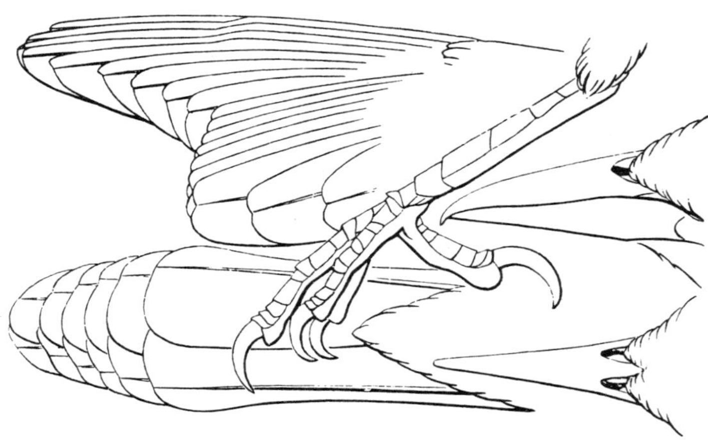

COMMON GRACKLE
Quiscalus quiscula

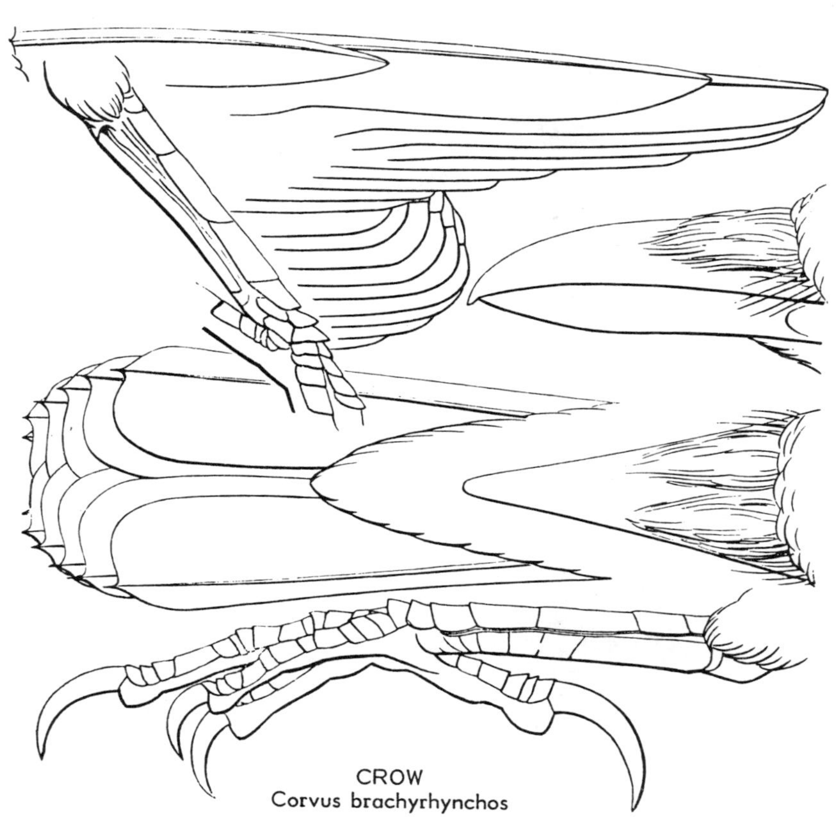

CROW
Corvus brachyrhynchos

TUFTED TITMOUSE
Parus bicolor

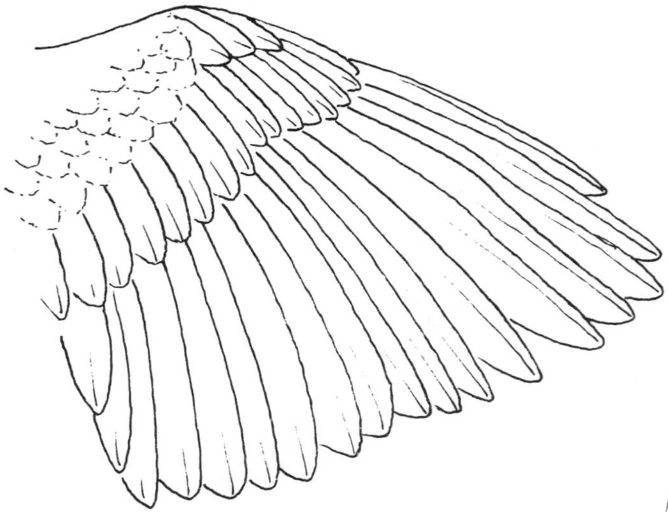

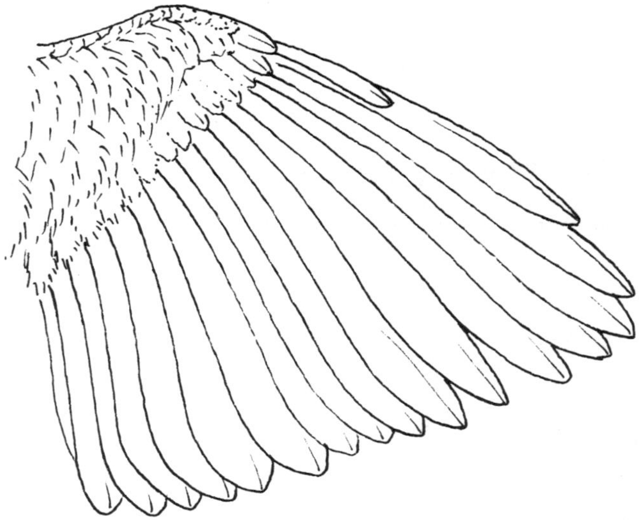

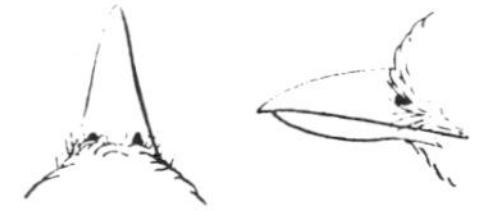

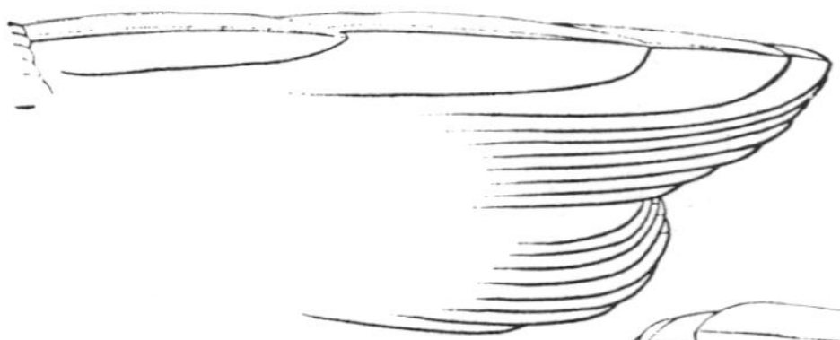

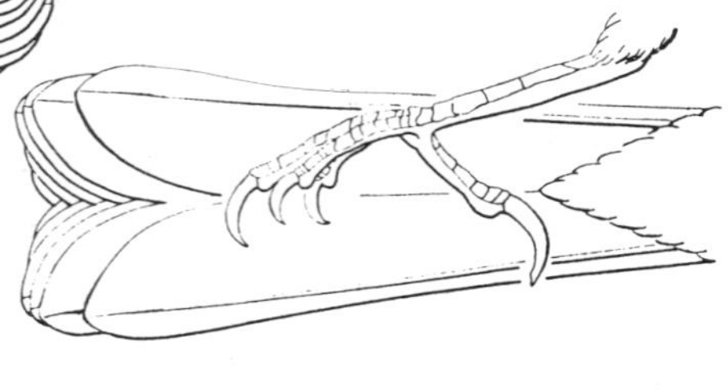

UNDERWING

underwing coverts may be separated by hand, but visually appear as a silky covering

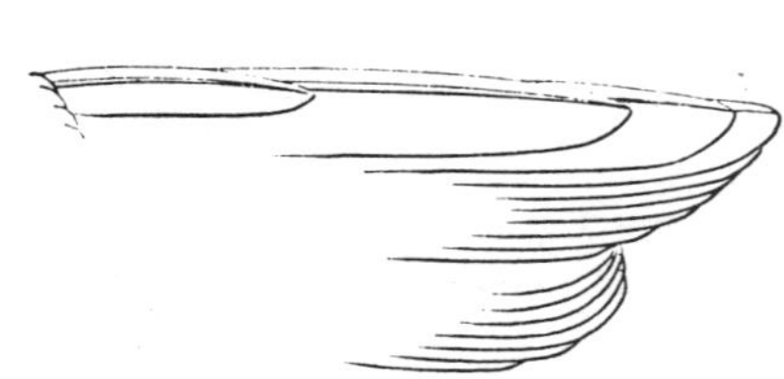

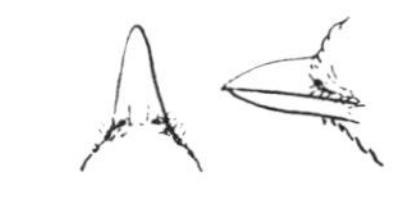

BLACK-CAPPED CHICKADEE
Parus atricapillus

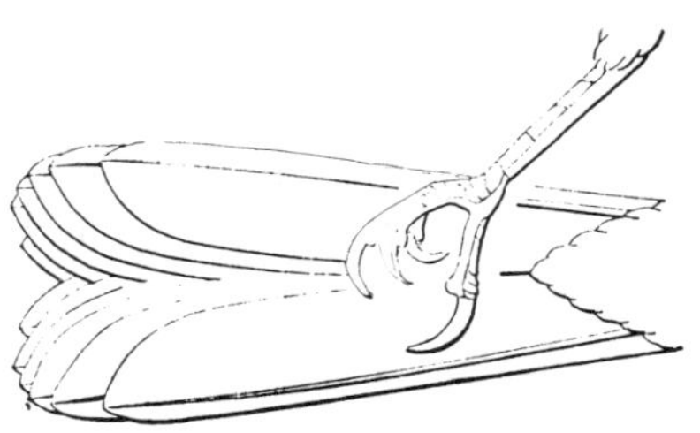

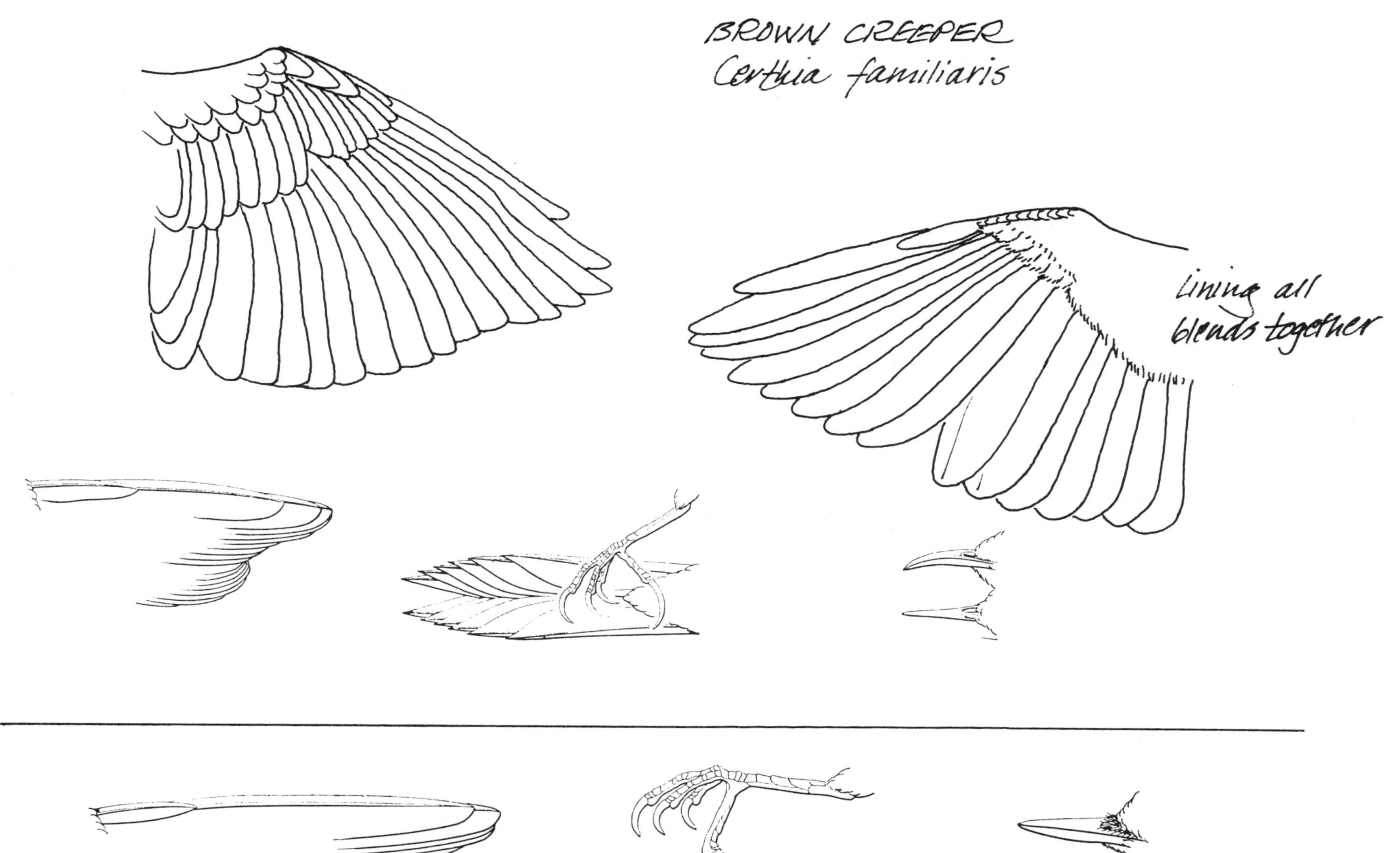

WHITE-BREASTED NUTHATCH
Sitta carolinensis

HOUSE WREN
Troglodytes aedon

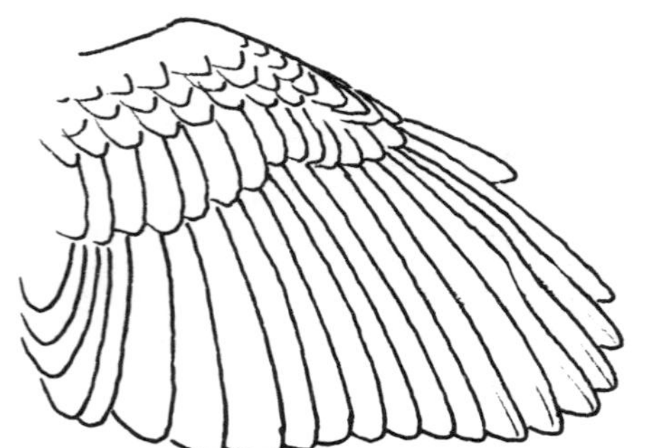

fifth thru tenth primaries have a hairlike leading edge

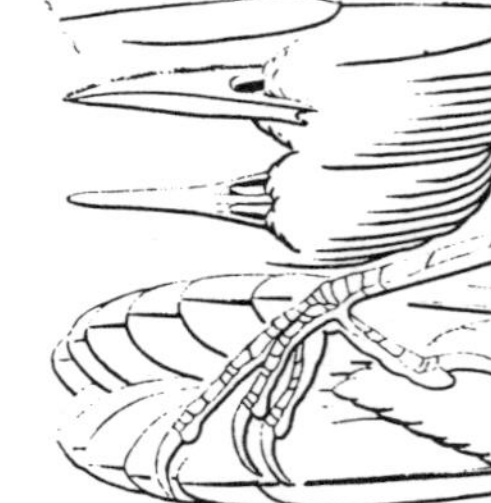

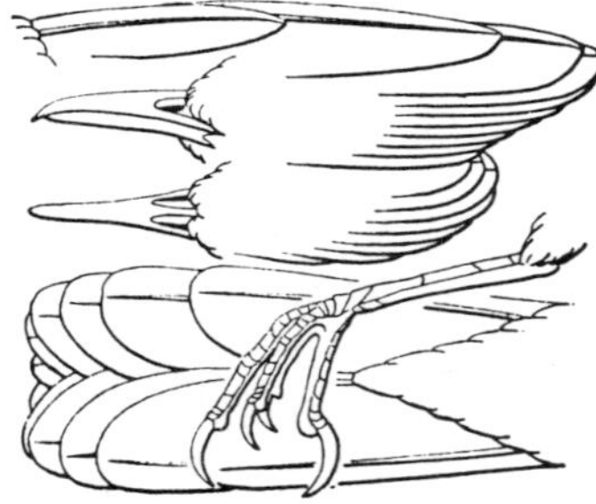

BEWICK'S WREN
Thryomanes bewickii

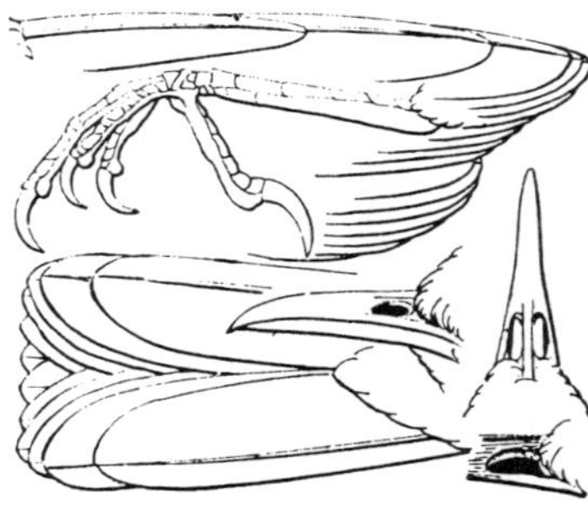

CAROLINA WREN
Thryothorus ludovicianus

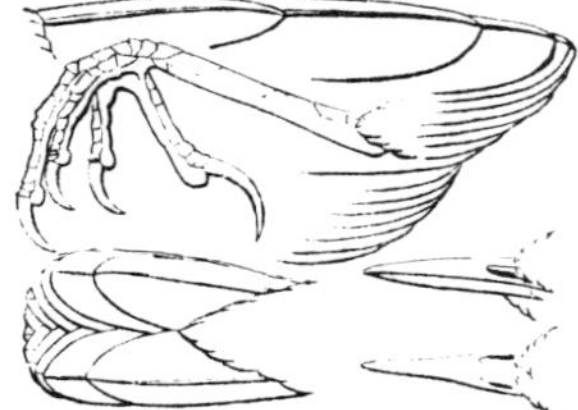

WINTER WREN
Troglodytes troglodytes

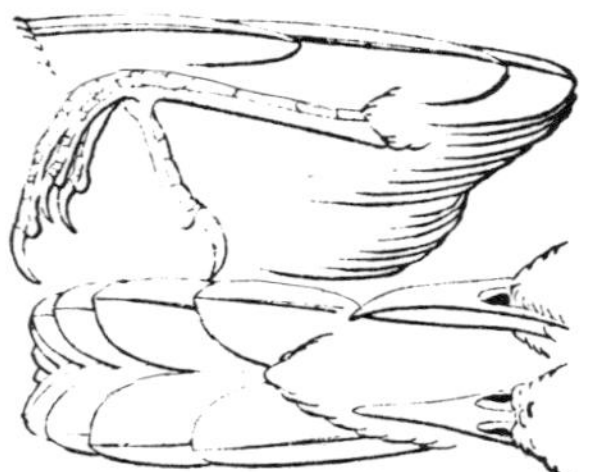

MARSH WREN
Cistothorus palustris

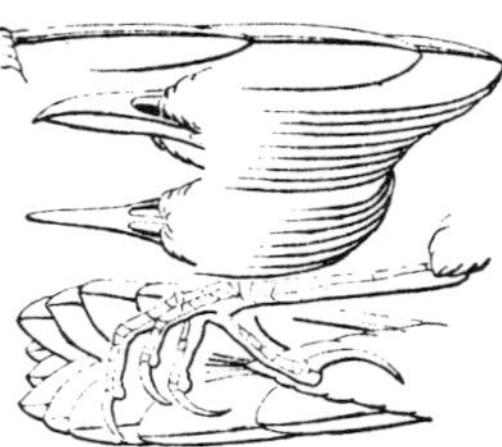

SEDGE WREN
Cistothorus platensis

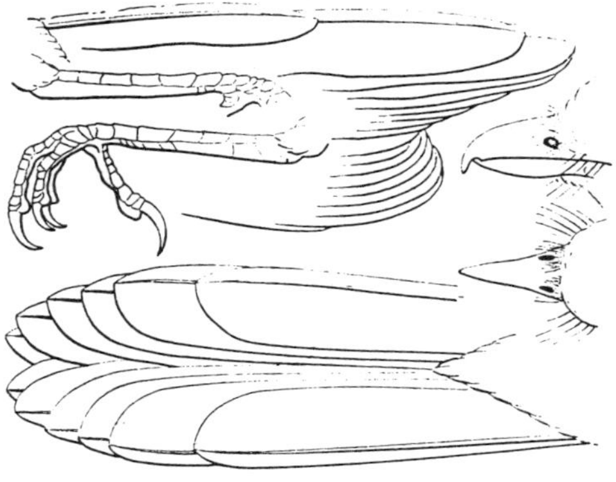

LOGGERHEAD SHRIKE
Lanius ludovicianus

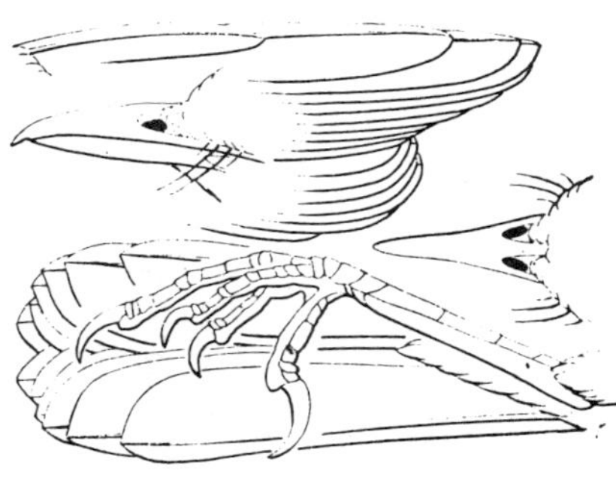

GREY CATBIRD
Dumetella carolinensis

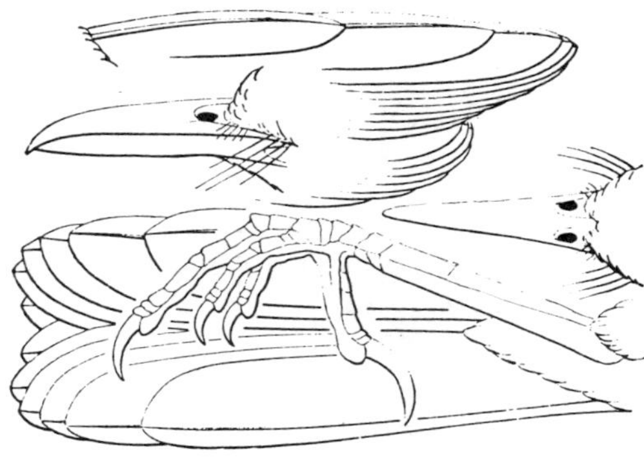

BROWN THRASHER
Toxostoma rufum

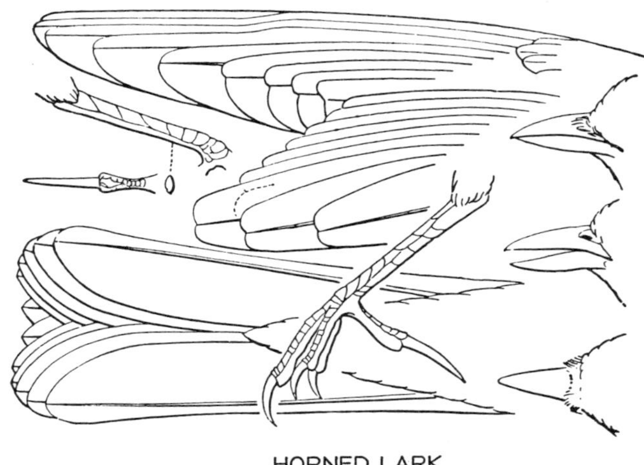

HORNED LARK
Eremophila alpestris

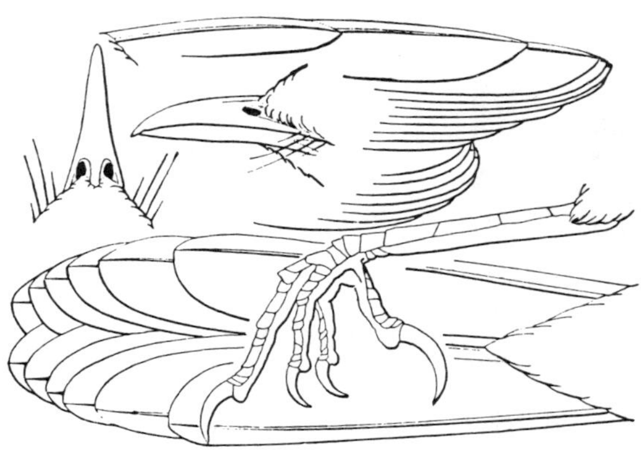

NORTHERN MOCKINGBIRD
Mimus polyglottos

SWAINSON'S THRUSH
Hylocichla ustulata

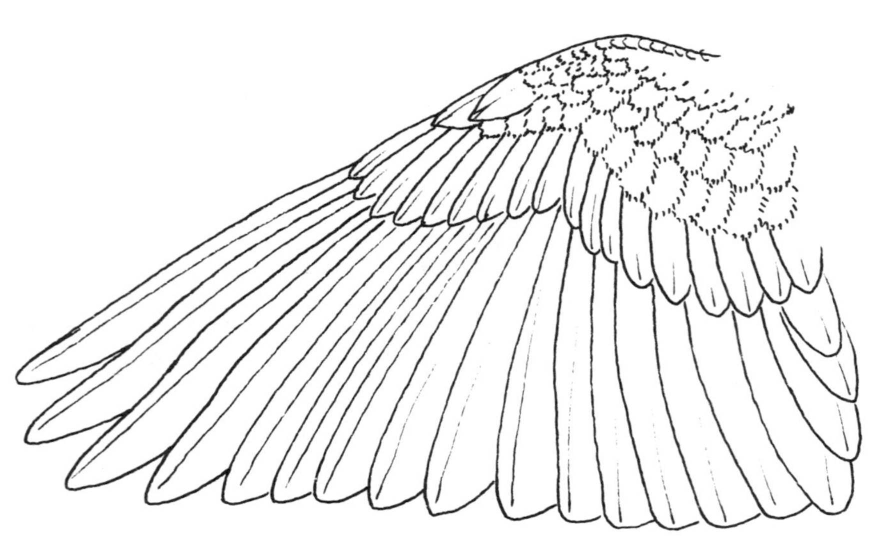

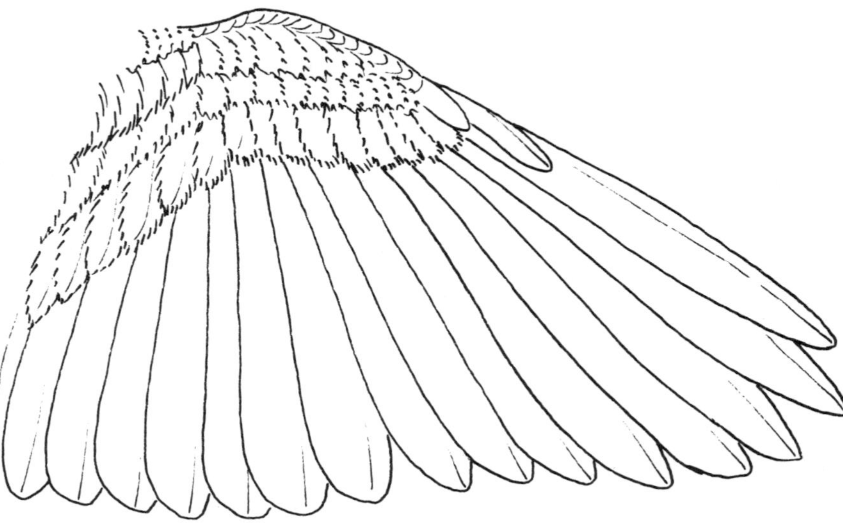

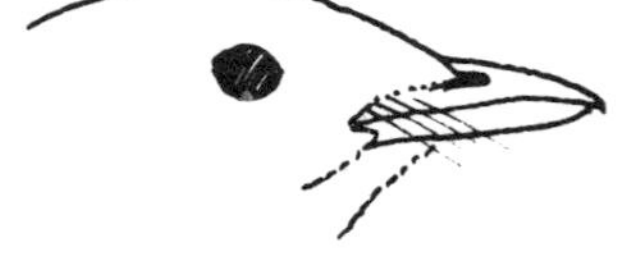

UNDERWING

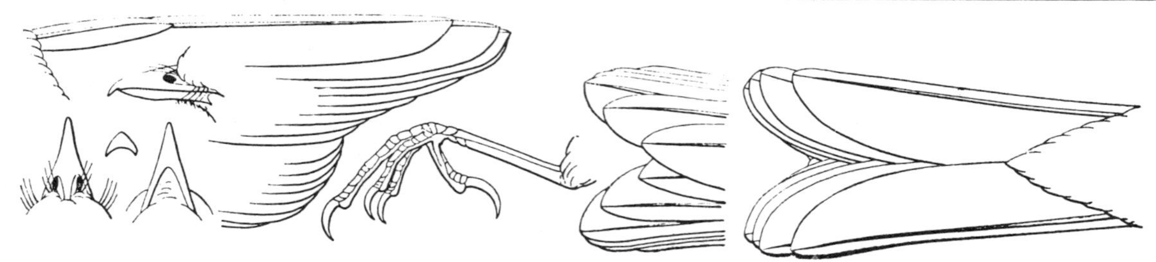

TOWNSEND'S SOLITAIRE
Myadestes townsendi

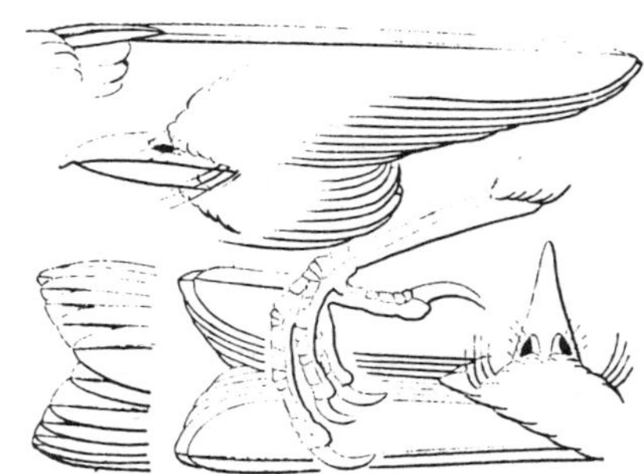

EASTERN BLUEBIRD
Sialia sialis

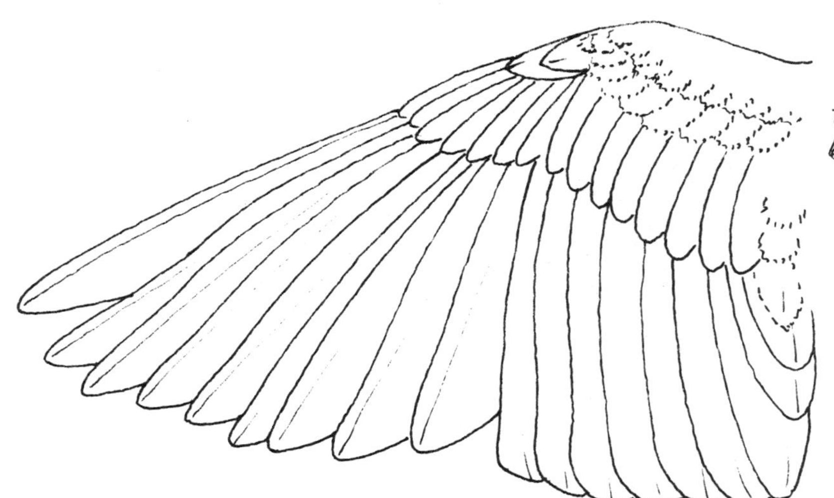

these coverts blend together

VEERY
Catharus fuscescens

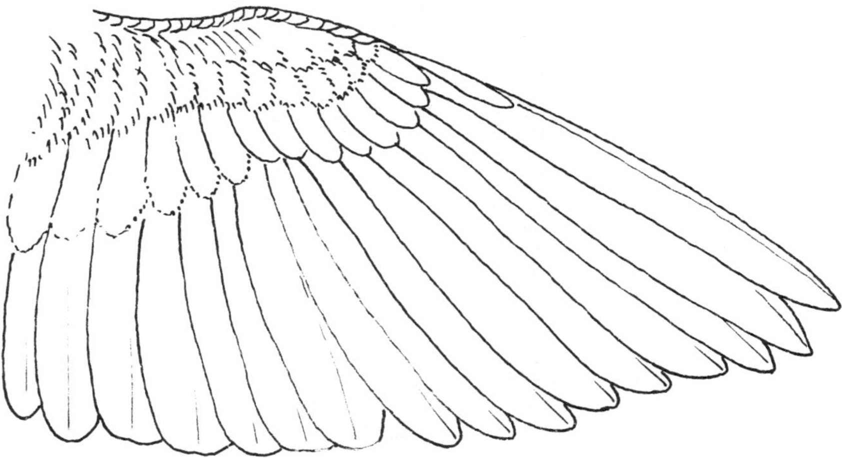

UNDERWING

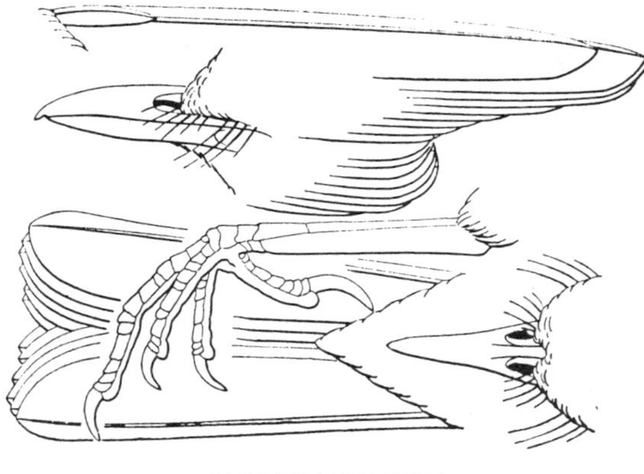

AMERICAN ROBIN
Turdus migratorius

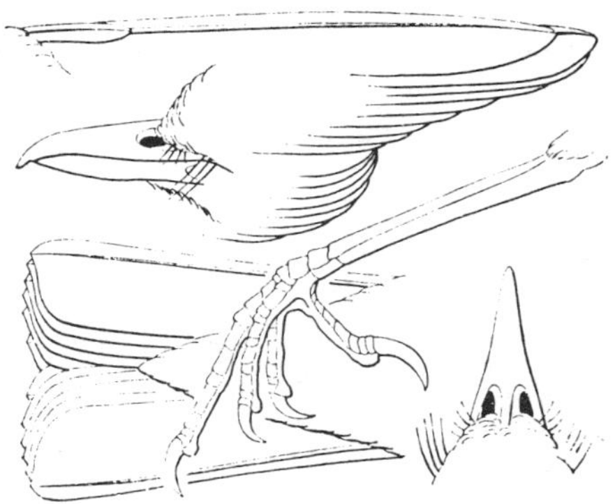

WOOD THRUSH
Hylocichla mustelina

GOLDEN-CROWNED KINGLET
Regulus satrapa

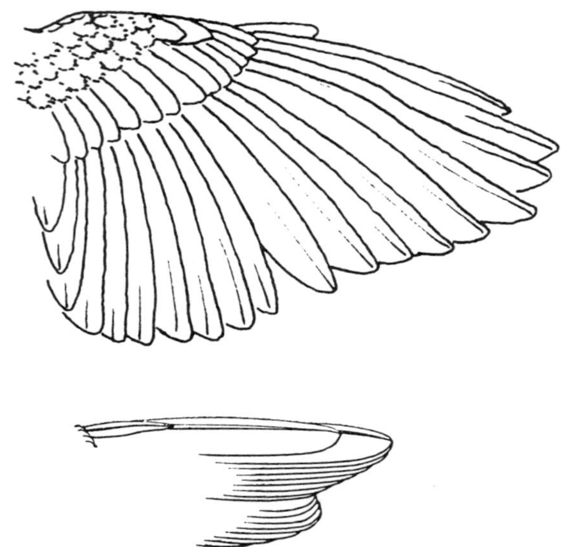

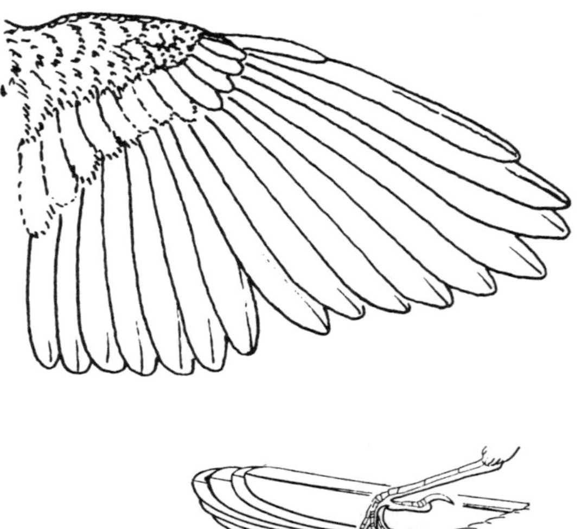

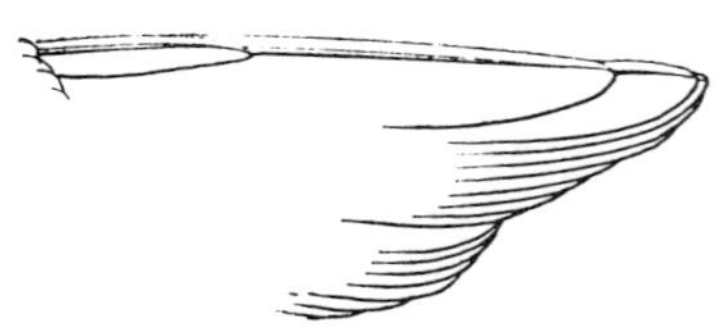

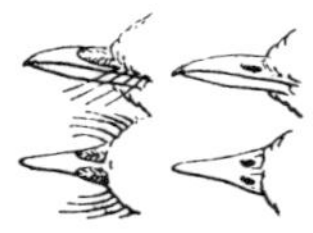

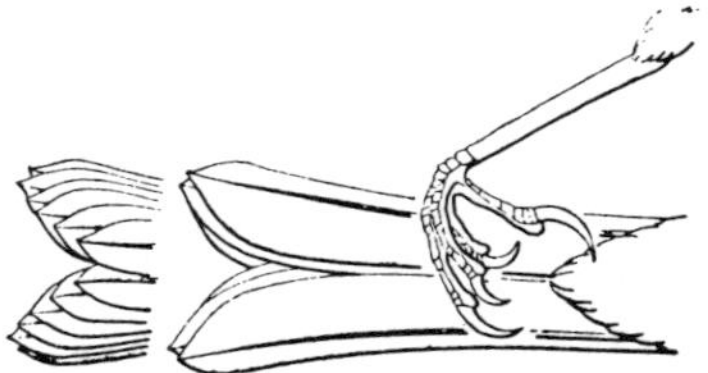

RUBY-CROWNED KINGLET
Regulus calendula

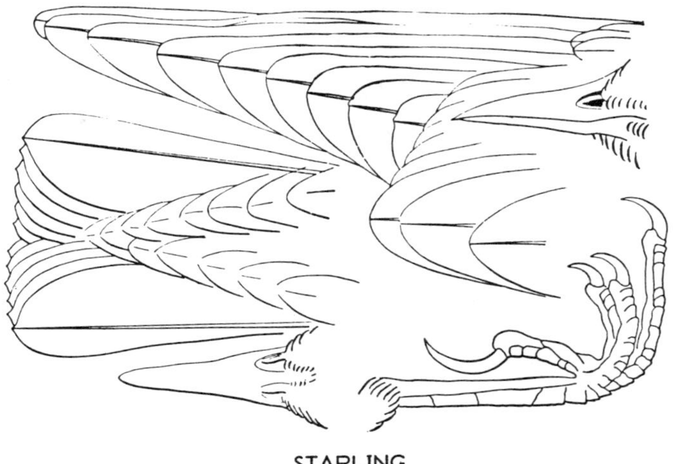

STARLING
Sturnus vulgaris

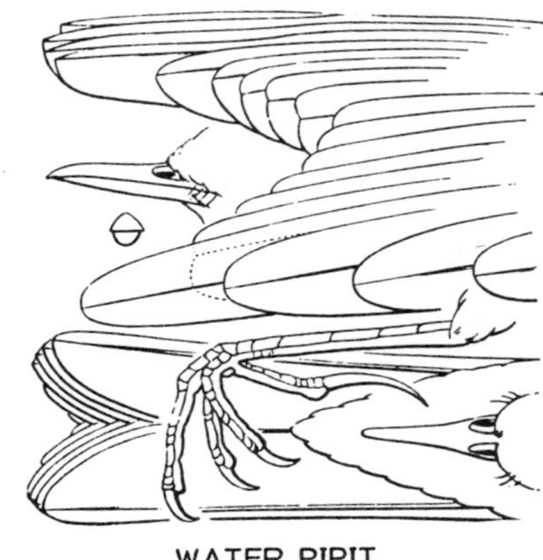

WATER PIPIT
Anthus spinoletta

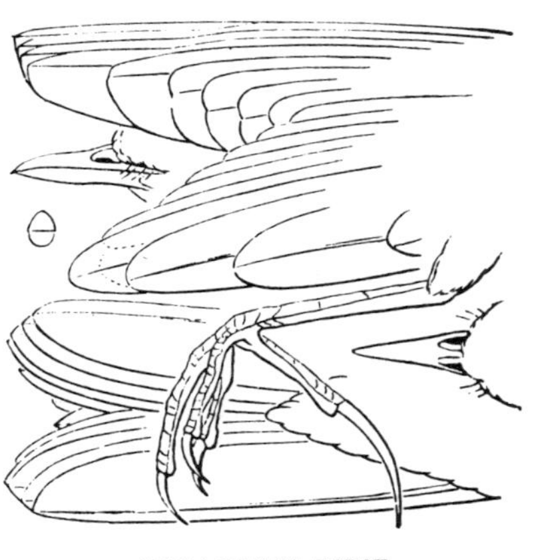

SPRAGUE'S PIPIT
Anthus spragueii

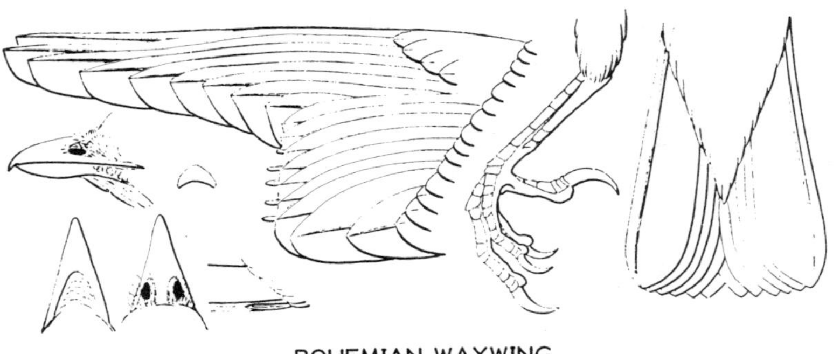

BOHEMIAN WAXWING
Bombycilla garrulus

BLACKBURNIAN WARBLER
Dendroica fusca

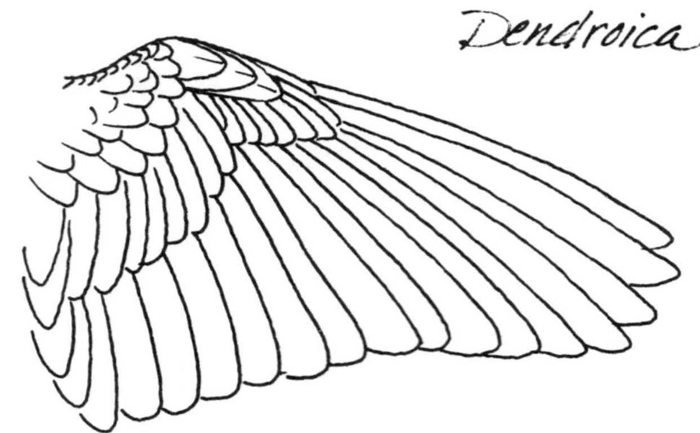

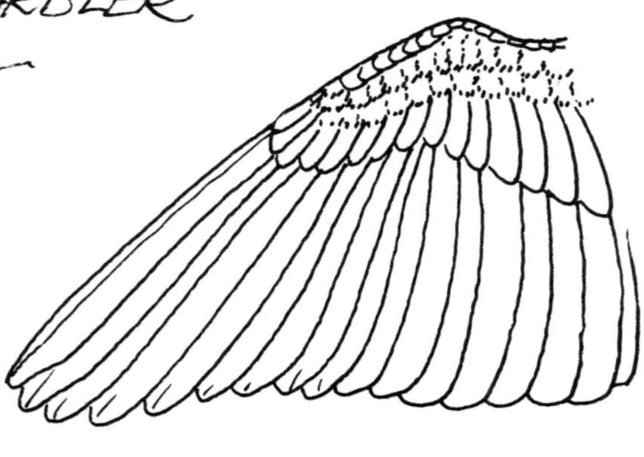

UNDERWING

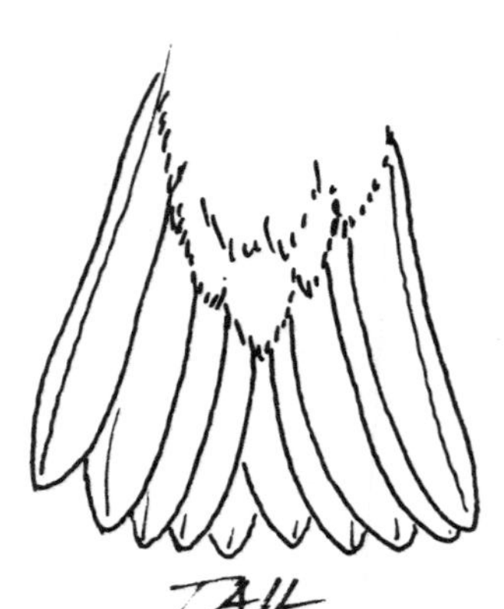

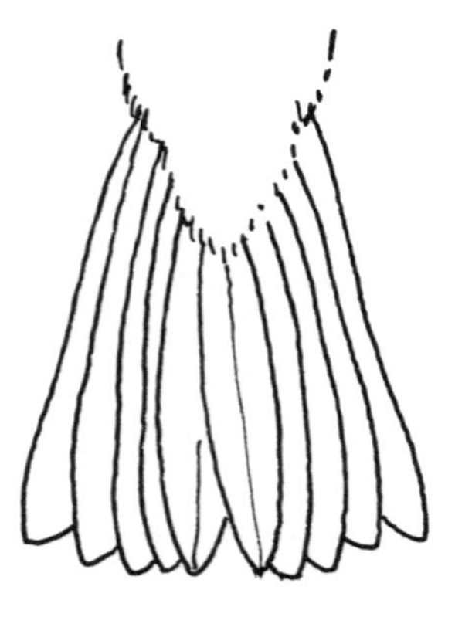

TAIL UNDERSIDE

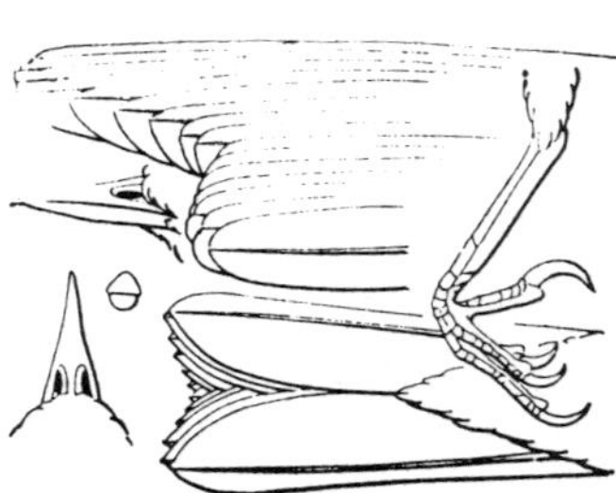

NASHVILLE WARBLER
Vermivora ruficapilla

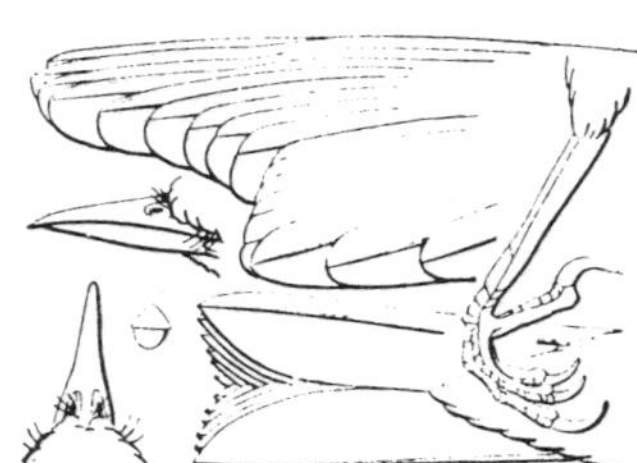

NORTHERN PARULA WARBLER
Parula americana

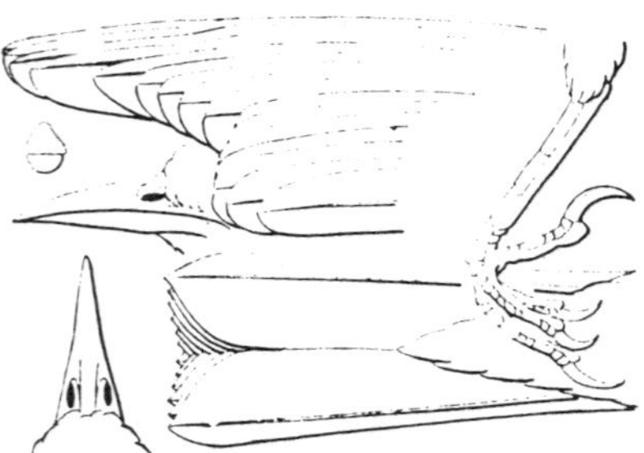

WORM EATING WARBLER
Helmitheros vermivorus

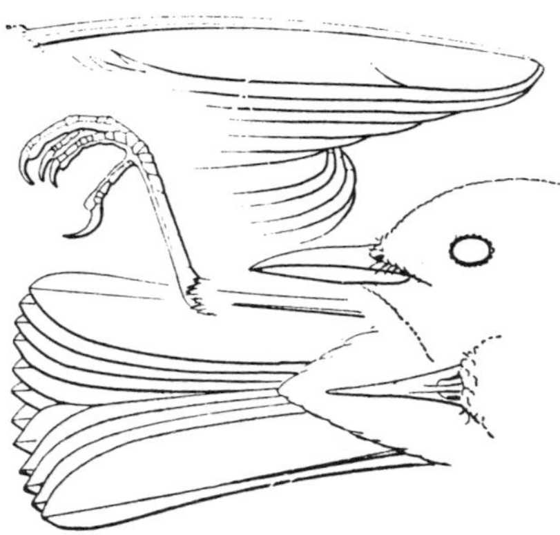

YELLOW-THROATED WARBLER
Dendroica dominica

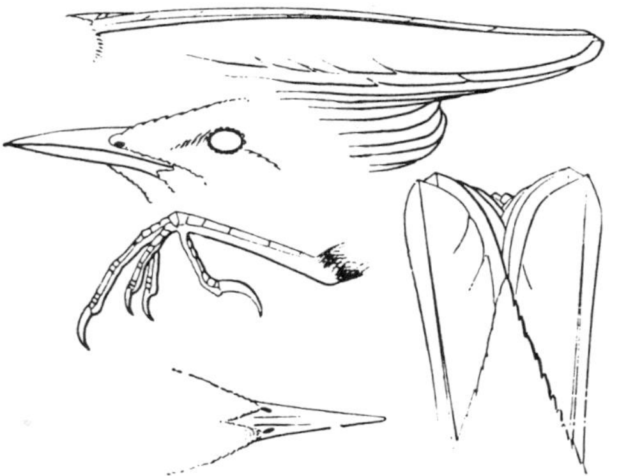
SWAINSON'S WARBLER
Limnothlypis swainsonii

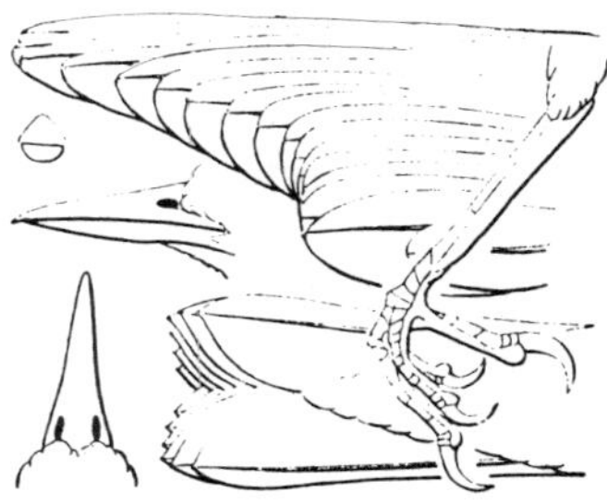
PROTHONOTARY WARBLER
Protonotaria citrea

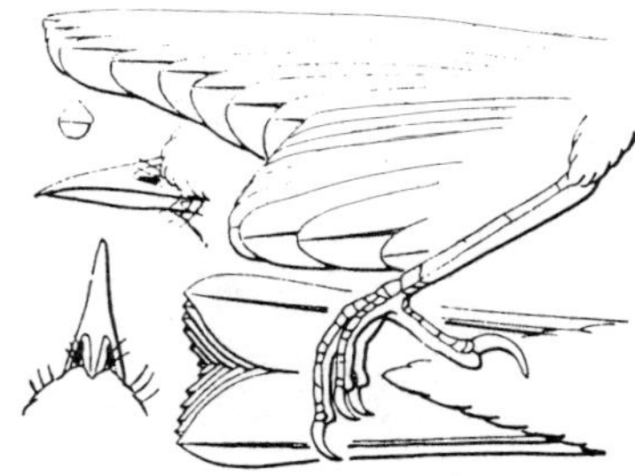
CAPE MAY WARBLER
Dendroica tigrina

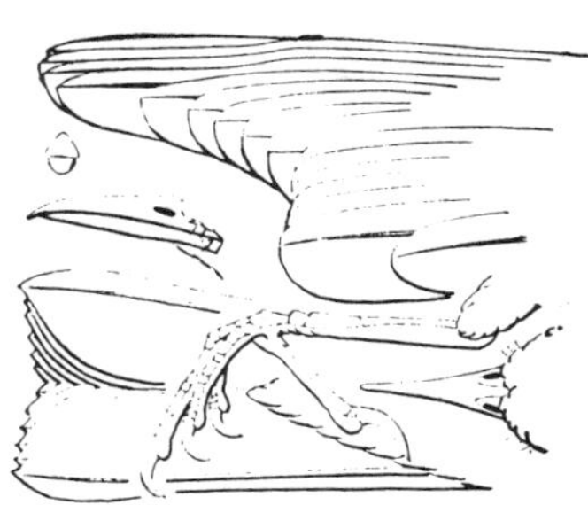
BLACK-AND-WHITE WARBLER
Mniotilta varia

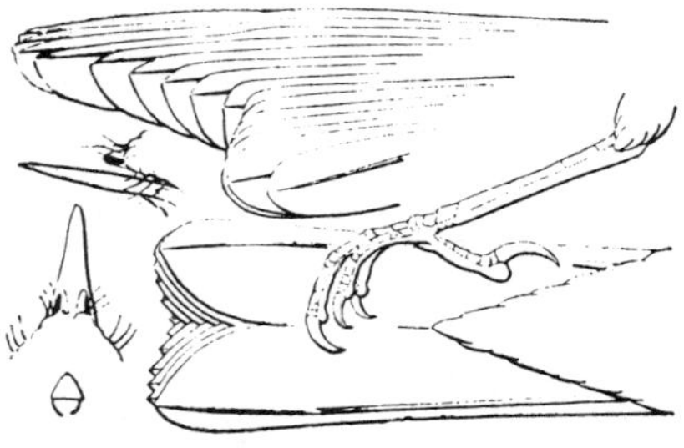
YELLOW-RUMPED WARBLER
Dendroica coronata

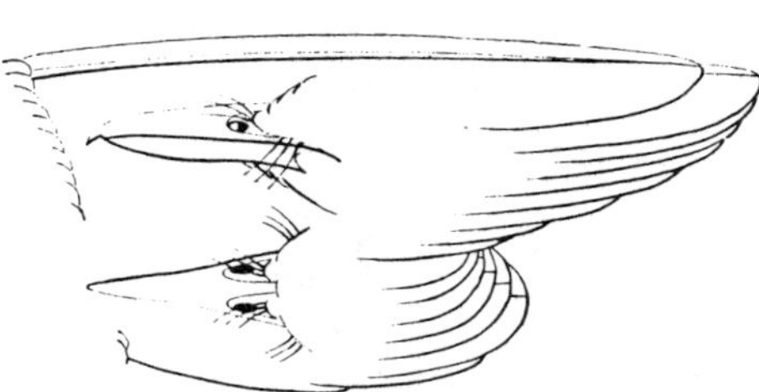
RED-EYED VIREO
Vireo olivaceus

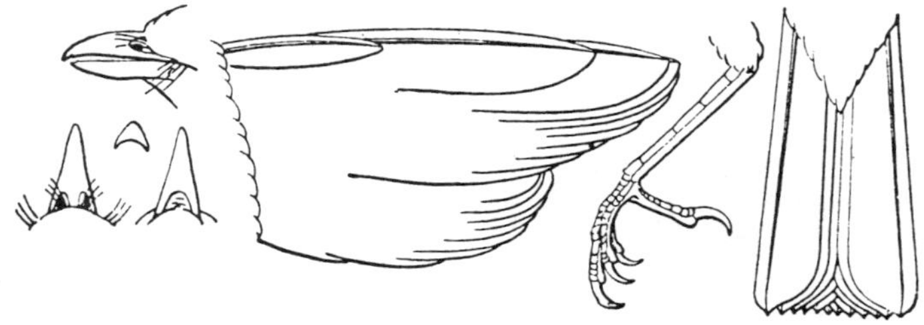
WHITE-EYED VIREO
Vireo griseus

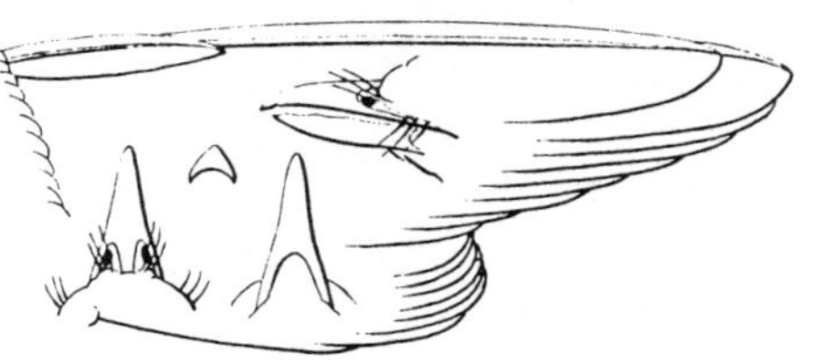
SOLITARY VIREO
Vireo solitarius

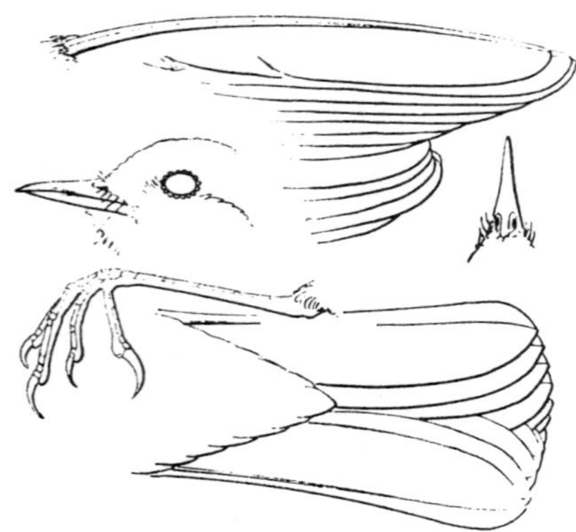

PALM WARBLER
Dendroica palmarum

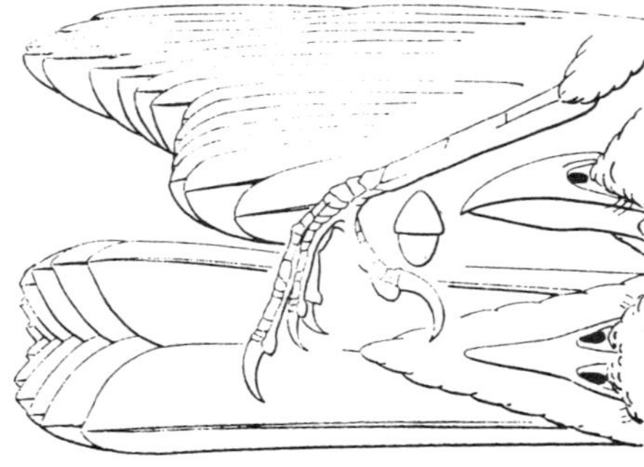

YELLOW-BREASTED CHAT
Icteria virens

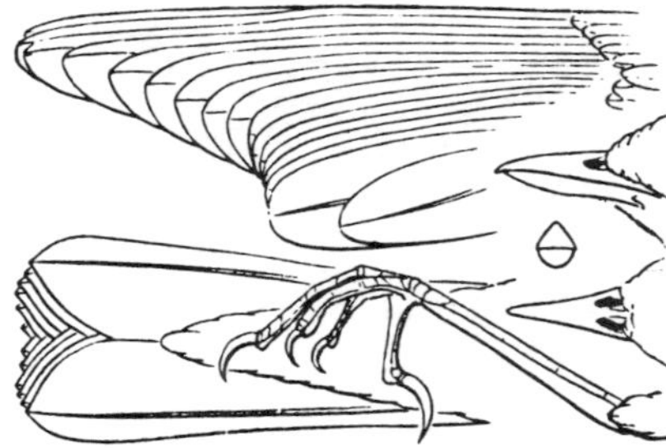

KENTUCKY WARBLER
Oporornis formosus

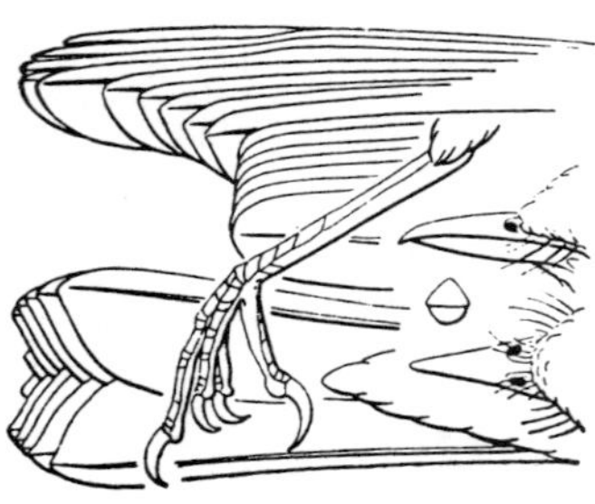

HOODED WARBLER
Wilsonia citrina

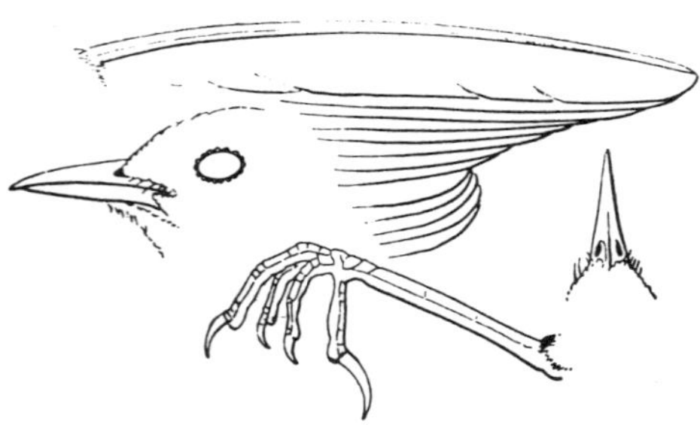

CONNECTICUT WARBLER
Oporornis agilis

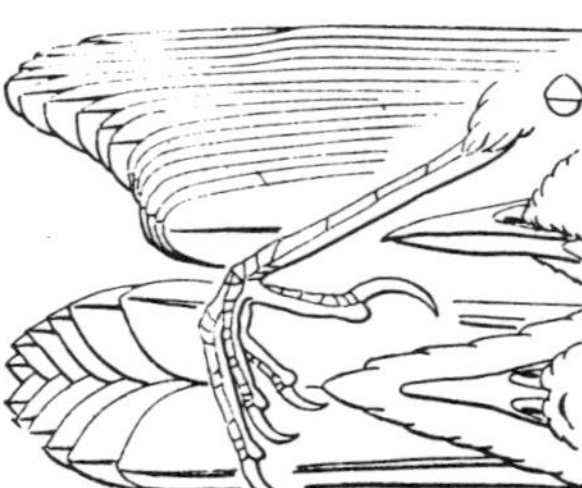

COMMON YELLOWTHROAT
Geothlypis trichas

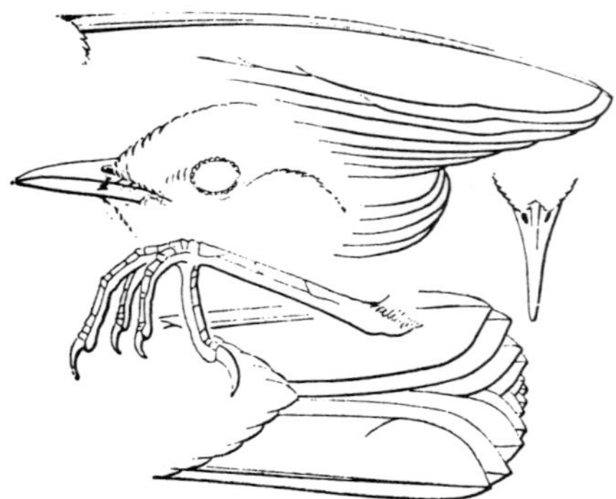

BLACK-THROATED GREEN WARBLER
Dendroica virens

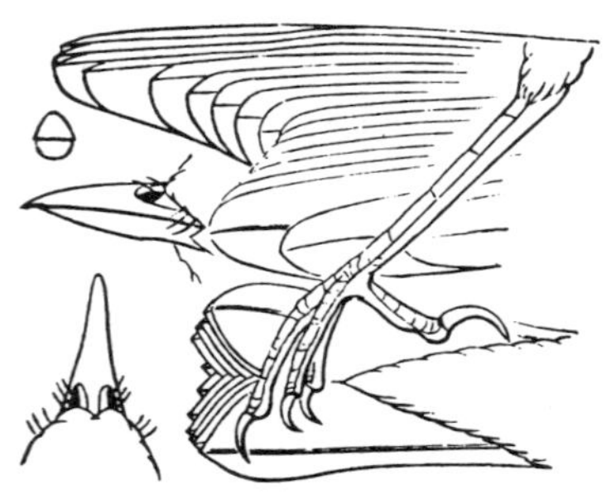

OVENBIRD
Seiurus aurocapillus

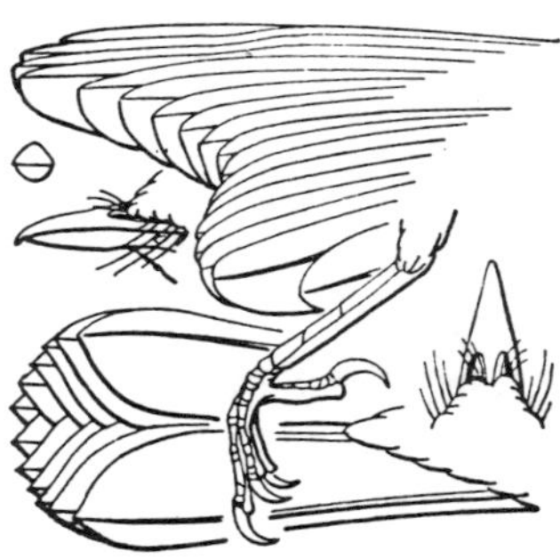

AMERICAN REDSTART
Setophaga ruticilla

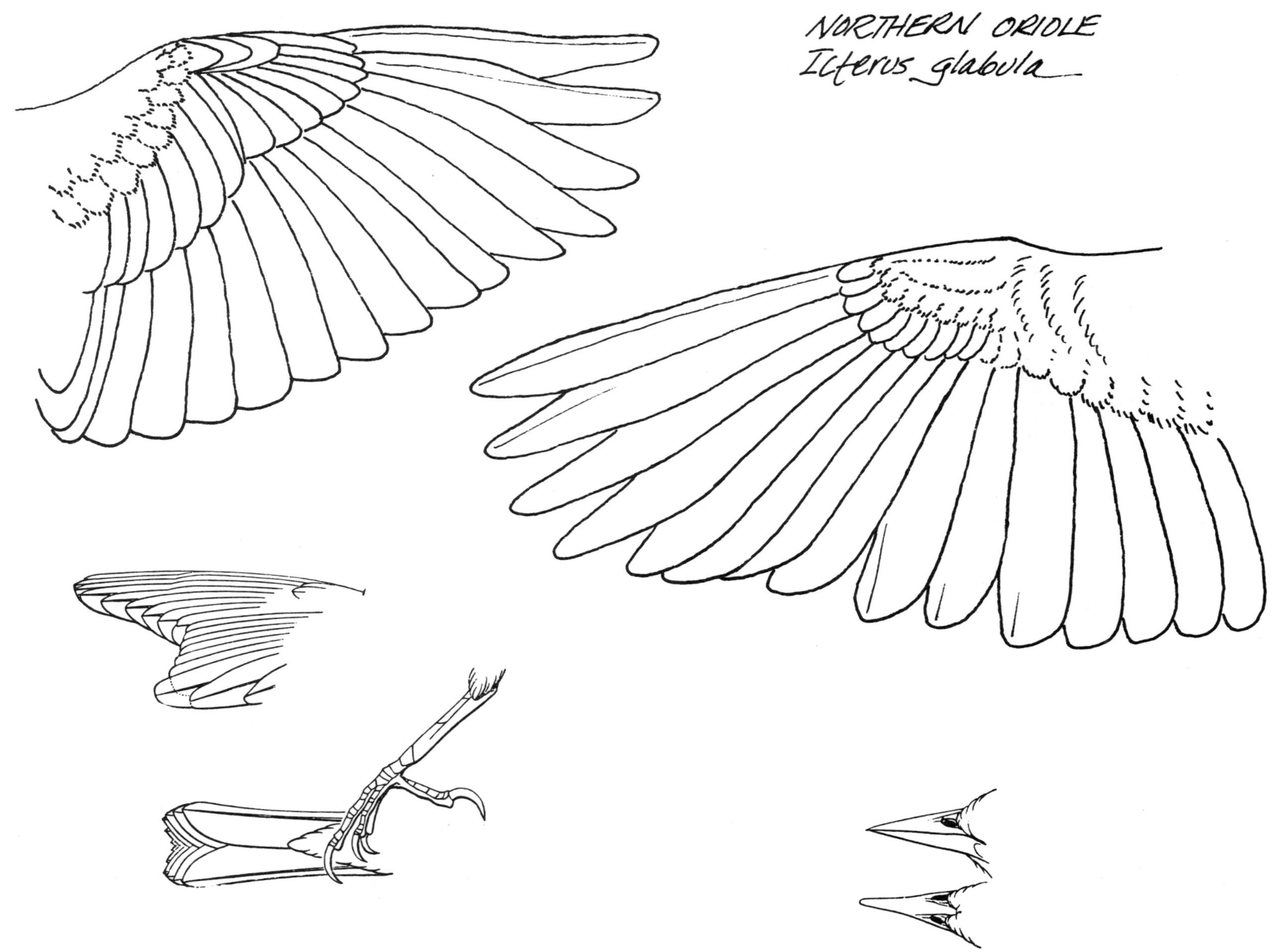
NORTHERN ORIOLE
Icterus glabula

SCARLET
SCARLET TANAGER
Piranga olivacea

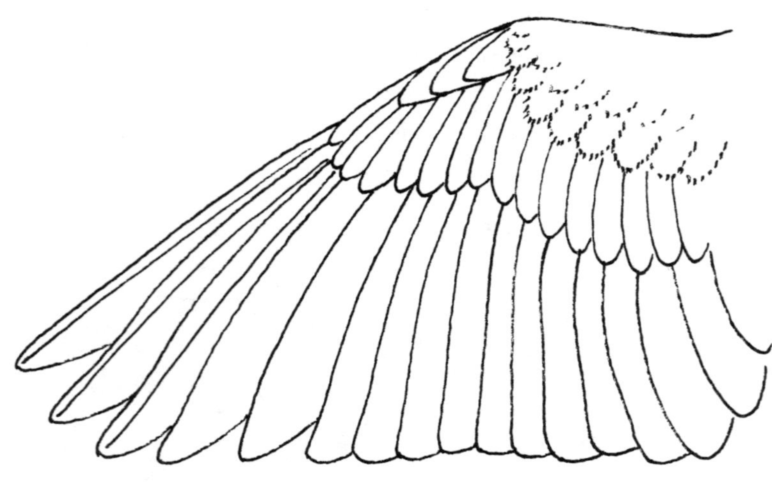

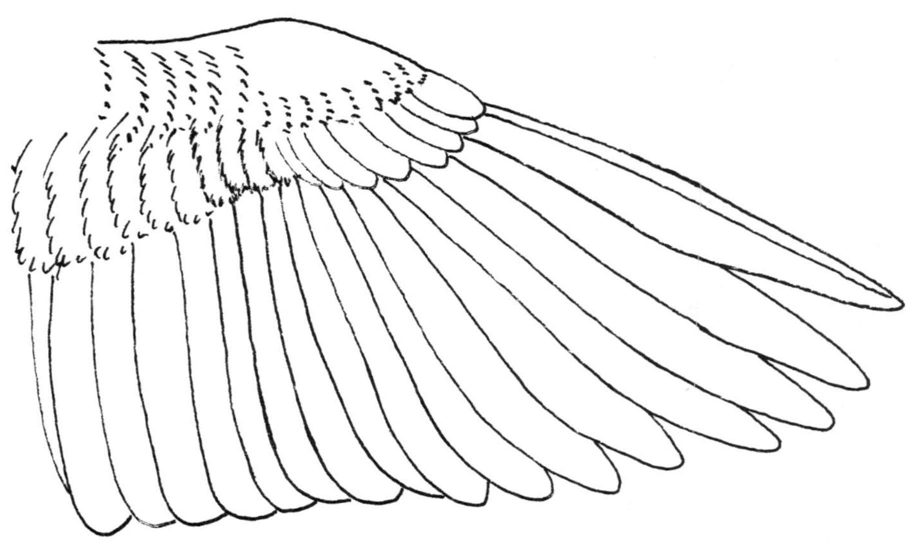

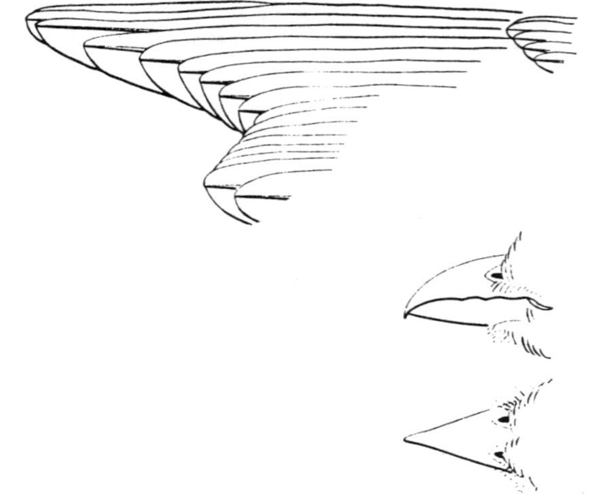

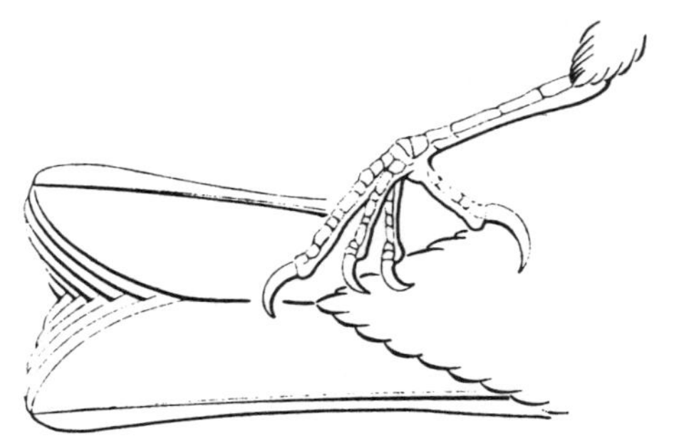

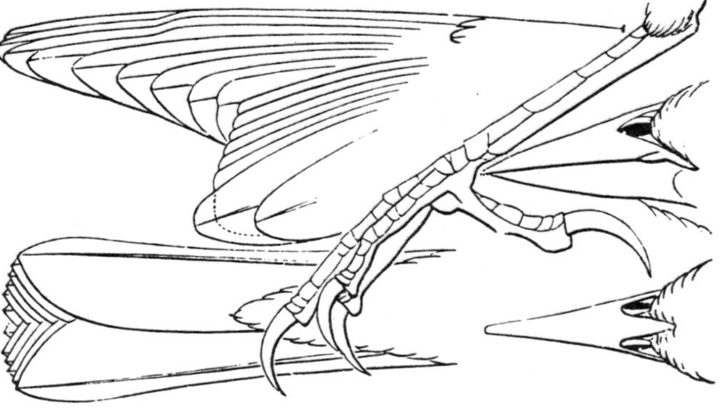

YELLOW-HEADED BLACKBIRD
Xanthocephalus xanthocephalus

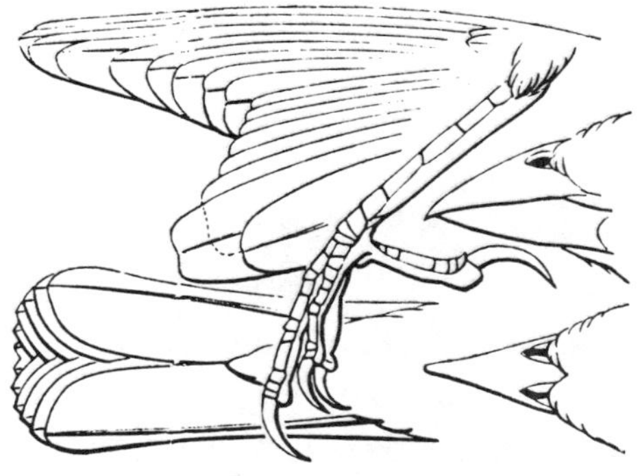

BROWN-HEADED COWBIRD
Molothrus ater

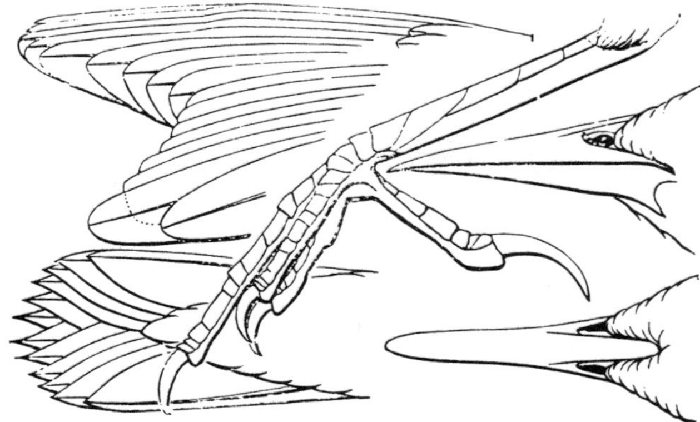

EASTERN MEADOWLARK
Sturnella magna

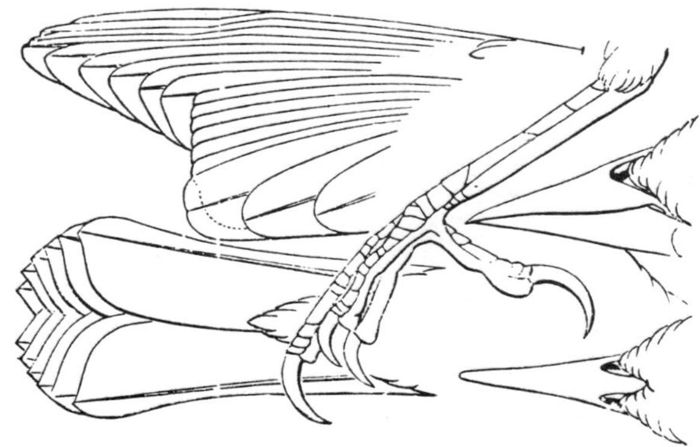

RED-WINGED BLACKBIRD
Agelaius phoeniceus

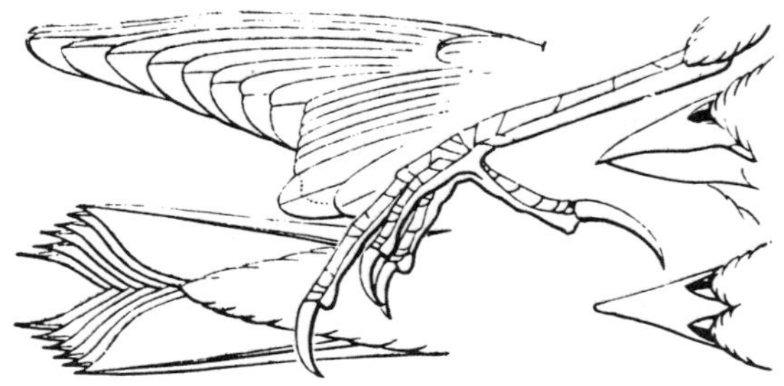

BOBLINK
Dolichonyx oryzivorus

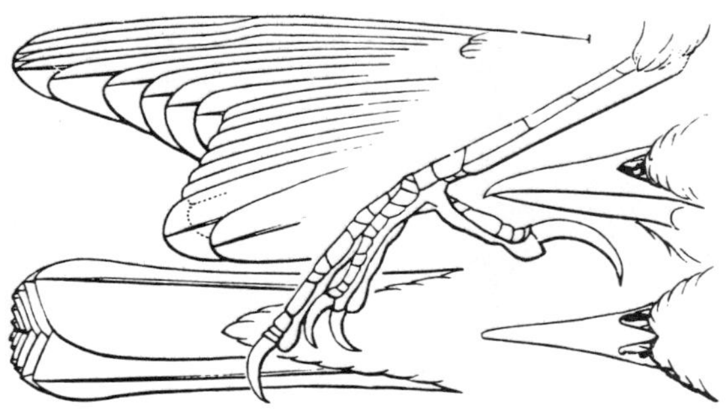

RUSTY BLACKBIRD
Euphagus carolinus

NORTHERN CARDINAL
Cardinalis cardinalis

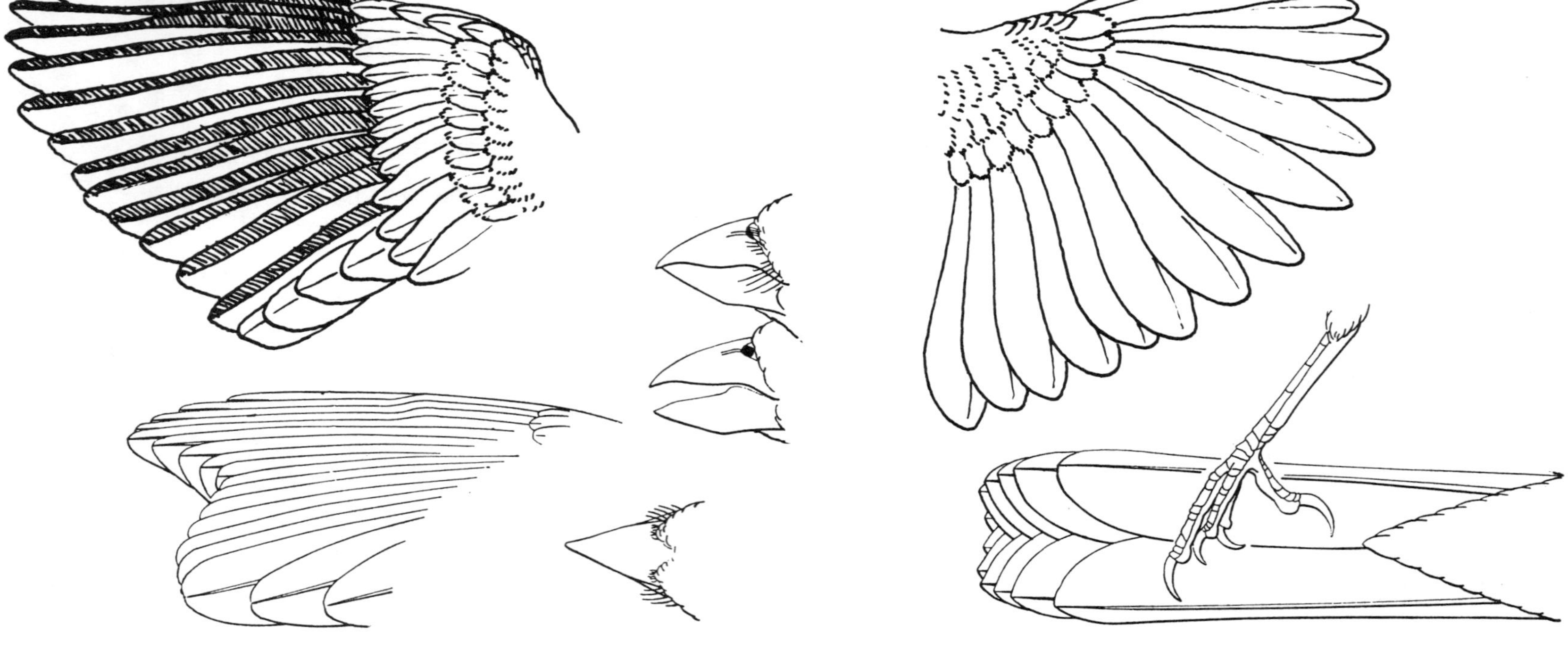

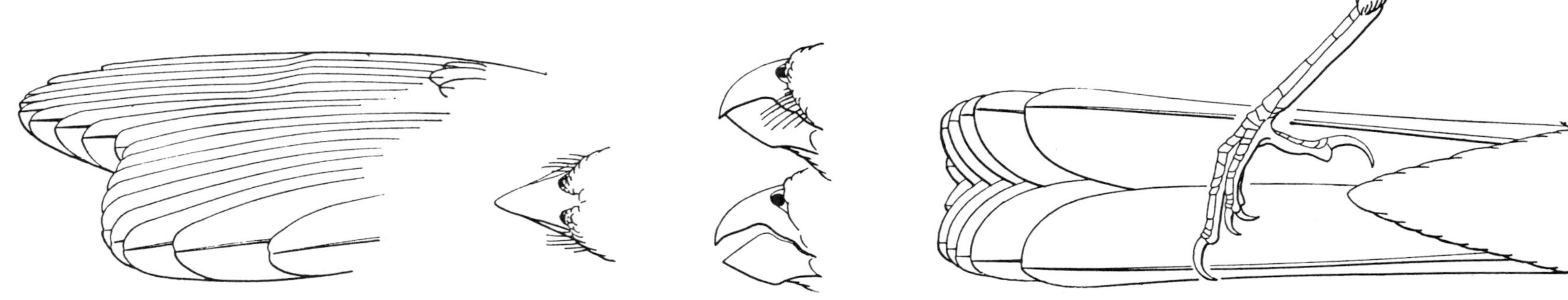

PYRRHULOXIA
Cardinalis sinuatus

INDIGO BUNTING
Passerina cyanea

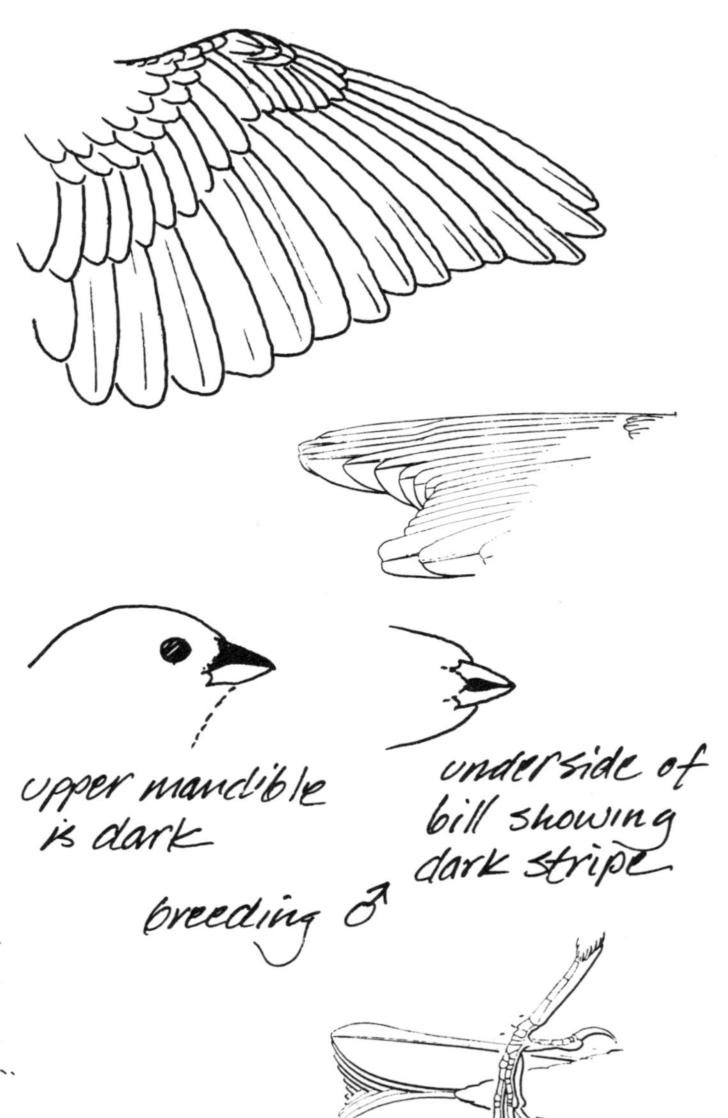

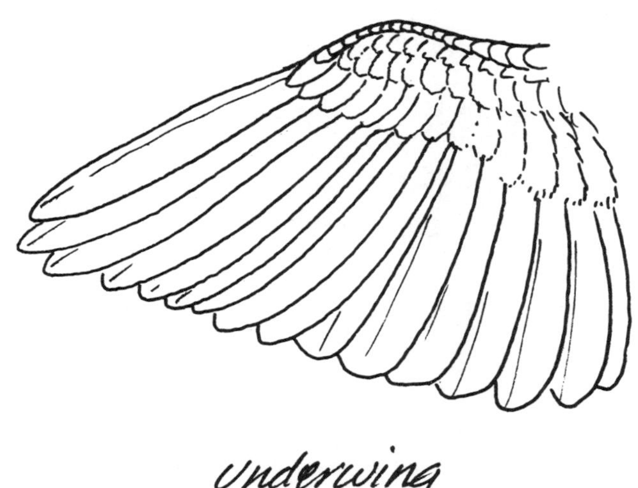

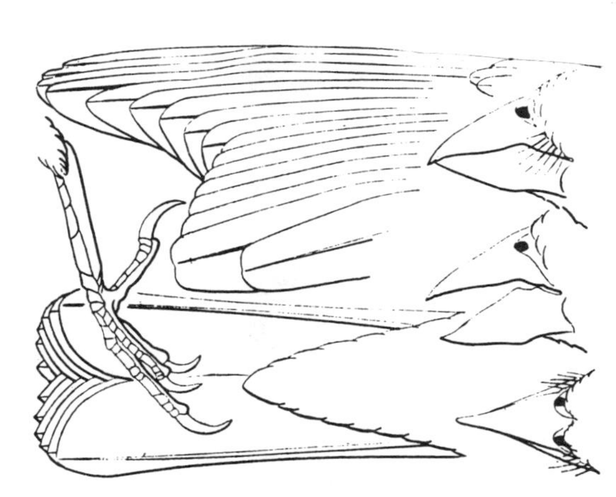

BLUE GROSBEAK
Guiraca caerulea

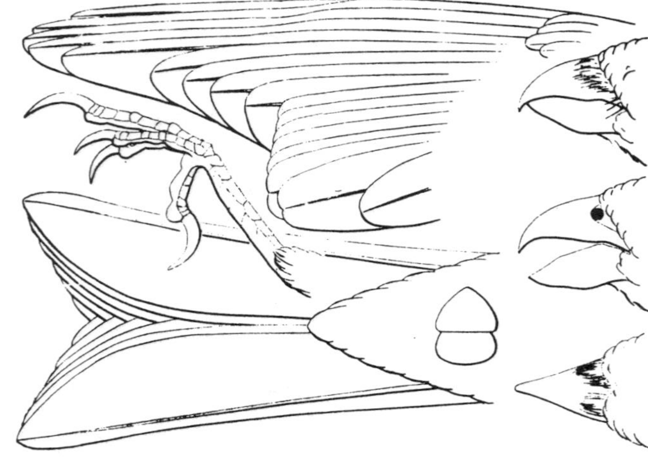

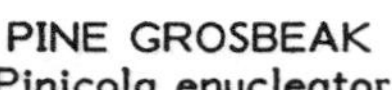

PINE GROSBEAK
Pinicola enucleator

EVENING GROSBEAK
Hesperiphona vespertina

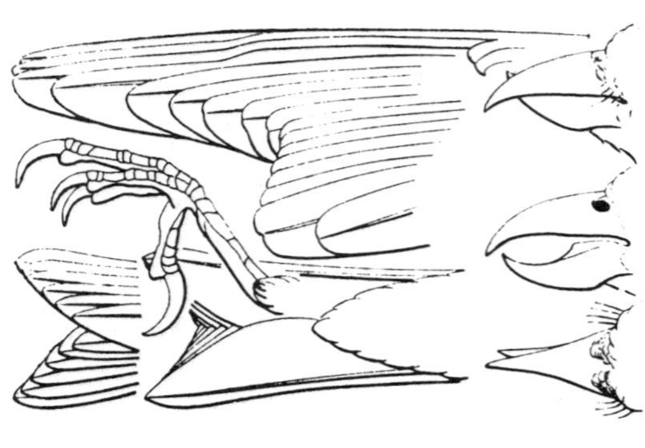

RED CROSSBILL
Loxia curvirostra

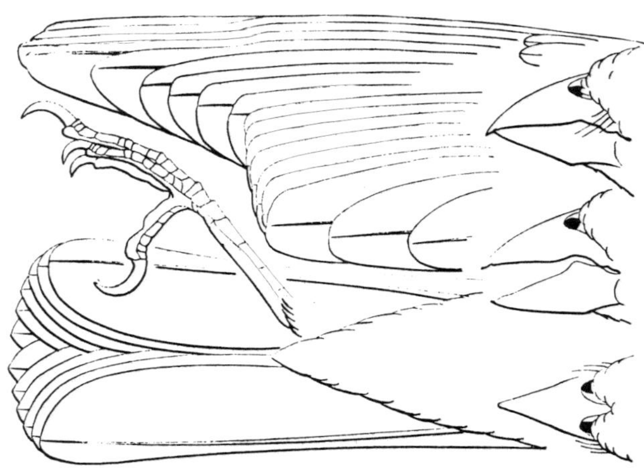

ROSE-BREASTED GROSBEAK
Pheucticus ludovicianus

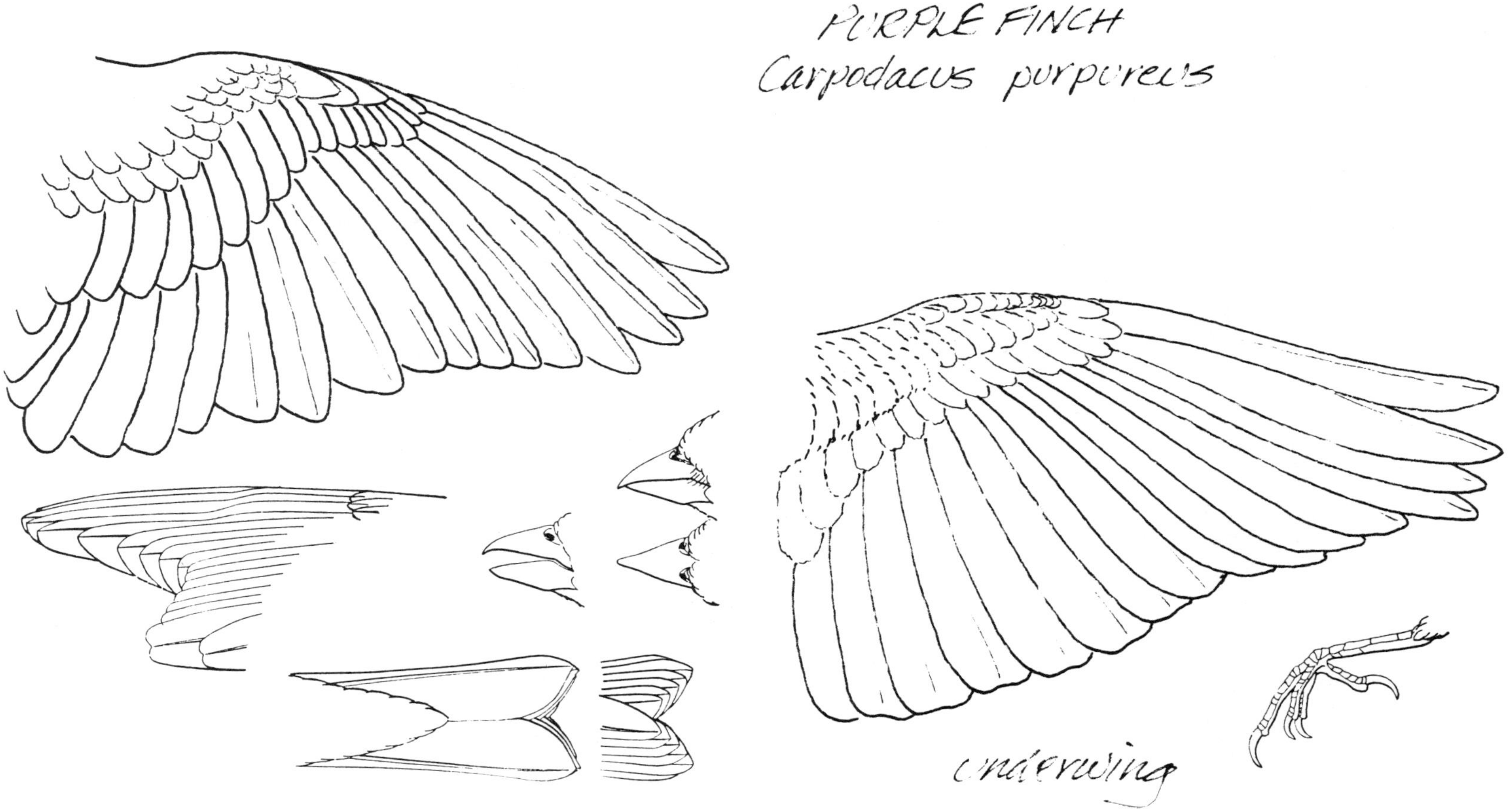

PURPLE FINCH
Carpodacus purpureus

underwing

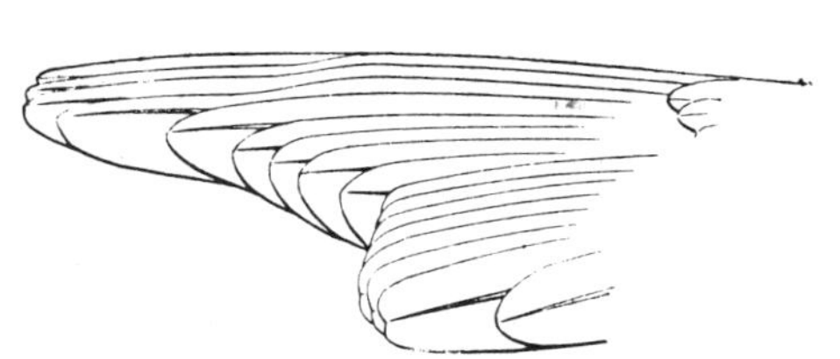

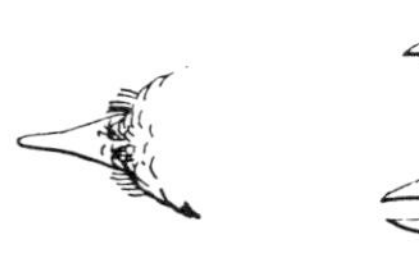

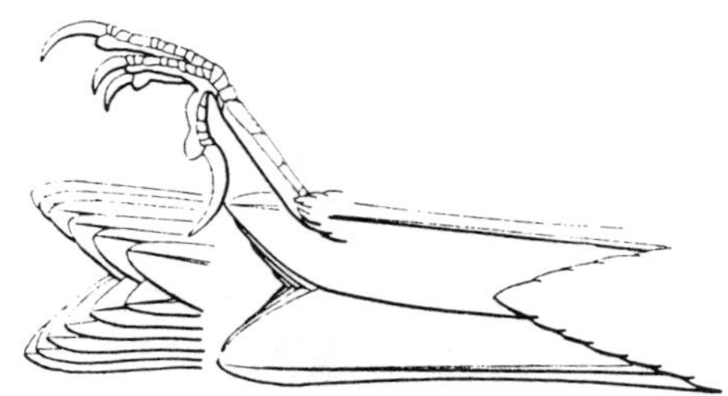

REDPOLL
Carduelis flammea

AMERICAN GOLDFINCH
Carduelis tristis

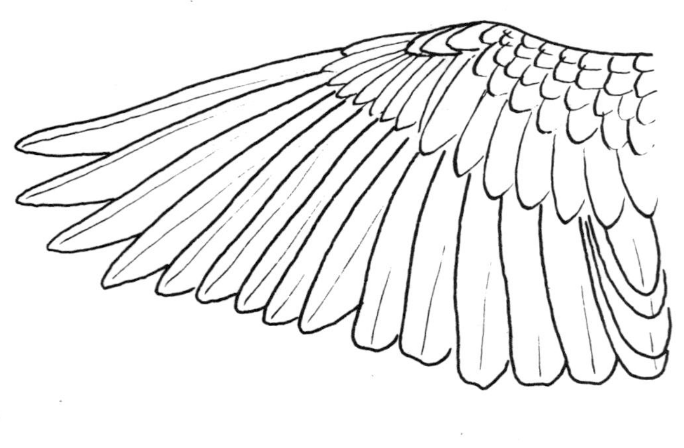

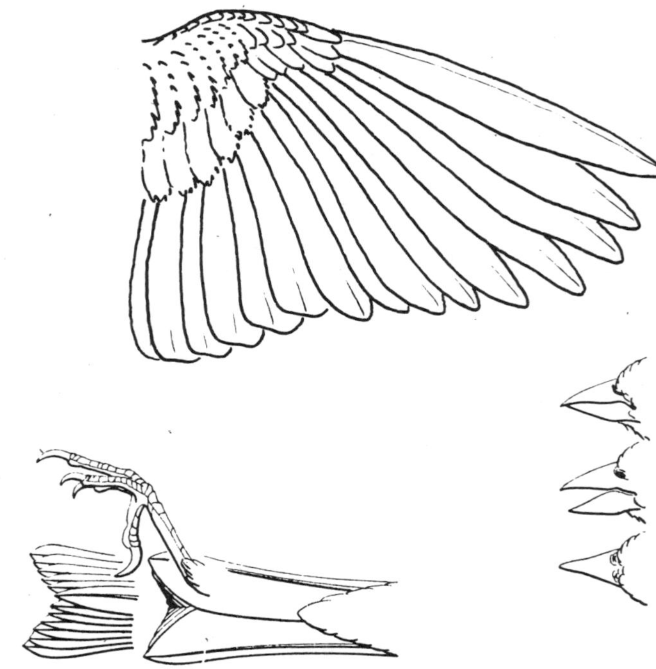

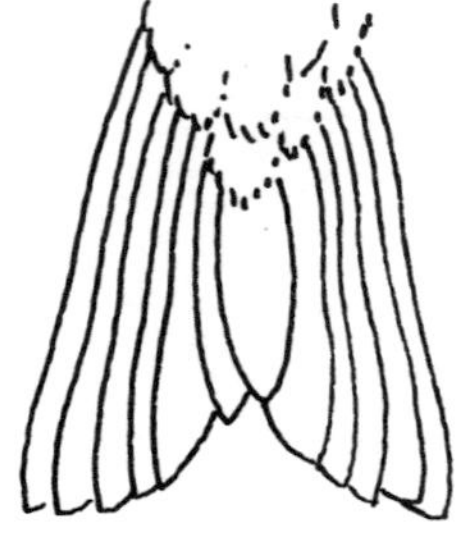

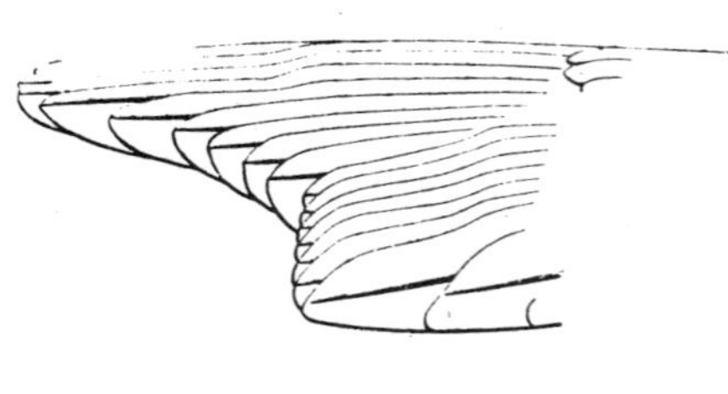

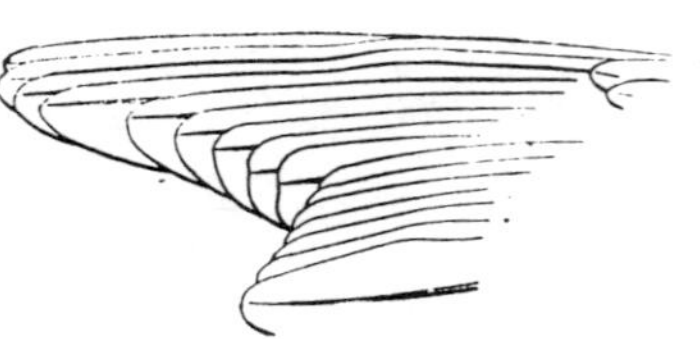

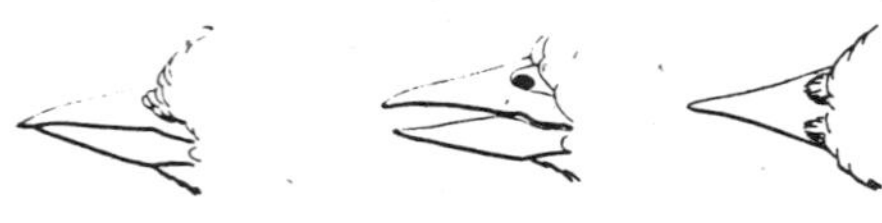

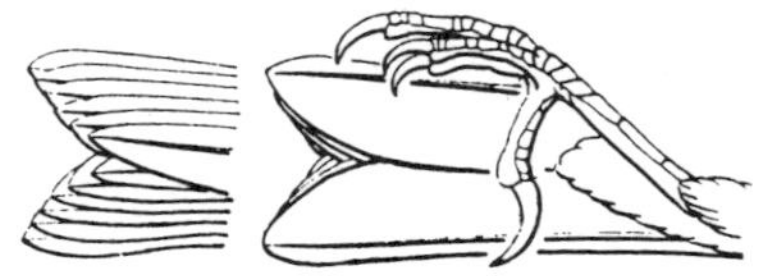

PINE SISKIN
Carduelis pinus

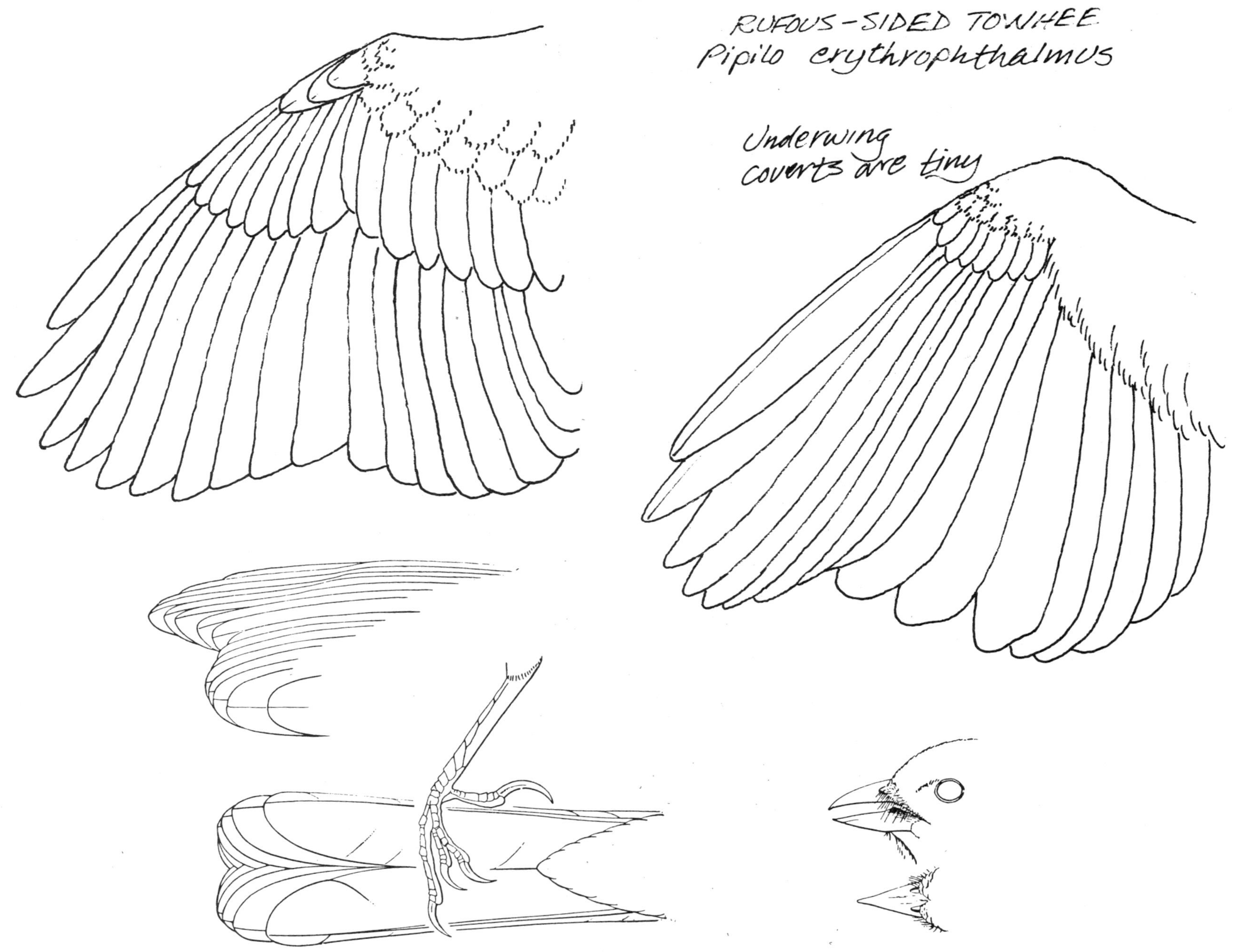
RUFOUS-SIDED TOWHEE
Pipilo erythrophthalmus
Underwing
coverts are tiny

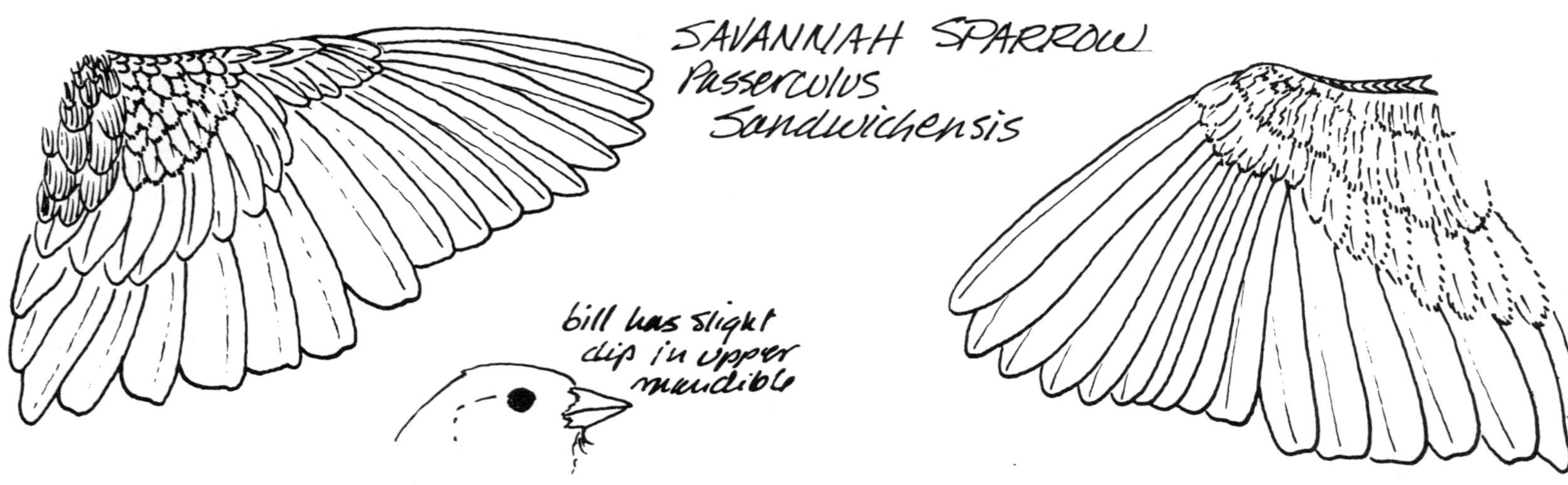

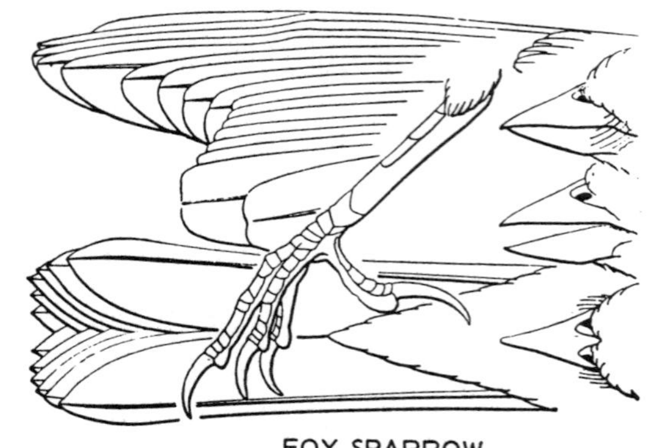

FOX SPARROW
Passerella iliaca

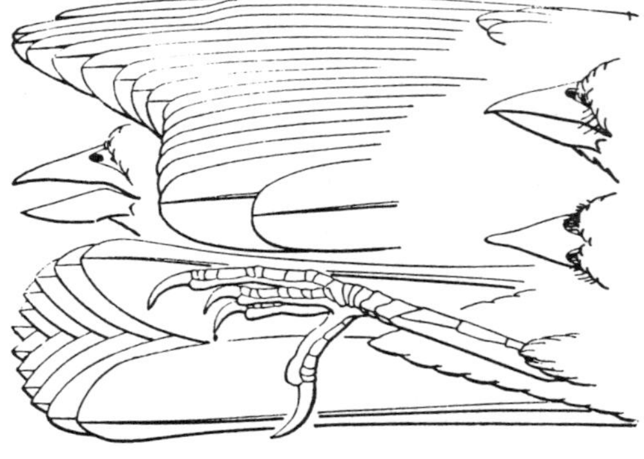

WHITE-CROWNED SPARROW
Zonotrichia leucophrys

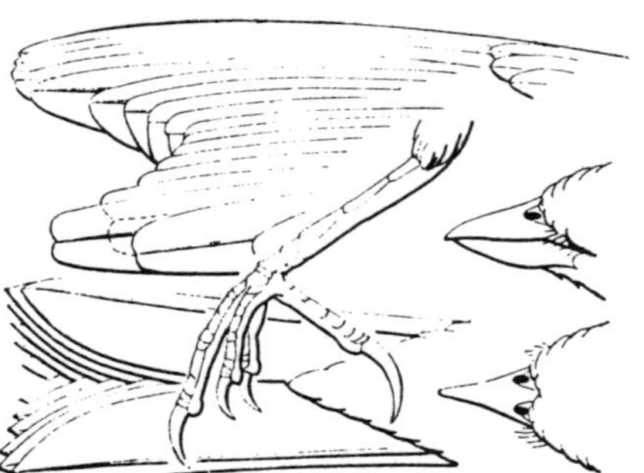

SAVANNAH SPARROW
Passerculus sandwichensis

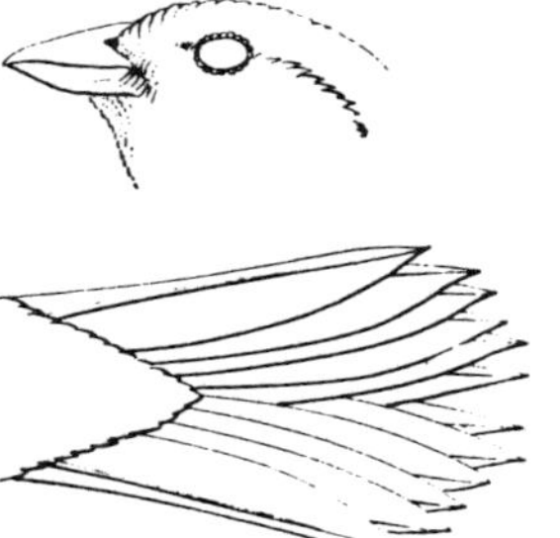

LECONTE'S SPARROW
Ammospiza leconteii

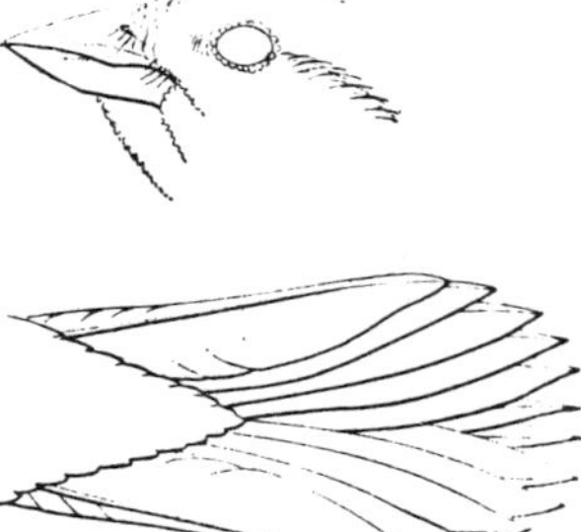

HENSLOW'S SPARROW
Ammodramus henslowii

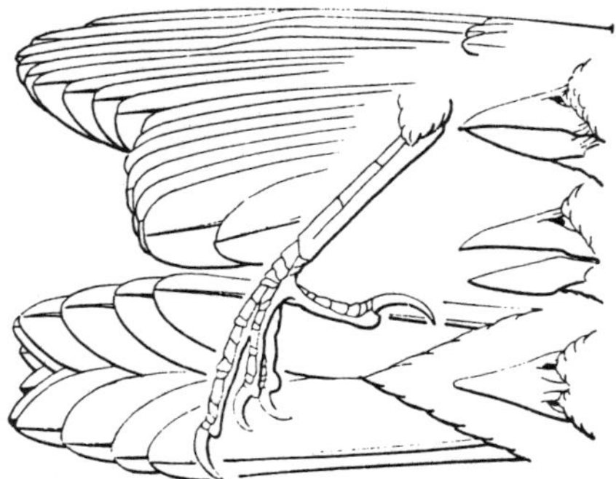

SONG SPARROW
Melospiza melodia

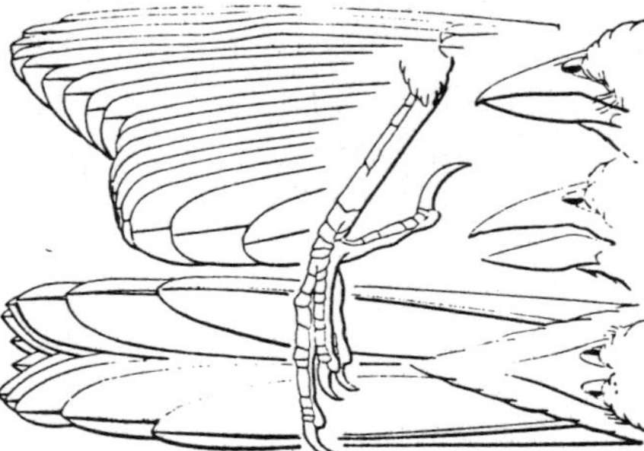

BACHMAN'S SPARROW
Aimophila aestivalis

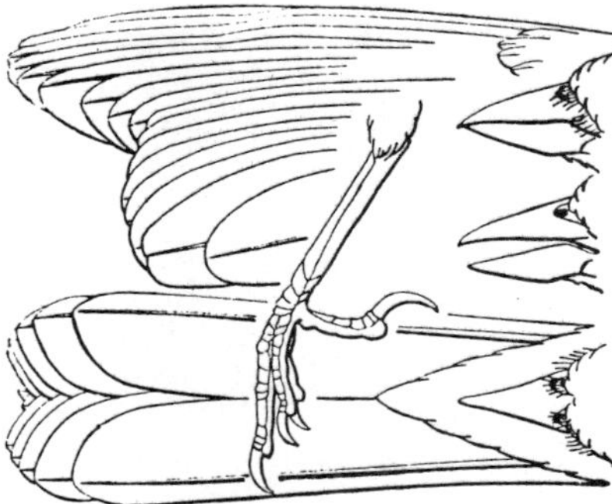

BLACK-THROATED SPARROW
Amphispiza bilineata

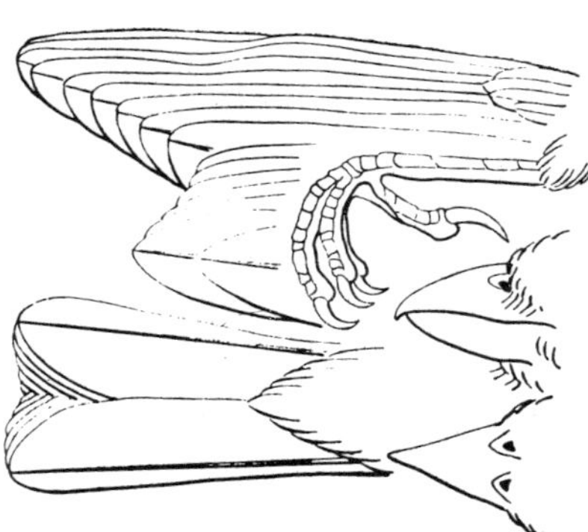

HOUSE SPARROW
Passer domesticus

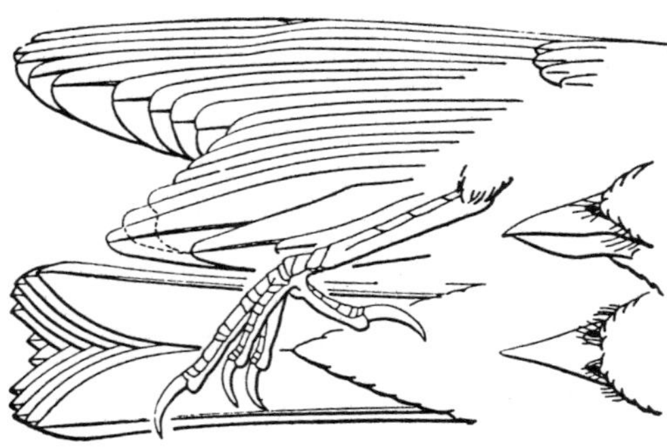

VESPER SPARROW
Pooecetes gramineus

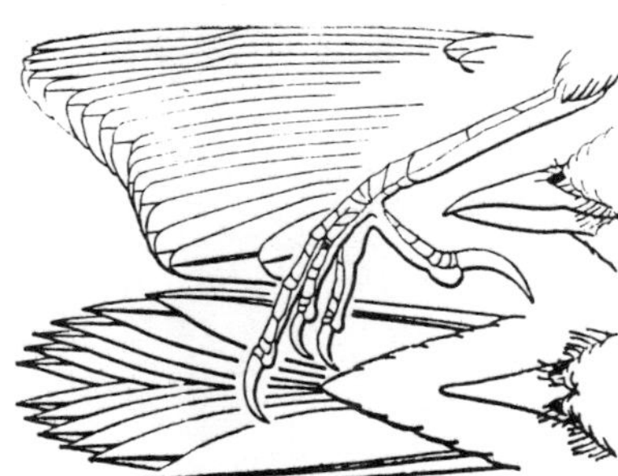

SHARP-TAILED SPARROW
Ammospiza caudacuta

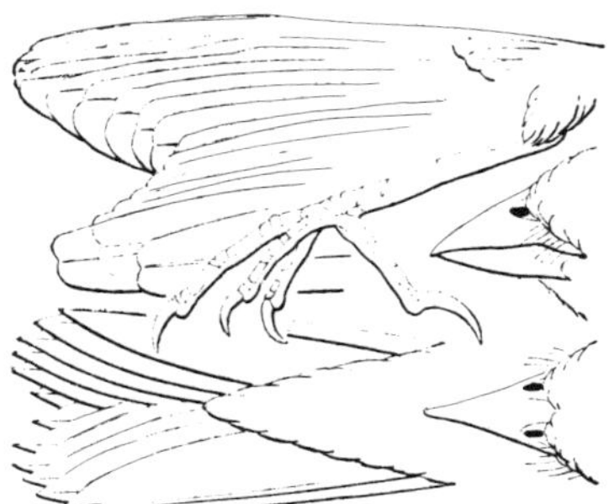

GRASSHOPPER SPARROW
Ammodramus savannarum

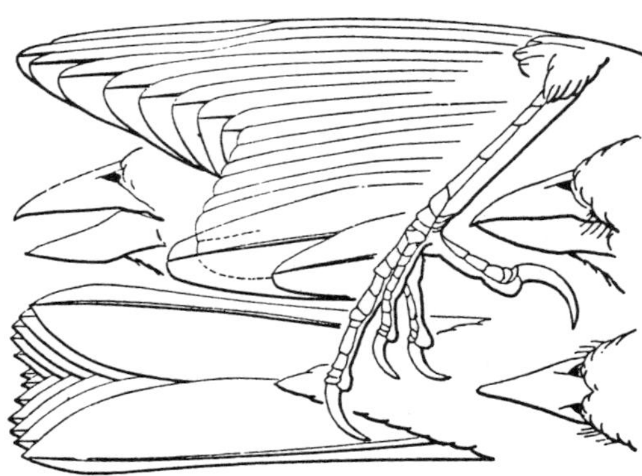

DICKCISSEL
Spiza americana

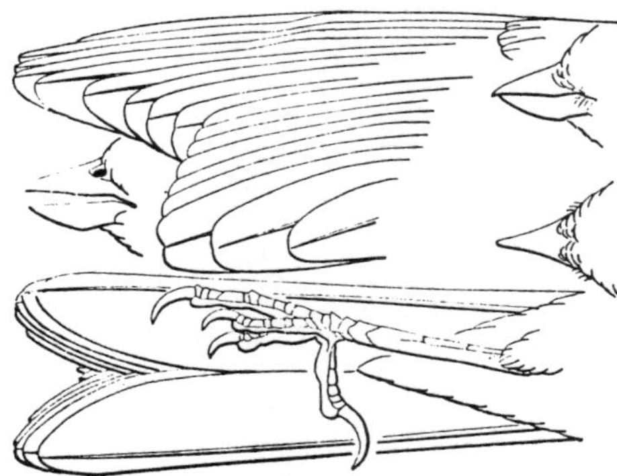

AMERICAN TREE SPARROW
Spizella arborea

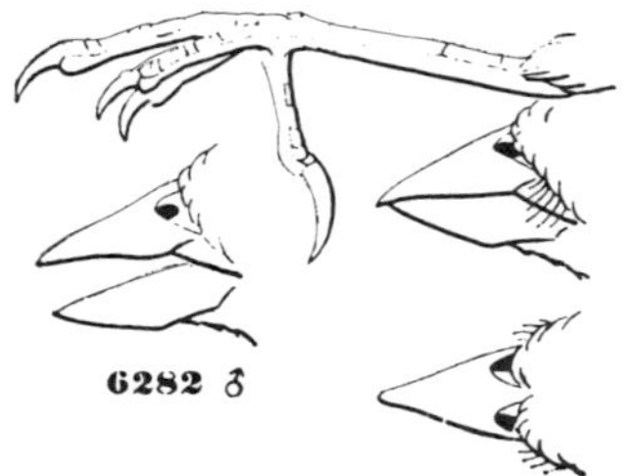

MC COWN'S LONGSPUR
Calcarius mccownii

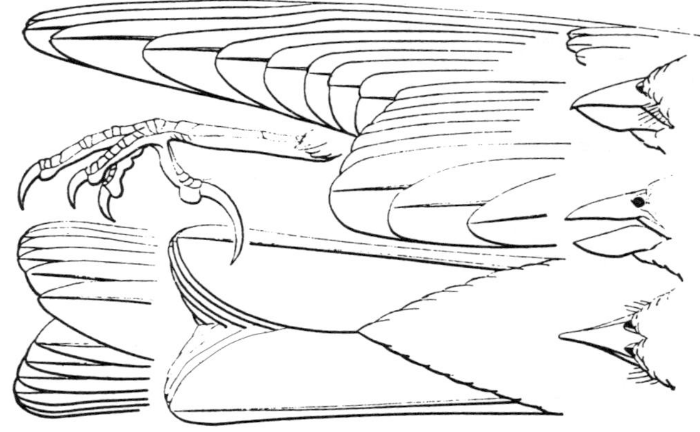

SNOW BUNTING
Plectrophenax nivalis

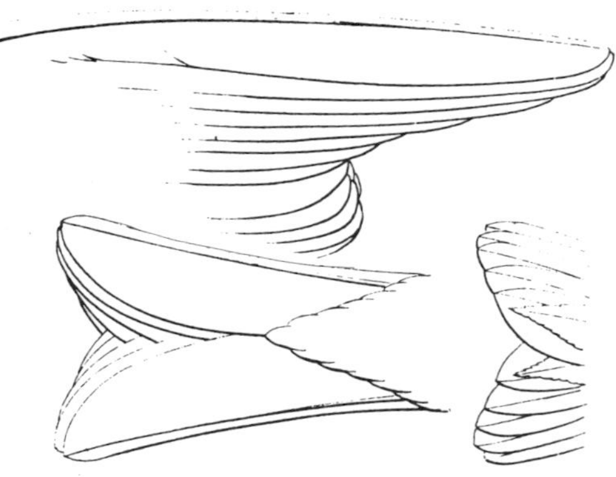

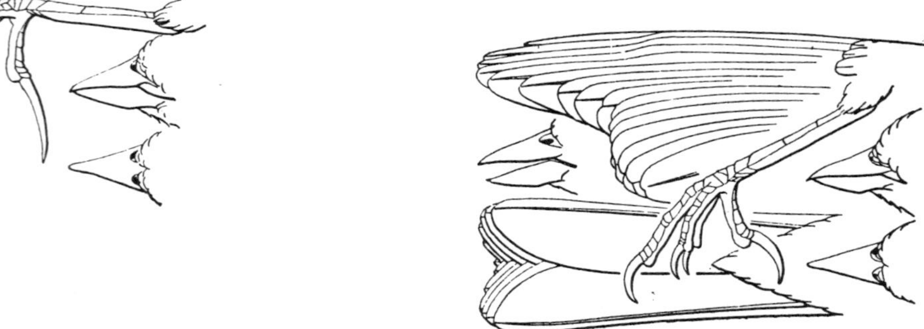

LAPLAND LONGSPUR
Calcarius lapponicus

NORTHERN JUNCO
Junco hyemalis

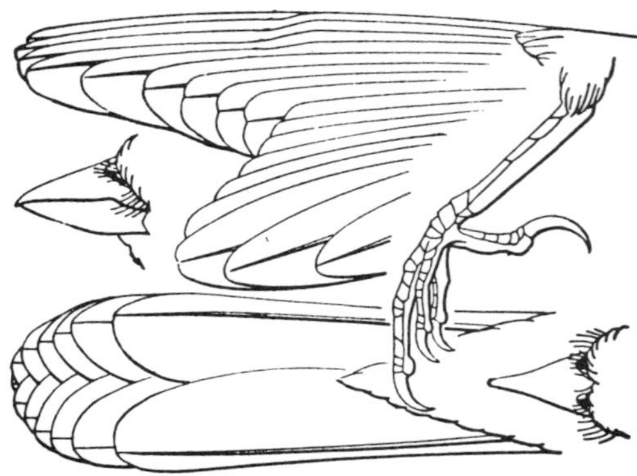

LARK SPARROW
Chondestes grammacus

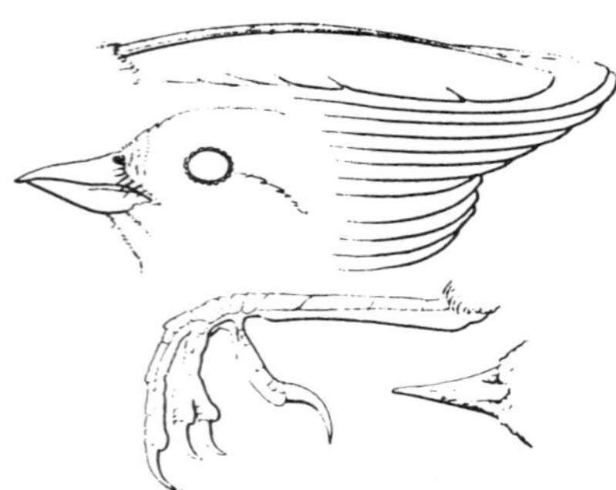

SWAMP SPARROW
Melospiza georgiana

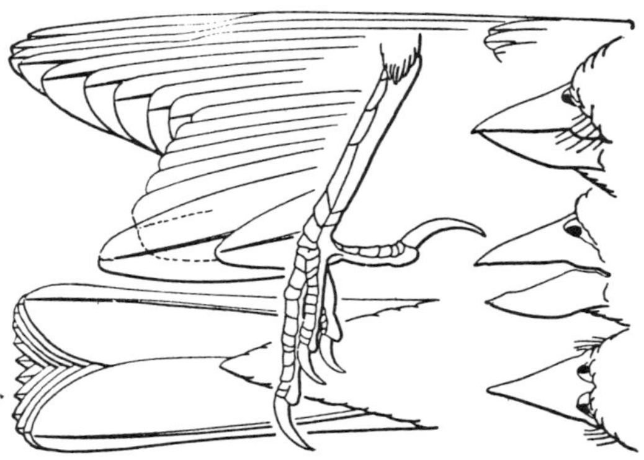

LARK BUNTING
Clamospiza melanocorys

INDEX

INDEX

Recommended Publications
for Woodcarving Artists

Woodcarvers' Favorite Patterns

Book Series by George Lehman

If you would like to start carving or further develop your carving skills, there is a good series of pattern and instruction books now available. Written by George Lehman , with 35 years experience as a commercial artist, each book contains detailed full size patterns complete with several different views of each bird to give a virtual blueprint of bird anatomy, attitude and position.

By special permission, we've reprinted a George Lehman pattern for a Cape May Warbler on the following page.
(Taken from "Nature in Wood", by George Lehman, copyright 1991 by Fox Chapel Publishing)

This pattern shows you the quality of the patterns in this series. Ordering a set of these books will increase dramatically the realism and life like quality of your carvings. See your favorite book supplier.

Woodcarvers Favorite Patterns Books

a collection of the best

"The different views of each bird, plus the sketches, give carvers almost a "360" degree perspective. Clear detailed patterns . Highly Recommended ."

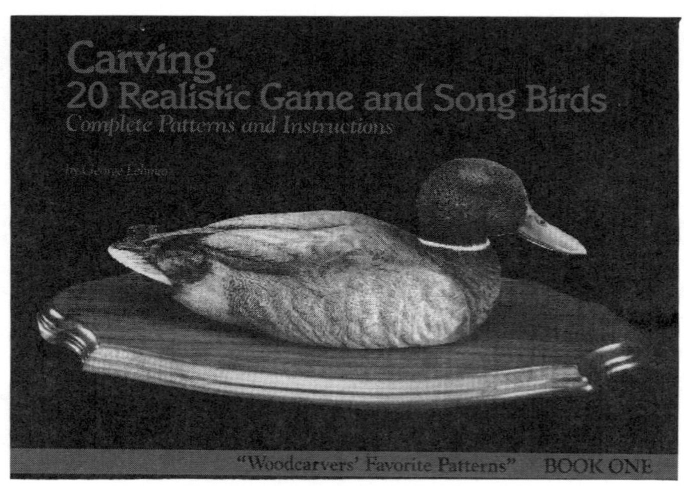

(BOOK ONE) "Carving 20 Realistic Game and Songbirds- Complete Patterns and Instructions" by George Lehman. This first title was enthusiastically received by carvers across the United States and Canada. Here, he pays particular attention to the questions of the beginning carver. In addition to the 20 full sized measured patterns, there are more than 70 additional photos , sketches and reference drawings. *Projects include : canvasback, pheasant, loon, chickadee, bluebird, robin, oriole, cardinal.*

Spiral bound, 14 x11 inches, full color laminated cover, 96 pages
includes Index , Appendix of suppliers clubs and publications
ISBN # 1-56523-004-3 **$19.95 retail**

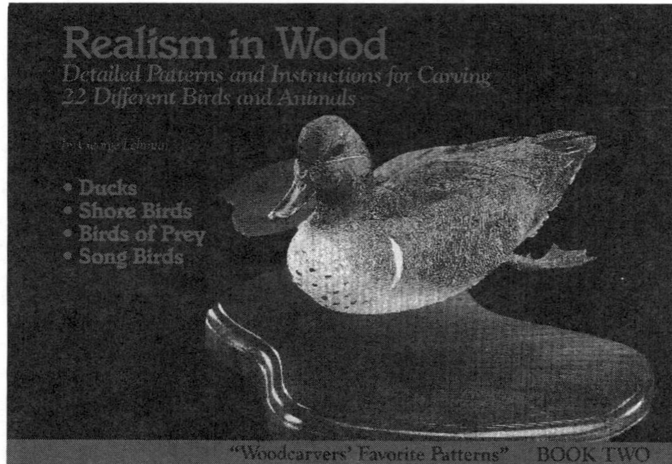

(BOOK TWO) "Realism in Wood- detailed patterns and instructions for carving 22 different birds and animals" by George Lehman. This volume features a strong selection of patterns for shorebirds and birds of prey in addition to some new duck and songbird patterns . Special sections on adding detail with a woodburning tool, inserting wooden feathers and building beautiful displays to show off your fine work.

Patterns include: bald eagle, sandpiper, sparrow hawk, great horned owl.

Spiral bound, 14 x11 inches, full color laminated cover, 112 pages
includes Index , Appendix of suppliers clubs and publications
ISBN # 1-56523-005-1 **$19.95 retail**

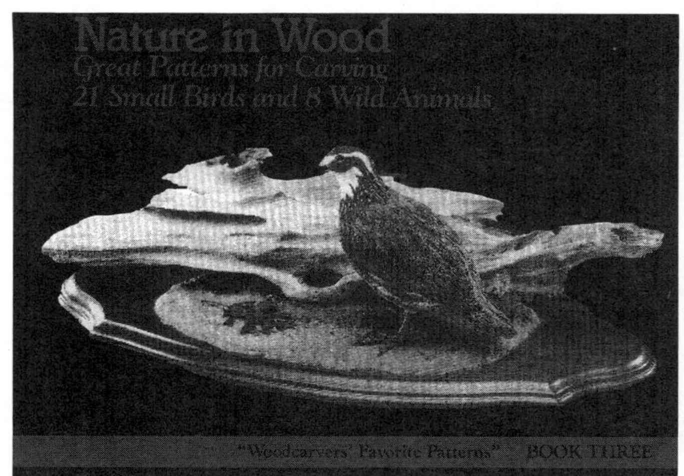

(BOOK THREE) "Nature in Wood - great patterns for carving 21 smaller birds and 8 wild animals" by George Lehman. In this book, George focuses on songbirds and the smaller game birds. numerous tips and hints are found throughout the book including how to give the appearance of soft, downy feathers to your carvings. A wonderful section on wild animal carvings, complete with measured patterns plus George has included a pair of country characters for your carving enjoyment

11 x 8.5 inches, perfectbound . Full color laminated cover. 128 pages includes Index , Appendix of suppliers clubs and publications

ISBN# 1-56523-006-X **$16.95 retail**

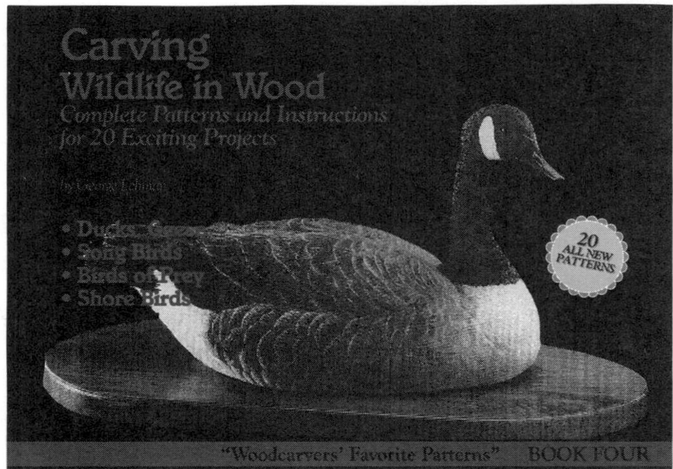

New Release ! " Carving Wildlife in Wood - complete patterns and instructions for carving 20 exciting projects" (BOOK FOUR) by George Lehman. Here is George's newest book for decorative woodcarvers. 20 projects illustrated with full page (oversize) patterns. Tremendously detailed, these patterns appeal to carvers at all skill levels. Includes instructions and reference photos. Contains a variety of plans to carve such birds as: Canada Goose, Blue Heron, Wild Turkey , House Wrens, Baltimore Oriole plus three animal carving subjects - Wild Horse, Mountain Lion and Brown Bear. *Carving Wildlife in Wood is a great addition to any carvers library and will be used again and again.*

14 inches x 11 inches , spiral bound , full color laminated cover , 96 pages including Appendix of Suppliers,clubs and publications

ISBN# 1-56523-007-8 October '91 title **$19.95 retail**

CAPE MAY WARBLER

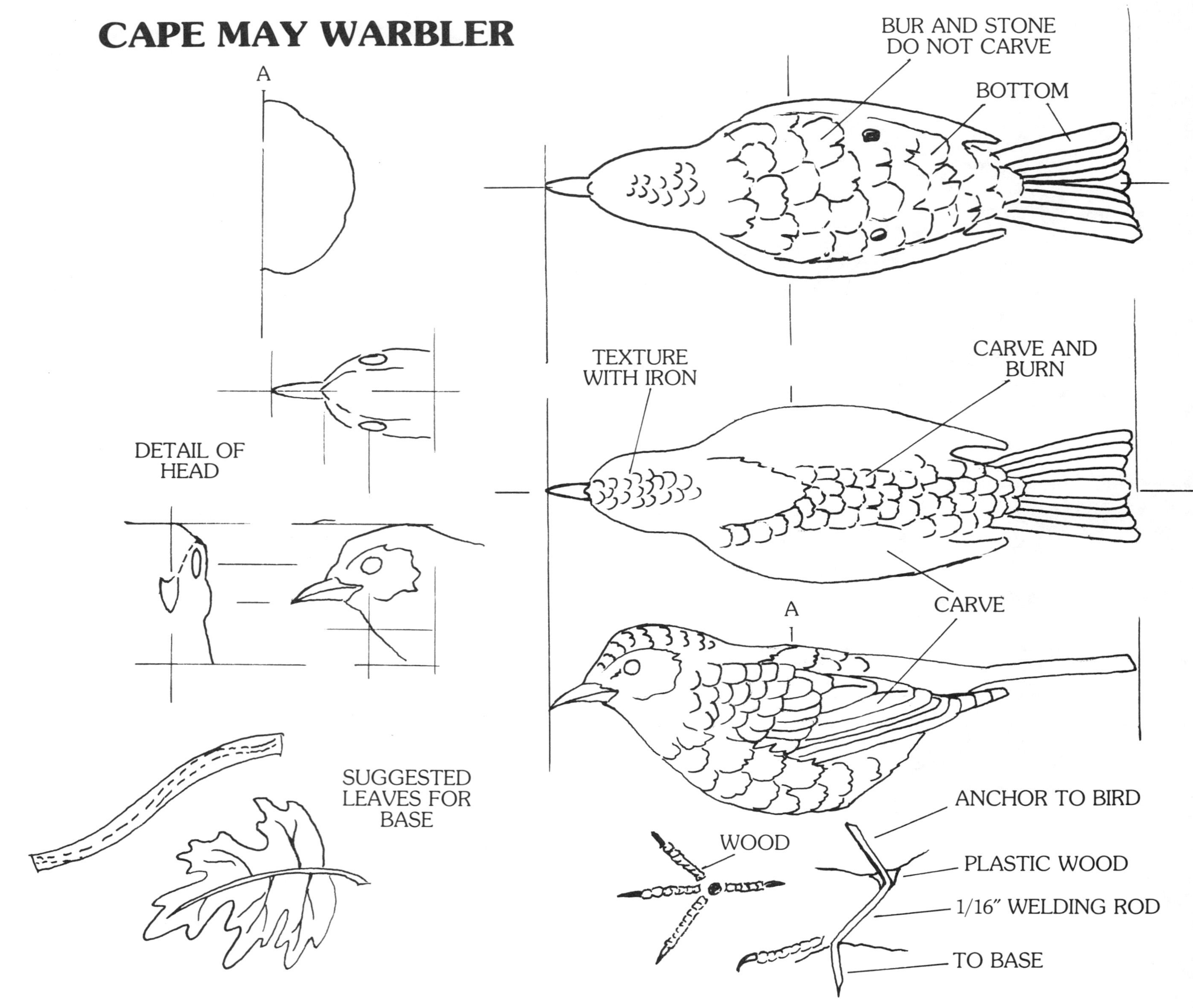

BOOK ONE

Carving 20 Realistic Game and Song Birds

Cardinal
Wood Duck (flying drake)
Hooded Merganser
Pintail Drake
Chickadee
Common Loon
Baltimore Oriole
Ruffed Grouse
Mallard (flying version)
Mallard (standing version)
Boreal Owl
Blue Bird
Hummingbirds
Canada Goose
Blue Jay (standing version)
Pintail (standing version)
Robin
Canvasback
Pheasant (wings outstretched)
American Widgeons, male/female

BOOK TWO

Realism in Wood

Bald Eagle
King Fisher
Upland Sandpiper
Redtailed Hawk
Wood Thrush
Wood Ducks, male/female
Great Horned Owl w/ mice
Spotted Sandpiper and sanderling
Mocking Bird
Sparrow Hawk (American Kestrel)
Common Bobwhite
Woodcock
Sharptail Grouse
Oystercatcher
Mallard Hen
Pheasants, male/female
Greenwing Teal
Pileated Woodpecker
Blue Wing Teal
Polar Bear
White Tail Deer

BOOK THREE

Nature In Wood

Bird Projects

Gambel Quail, male/female
Cliff Swallow
Bob o link
Cape May Warbler
Blue Jay
Cactus Wren
Evening Grosbeak
Scissor tailed Flycatcher
MacGillivray's Warbler
Eastern Meadowlark
Barn Swallow
Blackburnian Warbler
Scarlet Tanager
Red Poll
Great crested Flycatcher
Cardinal
Yellowheaded Blackbird
Greater Roadrunner
House Wrens
American Goldfinch

Animal Projects

Pronghorn Antelope
Canadian Lynx
Coyote
Tiger
Rabbit
Moose
Cheetah
Rocky Mountain Bighorn Sheep

Caricatures

Belle and Cactus Pete

BOOK FOUR

Carving Wildlife In Wood

Bird Patterns

Avocet, American
Bluebill
Bufflehead
Dove, Mourning
Goose, Common Canada
Goose, Snow
Grouse, Ruffed
Heron, Great Blue
Oriole, Baltimore
Osprey
Plover, Golden
Quail, Mountain
Redhead
Snipe, Common Jack
Turkey, Wild
Woodcock, American
Wren, House

Animals

Bear
Mountain Lion
Wild Horse

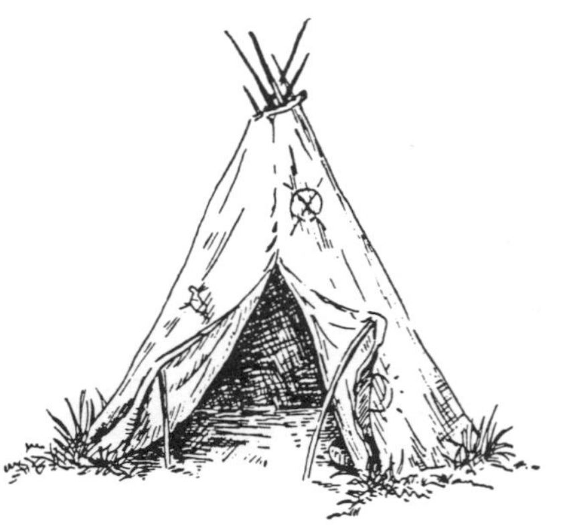

NATIVE INDIAN WILD GAME, FISH & WILD FOODS COOKBOOK

For the first time ever, a modern wild game cookbook written by Native Indian women.
Almost 400 recipes for all types of fish, game and wild foods, including:

Deer	Rabbit	Trout	Nuts
Moose	Turtle	Salmon	Berries
Bear	Squirrel	Bass	Wild Greens
Elk	Raccoon	Catfish	Baking Section

These simple, yet elegantly delicious recipes will appeal to all - from hunter to hostess.
Over two years of research and taste-testing thousands of recipes went into selecting the best of the best for this book .

Here's a sampling -

Salmon Rice Salad
Pheasant with Wild Rice Stuffing
Black Walnut Souffle
Curried Moose Burgers
Wild Blueberry Pancakes
Buffalo Jerky
Woodlands Wild Turkey
Apple Roasted Porcupine
Mad Bear's Elk Stew
Venison Pot Roast with Wild Cranberries
Wapiti Wild Rice Stew
Raccoon Delight

Special Sections on cleaning and skinning fish and game, natural tanning methods and herbal remedies.

NATIVE INDIAN WILD GAME, FISH AND WILD FOODS COOKBOOK
ISBN 1-56523-008-6 HARDCOVER, 304 PAGES $24.95

FOX CHAPEL PUBLISHING
BOX 7948, LANCASTER, PA 17604

REFERENCE BOOKS

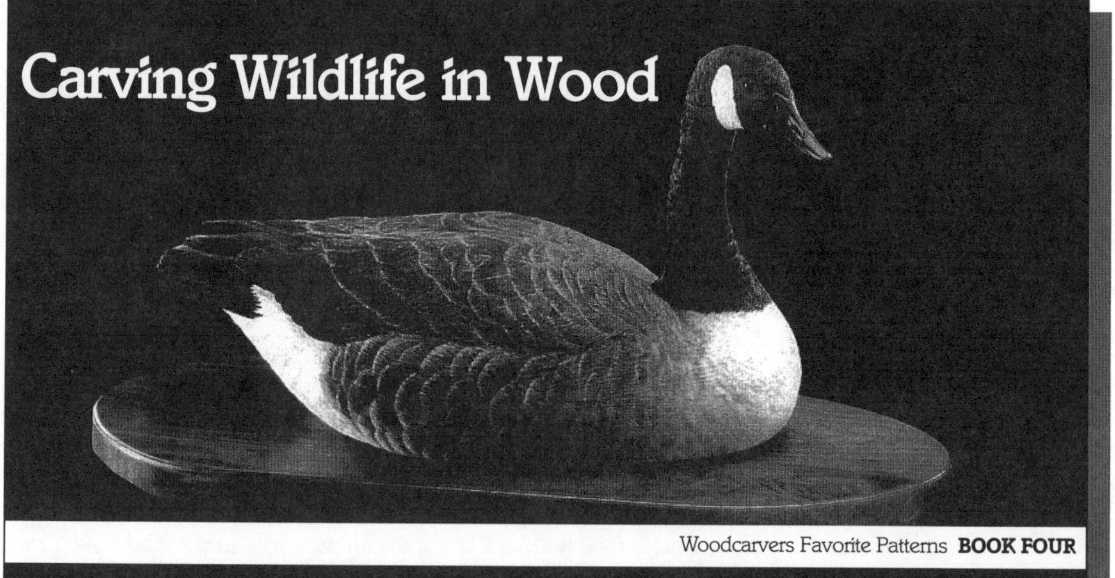

New! **" *Carving Wildlife in Wood*"** - by George Lehman, 20 patterns, sketches for an exciting variety of carving projects- ducks , geese, gamebirds, songbirds, shorebirds, an osprey - even a wild turkey! George's detailed patterns and drawings are a joy to use. Three animal patterns included for a change of pace. Huge 11x 17 inch format, spiralbound to lie flat. 100 pages.

(Book Four) only $19.95

"Different views of each bird, plus the sketches give carvers almost a "360 degree" perspective. Clear,detailed patterns. Highly Recommended."

Other titles available in the Woodcarvers' Favorite Pattern series:

"Carving 20 Realistic Game and Songbirds"
(Book One) contains 20 of your favorite projects including canvasback, pheasant , common loon, chickadee, bluejay. robin
100 pages, 11x 17 format spiral bound **$19.95**

"***Realism in Wood***"
(Book Two) contains detailed patterns and instructions for birds of prey, shorebirds, ducks and songbirds 100 pages, 11x 17 format **$19.95**

"Nature in Wood" (Book Three)
29 great patterns for small birds and animals . Examples: goldfinches, swallows, wrens, moose, bighorn sheep 128 pages, 11x 8.5 format **$16.95**

FOX CHAPEL

Mail orders , please add $2.00 per book shipping

Available from your favorite book supplier

Fox Chapel Publishing

Dept. 1 • Box 7948 Lancaster PA 17604

"ABA has done more to support and encourage birders than any other organization. Membership is a must for all active birders."

Victor Emanuel
President, Victor Emanuel Nature Tours

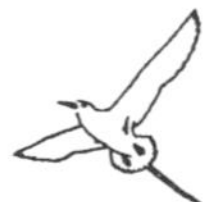

*"ABA is the bird club for everyone, where we can all share the excitement and the learning and the **fun**. ABA doubles my enjoyment of birding."*

Kenn Kaufman
author of the *Peterson Field Guide to Advanced Birding*

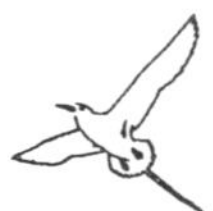

"ABA puts me in touch with the finest people on this planet—North American Birders"

Pete Dunne
Director, Natural History Information
New Jersey Audubon Society

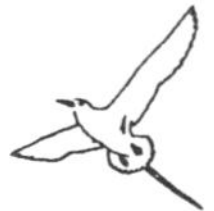

"ABA is the best value in the birding community today"

Roger Tory Peterson

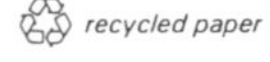
recycled paper

Membership Application

American Birding Association, Inc.

Membership entitles you to six consecutive issues of **Birding** magazine, monthly issues of **Winging It** newsletter, and member discounts offered by ABA Sales.

- ☐ New Member
- ☐ Renewal
- ☐ Gift

- ☐ Individual, $30/yr
- ☐ Family, $37/yr
- ☐ Century Club, $100/yr
- ☐ Life, $500*
- ☐ Family Life, $750*
- ☐ Patron, $1,000*

* May be paid in two annual installments; Patron includes life membership

Name & Address: ____________

Phone: ____________

- ☐ Check or Money Order enclosed (US funds only, please)
- ☐ Charge to MC/VISA No: ____________

signature ____________ expires ______

a $1.00 surcharge is added for credit card usage

Send to: ABA Membership, PO Box 6599, Colorado Springs, CO 80934 — (800) 634-7736 or (719) 578-0607 — (719) 471-4722 fax

Do You Want to Increase Your Birding Skills and Enjoyment?

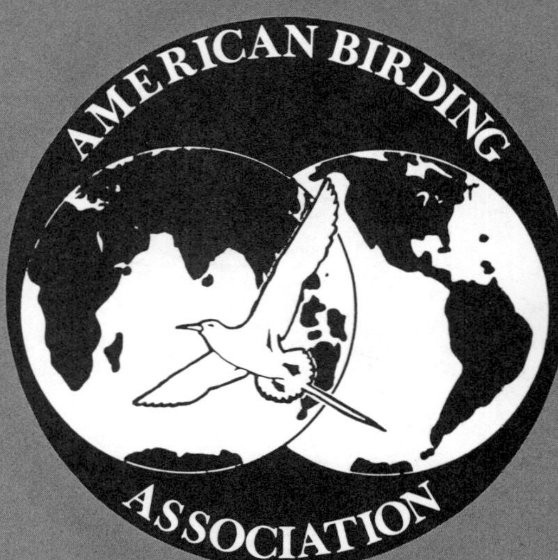

Join ABA ... The Only North American Association of and for Birders

FOR YOU

THE BIRD CARVING ENTHUSIAST

Educational.

WILDFOWL CARVING & COLLECTING is the only magazine that brings you the best of carving and collecting in its every form.

Informative.

You'll gain insight into the history of bird carving plus how-to details on this great craft.

Authoritative.

You'll glean expert advice from the renowned carving and collecting experts who regularly contribute to WC&C.

Fun.

You won't find such a wealth of information and entertaining reading anywhere else. Don't miss another exciting issue.

Mail your subscription today!

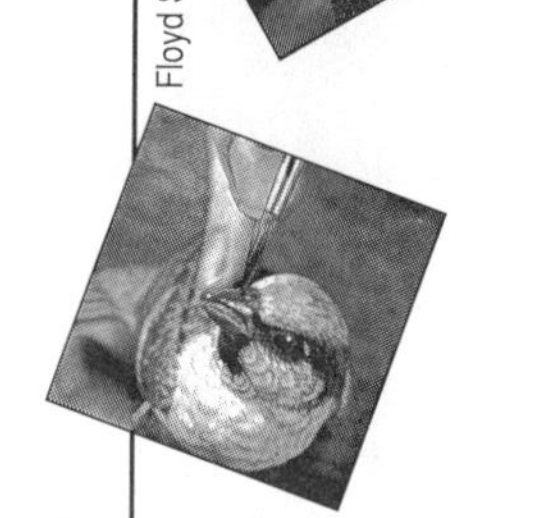

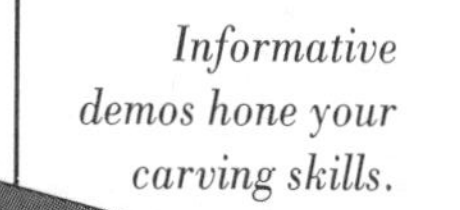

Floyd Scholtz

Informative demos hone your carving skills.

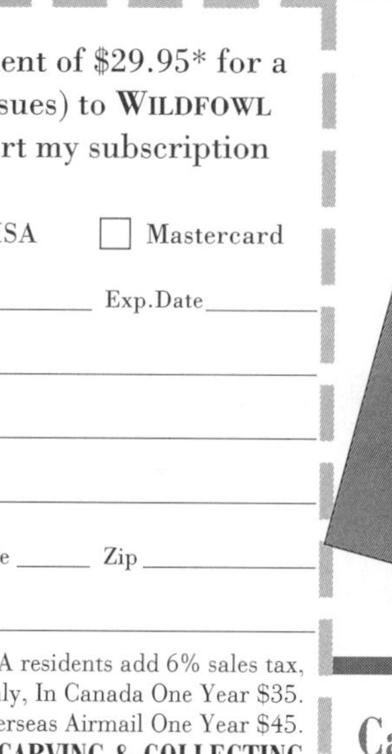

Guy Taplin

Pam McCoy

Yes! Enclosed is my payment of $29.95* for a full year's subscription (4 issues) to **WILDFOWL CARVING & COLLECTING.** Start my subscription right away!

☐ Check or Money Order ☐ VISA ☐ Mastercard

Card # ______________________ Exp.Date ________

Signature ______________________

Name ______________________

Address ______________________

City ______________ State ______ Zip ________

Phone ______________________

FCA2

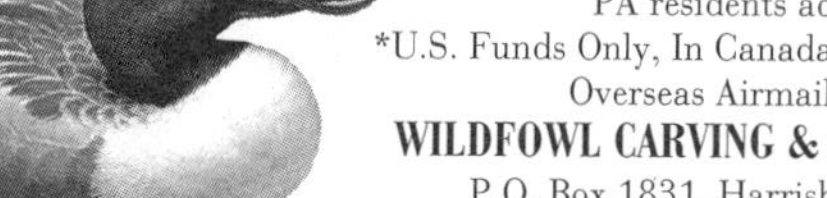

PA residents add 6% sales tax.
*U.S. Funds Only, In Canada One Year $35.
Overseas Airmail One Year $45.
WILDFOWL CARVING & COLLECTING
P.O. Box 1831, Harrisburg, PA 17105

Dennis Schroeder

Call 1-800-233-9015
Ext. 90 for Immediate Service!